The Last Secret

The Last Barrel

The Last Secret

THE DELIVERY TO STALIN OF OVER TWO MILLION

RUSSIANS BY BRITAIN AND THE UNITED STATES

Nicholas Bethell

INTRODUCTION BY HUGH TREVOR-ROPER

BASIC BOOKS, INC., PUBLISHERS

NEW YORK

CONTENTS

Illustrations vii

Introduction ix

Acknowledgments xv

1 The Decision to Use Force 1

2 The First Unpleasantness 31

3 Death on the Quayside 53

4 The Croats and the Cossacks 75

5 The Conference that Never Was 103

6 Mass Deportation from the Drau Valley 124

7 The Policy under Attack 166

8 The Last Operations—Dachau, Plattling, Keelhaul,
  Eastwind 188

Notes 212

Index 219

ILLUSTRATIONS

Between pages 98 *and* 99

The Yalta Conference in the Crimea, February 1945 (*Associated Press*)

A Russian Orthodox priest blessing recruits for the German army (*Gabriele Marvin*)

Part of a volunteer Cossack unit (*Imperial War Museum*)

German army prisoners in Northern France awaiting shipment to England (*Imperial War Museum*)

Cossacks surrendering their arms to the British 8th Army near Klagenfurt in Austria (*Imperial War Museum*)

Lieutenant-General Andrey Vlasov, photographed in German uniform in 1943 (*Robert Hunt Library*)

Cossacks on parade near their camp in the Drau Valley, Austria, in May 1945 (*Imperial War Museum*)

Commemoration ceremony at Lienz, June 1974 (*Author's collection*)

Stars and Stripes photograph of a Russian who attempted suicide at Plattling, March 1946

Field-Marshal Harold Alexander (*Imperial War Museum*)

Major-General Vyacheslav Naumenko, ataman of the Kuban Cossacks 1920-58

Lieutenant-General Charles Keightley at an observation post in Northern Italy, November 1944 (*Imperial War Museum*)

INTRODUCTION

by Hugh Trevor-Roper

WAR has its priorities which the longer perspective of peace
sometimes painfully deranges. In war one great aim obviously
over-rides others, and gives, for the time, an absolute validity
to the lesser decisions which it entails. Afterwards we may reflect
and, on reflection, think otherwise. But who can judge between
the two judgments? The comfortable after-wisdom of the historian
is a luxury: he has no responsibility: he can afford to be wrong.
Therefore he can only state the facts and, like the tragedian,
present rather than solve moral dilemmas.

This book is such a tragedy. It describes the consequences of
an over-riding war-time priority which, at the time, seemed
absolute. Today, those consequences will shock us. At the time
they did not. To many they were unknown. Those who knew of
them regarded them as necessary. In the context of the time,
perhaps they were necessary. And since they were judged
necessary, they were also judged moral. For men are not satisfied
with necessity: they must justify it with morality—sometimes with
a false morality which may outlast the real necessity.

The real necessity, in this story, was the alliance between
Soviet Russia and the West which alone, after the mistakes of
both partners in the 1930s, could defeat Germany and destroy
Nazism. That alliance was, in its origin, self-defensive. To each
party it was the sole means of survival. Apart from that one over-
riding need, there was no rational trust, no identity of aim.
Nevertheless, in the West, where public opinion was powerful,
the alliance of necessity had to be represented as an understanding,
a sympathy between peoples of similar ideals. By 1944 British
propaganda had for three years recorded the sufferings and extolled
the heroism of the Russian people. It had concealed the true
character of the Russian government. It had suggested that its
aims were similar to our own. Thereby it had created a public
attitude towards that government which made possible, and even
acceptable, certain great betrayals.

One such betrayal was the betrayal of Poland. The politicians could say that it was unavoidable. The German invasion of Russia, the victory of Russia in Eastern Europe, the hard facts of geography, made any other outcome impossible. But the betrayal was made morally digestible in the West by the public illusion which had been so sedulously spread about the character of Stalin's Russia. For was not Russia an ally, a virtuous anti-Nazi democracy, just like our own? Had not Stalin promised free and fair elections in Poland; and was not Stalin a man of his word?

Another such betrayal was the betrayal of the anti-Soviet Russians described in this book. Politically this can also be justified in the circumstances of the time. It too was made morally justifiable by propaganda: propaganda against those Russians who, through hatred of Stalinism, or mere physical necessity, had compromised themselves with the Germans; propaganda in favour of Stalin's supposed clemency. It was also a less public betrayal because it was kept secret. Indeed its true history was kept secret for twenty-seven years.

Of course, many of the facts were known at the time. They were known to the officials who handled the negotiations, to the soldiers who received the surrenders and manned the camps for 'Displaced Persons', to the journalists who visited those camps. But such facts were seldom published. The Russian government did not wish to admit that any Russian had fought against communism or was reluctant to return to 'a land where a man has no rights'. In deference to these wishes, the agreement whereby the British and American governments bound themselves to return even reluctant Soviet citizens to Russia was kept secret. So was its fulfilment. One of the few writers to declare in print that Russian prisoners and 'displaced persons' were refusing to return and were being 'repatriated against their will' was George Orwell.* He was promptly attacked for doing so.

The reality of the forcible repatriations to Russia in 1945 has been forced upon us this year by a great work of literature, Alexander Solzhenitsyn's *Gulag Archipelago*. Solzhenitsyn came

---

* In 'The Prevention of Literature' published in *Polemic 2* (January 1946). Orwell was attacked by the communist writer Randall Swingler in *Polemic 5* (September-October 1946) and justified his statements in marginal comments to Swingler's article.

upon that reality in the prison-camps of Russia in which the reluctant repatriates languished and died. From such sources he could discover individual histories: he could not discover the complex motives behind those histories, and those motives he unfairly simplified. He saw Churchill and Roosevelt as criminals who sent millions of Russian political refugees back into Russia to be persecuted and killed. But this is to ignore the political context and the intellectual climate of the time. It is to forget the reality of the war, the pressure of emotion and propaganda. Solzhenitsyn saw the repatriates as, at worst, 'dissidents' like himself, forcibly sent back from the countries in which they had sought asylum. He does not see the problem with the eyes of western statesmen and officials, locked in a long and desperate war. In order to see the story in its context, it is necessary to go to the archives of the western Allies. These were inaccessible to Solzhenitsyn. They were inaccessible to any historian till 1972. They have now been used by Lord Bethell, and form the solid historical basis of this book.

The story which Lord Bethell tells, from official archives, personal interviews, and other sources, covers almost three years, though most of the action takes place in the crowded spring and summer of 1945. The problem first forced itself on the western powers in June 1944, after the invasion of Normandy. It was then that Russian soldiers in German uniform began to fall into their hands, thus creating a difficult problem, both of diplomacy and law. Were such men, by virtue of their uniform, German soldiers entitled to the ordinary rights of prisoners-of-war, or were they Russian traitors, who should be handed over to Russian justice? The problem was not made easier of solution by the contradictory claims of the Russian government, which publicly insisted that no such 'traitors' could exist and yet simultaneously pressed for their return. Moreover, it soon appeared that the majority of these prisoners were not traitors in any ordinary sense of the word, but either political refugees seeking the traditional right of asylum, or victims of horrible circumstances, who, in a civilised country, could expect amnesty but who, in Stalin's Russia, would unquestionably be made to suffer for the mere fact of their presence in the West. It is interesting to follow the dialogue within the British government and to see the claims of inhumanity first advanced, then overtaken by the claims, first of necessity, then of politics, and both alike gradually clothed in the decent garment of morality—morality spun by helpful propaganda.

The claim of necessity was strong. If the western Allies, in France, were capturing Russian prisoners serving in and behind the German army, the Russians, in Poland and East Germany, would soon be taking charge of British and American prisoners held in German prison-camps. If the Russians refused to repatriate western prisoners from the East except in exchange for Russian prisoners from the West, how could the West do anything but comply? There might be a difference between western prisoners eager to return home and Russian prisoners equally eager to remain abroad; but what western government could sacrifice its own soldiers for the sake of those who had fought against them? Given that choice, the decision was inevitable. The traditional right of asylum must be sacrificed to an over-riding human necessity.

The sacrifice was confirmed by the agreement signed at Yalta in February 1945, and thereby became inextricably bound up with the other conditions of that treaty: conditions not of over-riding necessity but of political convenience. So, little by little, as the detailed story is unfolded, we see the policy of forcible repatriation extended to categories which at first can hardly have been envisaged, and justified by arguments not of humanity but of expediency. If the Yalta Agreement were broken by the West in this small matter, it could be argued, might not the Russians claim the right to break it in some larger matter, concerning (say) free elections in Poland? In fact, they would break it anyway: there would be no free elections in Poland, or anywhere else in eastern Europe; but meanwhile the reluctant Soviet citizens would have been forcibly sent home.

Nor was it only Soviet citizens who were thus returned. One of the most harrowing episodes recounted in this book is the story of the forcible repatriation of the 50,000 Cossacks who surrendered to the British in Southern Austria. They had fought for the Germans indeed, but their wives and children had not, and many of the men were anyway not Soviet citizens: they had been *émigrés* for a generation and had never acknowledged the authority of the Soviet state. Even by the terms of the Treaty of Yalta such men were not liable to repatriation. Nevertheless, in an excess of pro-Soviet zeal, the British authorities repatriated them. They were lured by the false promises of their supposed protectors, and forcibly delivered into Soviet hands. After repatriation, 50% of them perished in Soviet labour camps. Of the six leaders whose execution was publicly announced only one had been liable to repatriation under the Yalta Agreement. The others should unquestionably have remained as prisoners of the western powers and, ultimately, have secured political asylum.

The crux of the matter was that the western Allies were determined, above all, not to exasperate Stalin, and Stalin was determined, now as in the Great Purge, to lay his hands on all those Russians who had so far eluded him. To gratify him the western Allies sacrificed not only the Cossacks but also the strict terms of the Yalta Agreement itself, and the distinction between treason and political dissent. 'We consider,' wrote Ernest Bevin, then Foreign Secretary of Britain, 'that it would be difficult in practice to draw a line between traitors and political refugees'; and he added, somewhat inconsequently, 'the Cossacks are acknowledged traitors.' They were traitors in the sense in which the Huguenots who fought for William of Orange were traitors to Louis XIV.

If the diplomatists were conditioned by their abstract reason of state, the soldiers were conditioned in an opposite sense by their personal contacts. They were not familiar with the mysteries of state but they did know their Russian prisoners and came to sympathise with them in their predicament. They found it repugnant to obey orders to deceive those who trusted them and to send them, in cold blood, to their destruction. They witnessed the scenes of anguish and suicide which invariably accompanied repatriation. Naturally they hated the whole policy and it was they who protested against it—indeed, in the end, nearly mutinied against it. The strongest champion of those who resisted the policy of forcible repatriation was a soldier, Field-Marshal Lord Alexander. He positively evaded the explicit orders of his government. Less highly placed officers could hardly do this. They complied with reluctance. To some, hardened by war, it was 'just another unpleasant job'. Others reasoned that if they did not obey the orders, they would simply be replaced by more pliant successors. Or they fell back on the duty of soldiers to obey without question. We have heard all these arguments from

German soldiers; perhaps it is salutary to hear them also from our own countrymen: it brings the dilemma nearer home.

To me, the great value of this book, apart from its documented and dramatic historical record, lies in its presentation of that dilemma: a dilemma that was solved brutally at the time and which cannot be solved again, retrospectively, by any easy formula. That is why I have called it a tragedy. Lord Bethell has given it its tragic quality by abstaining from facile judgments and re-creating, in exact detail, the particular context of those years which prevented a humane solution—although it did not justify the over-compliance with unwarranted Russian demands.

How simple the problem seemed to many at that time: to the doctrinaires imprisoned by their doctrine, to the officials imprisoned by their offices, to the public lulled by comfortable propaganda! The Russian deserters, said John Strachey, were quislings and 'deserved everything that was coming to them'. Strachey was a Marxist and 'as usual, he was excusing the Russians for everything they did'. The officials of the Foreign Office saw the Russian 'traitors' as an inconvenient 'element' which jeopardised their own tenuous but essential diplomatic constructions. The public, as always, heard only these public voices. Now that the facts are revealed and the context has changed, we shall no doubt be told that the problem was indeed simple but should have been solved in an opposite sense. We can only reply that such an answer would be unhistorical. It is better to admit the dilemma, to be chastened by the tragedy, and to respect those who, at the time, saw beyond immediate propaganda and political orthodoxy. To me the heroes of this book are Ethel Christie, the Quaker lady who, single-handed, forced the British govern-ment to save one Russian couple from repatriation, and the anonymous British officer who, when faced by Russian prisoners in German uniforms, thought that 'it would be an impertinence for an outsider to set himself up lightly in judgment of their actions during the war'. This is not a book which calls for judgment: it calls, as good books do, for reflection.

ACKNOWLEDGMENTS

MY FIRST thanks are due to the dozens of people who spoke to me about their personal experience of forcible repatriation. Their names appear in the body of the book and I would like them to know how much I appreciate the frank way in which they talked about this controversial matter, the discussion of which often caused them deep emotion. I can only hope that this book will do something to heal the mental wounds suffered by the victims as well as to mitigate the worry and the self-questioning of the soldiers who took part in the operations.

An equally important source for this book has been the documents now lying in the Public Record Office, London, and in the National Archives, Washington. The staff of the National Archives, both in Washington and in Suitland, Maryland, were impeccably helpful in answering my queries both in person and by post. I must also thank James Boyle who assisted me with research into these American documents. For the London archives I am very grateful to all the staff of the Public Record Office for helping me to trace documents and to have them photocopied, and to James Lucas of the Imperial War Museum for his help with the book's photographs.

Edward Greenland, Records Officer of the Ministry of Defence, London, was amazingly helpful. I had thought that he and his Department might view the idea of a book on this difficult subject with some apprehension. In fact, the Ministry of Defence did all it could to help me. Clifton Child, Records Officer of the Cabinet Office, was also very kind, putting me onto the track of several items which I might otherwise not have found. I must also thank Harry Harcombe, Records Officer of the Foreign Office, for reading the text and for making useful observations.

Grateful acknowledgement is made to Harper & Row, Publishers, Inc. for permission to quote from *The Gulag Archipelago* by Aleksandr I. Solzhenitsyn, Copyright © 1973 by Aleksandr I. Solzhenitsyn. English language translation copyright © 1973, 1974 by Harper & Row, Publishers, Inc.

The Last Secret

THE DECISION
TO USE FORCE

At the end of May 1944, a few days before the D-Day landings, intelligence reports available to General Eisenhower and his staff showed that large numbers of Russians under German command were being sent to man the 'Atlantic Wall', the western coastline of France which the Allies were about to attack. These reports caused great concern in Britain and the United States. It was known that since the German invasion of the Soviet Union on June 22, 1941, many millions of Russians had become prisoners of the Nazis. Some of these hated Stalin, Bolshevism and the Soviet system with a deadly loathing. They were only too ready to take up arms on the German side, and having done this, although they had no quarrel with Britain and America, they were available to fight on the western front as well as on the eastern. They had joined the German army to fight against Stalin, but they were now soldiers, and soldiers cannot in wartime pick and choose where or against whom they fight.

As well as those who volunteered to fight for the Nazis there was a much larger group of Soviet citizens who were forced by hunger, overwork or threat of imminent death to abandon their prisoner-of-war status and put on German uniform. The Soviet Union was not a member of the Geneva Convention. Soviet prisoners in Germany did not receive parcels of good things through the International Red Cross. They were regarded by the Nazis as sub-human and treated abominably. It was a very steadfast and patriotic Russian indeed who would in these circumstances refuse an invitation to work in a German labour battalion, where food and conditions were a little better.

The work he was required to do was not, on the face of it, traitorous. He might be asked to help gather the harvest or build roads or, in the case of Russian women, to work as a domestic servant for a German officer. But once he had agreed to serve the enemy in whatever capacity, the slope was a slippery one, and it was only a matter of time before he was asked to do work more closely related to the German war effort. Many Russians were put to work in munitions factories, particularly in the dangerous work which involved the handling of volatile materials or poisonous chemicals. From this it was but a small step to active service in the German armed forces.

Again, there were promises of improvement in conditions, and if these were not enough other more crude methods of conscription were available. There were many cases when a Russian was presented with a straight choice—either join or be shot on the spot. By 1944, when the German army was in dire straits and reduced to such methods, many Russian prisoners had been in German hands for several years, and however much they loved their country and hated the foreign invader they were reluctant to martyr themselves in the cause of Stalinist communism.

On May 28, 1944, Archibald Clark Kerr, British Ambassador in Moscow, wrote to Stalin's Foreign Affairs Commissar:

> Dear Mr Molotov—I hear from London that the Anglo-American Combined Chiefs of Staff have information that shows that there is a large Russian element that has been forced to serve with the German armies in the West. The Supreme Headquarters of the Allied Expeditionary Force is anxious that a statement should be made promising an amnesty or considerate treatment to these Russians, provided that they surrender to the Allies at the first opportunity. The promise it has in view would not include persons known to have intentionally performed traitorous acts, or volunteers, or members of ss formations, but would be confined to those Russians serving as a result of German compulsion. The power of such a statement would be to induce Russian desertions from the German armed forces and to provoke German mistrust of Russians serving with those forces.

The Ambassador's letter concluded that such a statement would have the greatest value if it were issued in the name of Stalin himself.

The fact that such a letter could be written shows how deep was the western Allies' lack of appreciation of the true nature of Russia under Stalin. The Soviet government could not forgive any Soviet citizen who had in any way collaborated with the Nazi Germans, let alone actively fought for them. No degree of duress, threat or hardship could excuse such an act in Soviet eyes. A man who had done this was not only a traitor who must be punished as an example to others, he was also a security risk, a man who had spent time outside the control of the total state and might therefore have developed disloyal tendencies, who had seen the outside world and must not be allowed to go about Russia describing the comparative affluence in which the German people lived, even in wartime. The Soviet Union had for more than a decade been a closed country, empty of non-communist influences and purged of dissidents. That so many ordinary citizens should spend a number of years in a foreign country was in itself a mind-racking worry to the blinkered, security-obsessed men who ran the country. To such 'policeman minds' they were all dangerous, every one of them, even those who had resisted the Nazi blandishments or threats and remained in prisoner-of-war camps on starvation rations. Stalin was resolved to isolate every one of them from the community, the innocent as well as the guilty, the loyal as well as the traitorous.

In any case, his security men would never be able to work out exactly who had collaborated. Those who had fought for the Germans were of course guilty, but what of the others who had refused all temptations and remained as prisoners-of-war? Might not the Germans have left some of the traitors in the camps to spy on their fellow prisoners? Thousands might have been recruited. It would take dozens of years to consider each case and to 'clear' every former prisoner-of-war. Also, the mere fact that a man had fallen into captivity was taken as evidence of a lukewarm attitude to Soviet Russia. Why had he not fought to the death? Perhaps because he *wanted* to be taken prisoner. The security men could of course examine every case in detail, take evidence, conduct interrogations, hold trials. By skilled, pain-staking work they would be able to sort the sheep from the goats. But then, what if they made a mistake and allowed a foreign agent to slip through their fingers? Stalin and his men concluded that there was a simpler and more secure way of dealing with the problem—to imprison the lot.

The Ambassador's letter contained a second misunderstanding. While it was undoubtedly true that 'a large Russian element' was helping the German army in the West, it was quite impossible for the Soviet government to admit this fact. Any such admission would lower the Soviet Union in the estimation of her allies and would embarrass her communist government in the eyes of her population. After all, there were hardly any American or British troops fighting on the German side. Why then were there Russians? Why was it only in the camps for *Soviet* prisoners-of-war that the Germans had induced large numbers to turn traitor? The situation was a humiliating one for Stalin, and he was resolved to deal with it in the classic way of dictators, by pretending that it did not exist.

Molotov wrote back to Clark Kerr on May 31:

> According to information at the disposal of the Soviet authorities, the number of such persons in the German forces is very insignificant and a special appeal to them would not be of political interest. Under these circumstances the Soviet Government sees no particular reason to make the statement suggested in your letter either on behalf of J. V. Stalin or of the Soviet Government.[1]

The American and British armies, invading France on D-Day a week later (June 6), found nevertheless a number of Russians in German uniform which was far from insignificant. A British intelligence report dated June 17 noted that of enemy prisoners captured and brought to Britain nearly 10 per cent were Russian. Together with other non-Germans, they had been formed into special battalions under German officers and sent to strengthen existing units. The foreigners were not concentrated in any one area, but were scattered right down the western coast of Europe, from Holland to the Pyrenees. The German Command considered the foreign units to be unreliable and was frightened that they would rebel if they came together in any strength.

The Russians were more ready to surrender than the Germans. A British report notes that when the Allies began to bombard the beach the Russians 'just sat and waited for things to happen'. Under British or American interrogation they painted a consistent and tragic picture of how it was that they came to fight for their country's enemy. One unit captured only a few hours after the invasion possessed no motor transport or machine guns. Their only weapons were rifles and their only transport consisted of

twenty horses for each company. They were ready enough to
tell their sad story:

> After working on roads and fortifications for many months in
> Russia as prisoners of war they were sent in batches of 50 to 150
> men to France, where they continued the same type of work. They
> were never asked if they would like to join the German army, but
> simply given German uniforms and issued with rifles ... The
> Russians never considered themselves anything but prisoners.
> Speaking only Russian, they were entirely cut off from the outside
> world. On the other hand, when asked if they would like to go back
> to Russia, most of them were just indifferent or even said no. None
> of them seemed to have any political convictions. Most of them
> were too ignorant to possess any. Many seemed to feel however
> that after having served in the German army, even though forcibly
> conscripted, they would be treated as traitors by the Russians and
> probably shot.

The Russians in France were between the devil and the deep
blue sea. To save their lives they put on German uniform, but
by doing this they compromised themselves irrevocably with
their Soviet government and (though they did not realise this at
the time) with the Americans and British as well. The Nazi
Germans were quick to exploit the situation, assuring them that
if they fell into the hands of the Allies they would undoubtedly
be executed and that their only hope was to fight furiously on
the German side. They were also able to make propaganda out
of the situation, for the presence of Soviet citizens in their army
was evidence of disunity among the Allies. This was important
now, because realists among them knew that they were rapidly
losing the war and that their only hope was the collapse of the
Grand Alliance.

The western Allies realised the delicacy of the situation and,
while they were angry at having to fight against Soviet soldiers
and then feed them after they had surrendered, they were
anxious to do nothing that would offend the Soviet Union, which
was still bearing the brunt of the war on the eastern front. Large
numbers of prisoners were being ferried across the channel from
France and, since Britain did not have the facilities to hold them
all, many were being sent on by boat across the Atlantic to camps

in the United States and Canada. The Allies realised that the
Soviet government would object to its citizens being held in the
same camps with Germans and would probably want access to
these sheep who had gone astray.

They were ready to oblige Stalin in this and as early as June
24 Patrick Dean, a legal adviser to the Foreign Office, wrote of
the importance of keeping Soviet citizens in camps separate from
the ordinary German prisoners-of-war. He indicated that there
was no legal right to imprison such people in Britain. They were,
after all, citizens of an Allied country and unless they had
committed some specific crime they ought to be treated as
friendly. The Soviet Embassy and Military Mission would be
asked to help in administering the camps and in arranging for
the people to return to the Soviet Union as soon as shipping was
available. Meanwhile they would be able to work in Britain and
assist the war effort.

But those who had helped the Germans, either as workers or
as soldiers, were according to Dean in a different position. In
his view they 'may have committed offences under Soviet law,
e.g. treason, unless they can prove to the satisfaction of the Soviet
authorities that they were acting under such compulsion that no
punishable offence has been committed.'[2] What concerned Dean
was the reaction of Germany if the men were handed back to the
Soviet authorities and punished. After all, the men had been
captured in German uniform, and there were many lawyers who
held that it was the uniform which determined a soldier's allegi-
ance. Germany would have reason to complain through her
protecting power if she discovered that Britain and America
were handing members of her army over to almost certain execution. She might take vicious reprisals against British and American
prisoners-of-war.

The Foreign Office was careful to point out that, although
unwilling to hand over the Russians for the moment, it had no
intention of protecting them. It merely wanted to wait a little,
wrote Dean, and 'the effect of this would not be to deny the
Soviet authorities the right to try and punish their own nationals
in due course if they think fit, but merely to delay such steps
being taken until all fear of reprisals against British and United
States prisoners has been removed.' The Foreign Office's view
of the matter he set out in stark terms:

This is purely a question for the Soviet authorities and does not concern His Majesty's Government. In due course all those with whom the Soviet authorities desire to deal must be handed over to them, and we are not concerned with the fact that they may be shot or otherwise more harshly dealt with than they might be under English law.[3]

Thus was the basic thesis formed, only eighteen days after the Allied invasion of Normandy and the beginning of the problem, that the Soviet government had the right to deal with its citizens as it thought fit, and that the British or American governments had no right to deny their ally the chance to exact retribution. It was as yet too early to know what this policy might involve, what would happen if Russians refused to go home and demanded the asylum traditionally granted in Britain and America to the politically oppressed. Allied officials did not realise how many Soviet citizens would resist repatriation, many of them violently, some to the point of suicide.

On July 20, 1944, the British Foreign Secretary, Anthony Eden (now Lord Avon) wrote to the Soviet Ambassador in London to inform him that Soviet citizens had been captured in France and were arriving in Britain by the thousand. What was to be done with them? Eden continued:

The Soviet Government will no doubt wish to ascertain in detail the circumstances in which these Soviet nationals came to serve in enemy military or para-military formations and the conditions under which they are at present being detained. For this purpose His Majesty's Government are anxious to make arrangements whereby the Soviet authorities in the United Kingdom may be put in direct contact with these Soviet nationals.

He pointed out that all prisoners from France were being sent across the Atlantic to camps in America and advised the Ambassador to do his best to come to some swift agreement. Obviously, the farther away these Soviet citizens were sent, the longer it would be before they could be repatriated.

On July 17, the British War Cabinet accepted the principle that the prisoners would have to be handed over, if this was what the Soviet government wanted. They did not discuss the problem in detail or consider what would happen if large numbers refused

to go. But there the decision might have rested had not Lord
Selborne, then Minister for Economic Warfare, protested in strong
letters to Eden and to Winston Churchill. 'I am profoundly
moved by the decision of the Cabinet,' he wrote to Eden. His
letter to the Prime Minister began:

> I greatly regret the Cabinet's decision to send these people back to
> Russia. It will mean certain death for them. There are many
> thousands of Russians and a lesser number of Poles and Czechs
> serving in the German Army in France, and I believe that if the
> prospect of merciful treatment could be held out to them there is
> every chance of their joining the Maquis. A few have already done so.
>   My officers have interviewed 45 of these prisoners and in every
> case their story is substantially the same. After weeks of appalling
> maltreatment and such starvation that cannibalism was not un-
> common in their camps, their morale was pretty well broken. They
> were paraded and addressed by a German officer, who asked them
> to join a German labour unit. They were then asked individually
> whether they accepted the invitation. The first man replied no
> and was immediately shot. The others consequently said yes in
> order to save their lives. As soon as they were in the German labour
> unit they were given weapons and told that they were now in the
> German Army. None of them have any doubt that if they are sent
> back to Russia they will be shot and their families disgraced and
> maltreated.[4]

Eden's reaction to all this was immediate and crucial to the
decision which was about to be taken. On July 22 he scribbled on
Selborne's letter, 'It does not deal with the point, if these men do
not go back to Russia, where can they go? We don't want them
here.' Churchill's reaction was more sympathetic. He wrote to
Eden: 'I think we dealt rather summarily with this at Cabinet, and
the point put by the Minister for Economic Warfare should
certainly be reconsidered. Even if we are somewhat compromised
[with the Soviet Government], all the apparatus of delay may be
used. I think these men were tried beyond their strength.'
    Eden wrote back to Churchill on August 2. 'I have considered
this difficult question more than once recently,' he wrote. But he
had come to a firm conclusion, that it was vital to allow the original
decision to stand and to send all the Russians home, whether they

wanted to go or not and by force if necessary. Unlike Selborne and Churchill, who seemed to appreciate the sufferings which the Russians had endured and the pressures which had induced them to serve Nazi Germany, Eden expressed little sympathy towards them. 'They were captured while serving in German military or para-military formations, the behaviour of which in France has often been revolting,' he wrote. His conclusion was that 'we cannot afford to be sentimental about this.'

'We surely do not wish to be permanently saddled with a number of these men,' Eden continued. To refuse to return them would cause serious trouble with the Soviet government: 'We have no right whatever to do this and they would not understand our humanitarian motives. They would know that we are treating them differently from the other Allied governments on this question and this would arouse their gravest suspicions.' He felt that Britain would be in an indefensible position if she tried to dictate to the Soviet Union about the punishment of traitors and that 'it is no concern of ours what measures any Allied government, including the Soviet government, takes as regard their own nationals.'

Eden's final argument was a more compelling and valid one. There were, he pointed out, large numbers of British and American prisoners-of-war held in eastern Germany and Poland. The Red Army was advancing quickly towards these areas and it was probably they who would shortly overrun and release them. It was a situation which many people in the West found worrying. Eden wrote: 'It is most important that they should be well cared for and returned as soon as possible. For this we must rely to a great extent upon Soviet goodwill and if we make difficulty over returning to them their own nationals I am sure it will reflect adversely upon their willingness to help in restoring to us our own prisoners.'[5]

Churchill decided nevertheless to put the matter before the Cabinet again. Meanwhile, on August 23, the Foreign Office received a letter from the Soviet Ambassador, M. Gousev, confirming that his government did indeed want the prisoners and wanted the British to provide ships for their repatriation as soon as possible. This last request did not appeal to Britain, whose ships were then heavily committed, carrying men and material across the Atlantic and the Channel. Then the next day a further difficulty arose. Another senior minister, the Secretary of State for War, P. J. Grigg, was worried about the whole business. He wrote to Eden:

> We are in an obvious dilemma. If we do as the Russians want and hand over all these prisoners to them whether or not the prisoners are willing to go back to Russia, we are as Selborne's minute of July 25th suggests, sending some of them to their deaths. And though in war we cannot, as you point out, afford to be sentimental, I confess that I find the prospect rather revolting and I should expect public opinion to reflect the same feeling. There is also the danger that if we hand the men back there may be reprisals on our men in German hands. But I think that that risk is probably growing appreciably less, and that the Germans have problems enough to think about without keeping an eye on what happens to Russians whom they forced into the German armies.
>
> On the other hand, if we don't do what the Russians want there may be the danger that they may not be ready to co-operate in sending back speedily to us the British and other Allied prisoners who fall into their hands as they advance into Germany. Obviously our public opinion would bitterly and rightly resent any delay in getting our men home, or any infliction of unnecessary hardship on them, and if the choice is between hardship to our men and death to Russians our choice is plain. But I confess that I am not at all convinced that, whatever we do, the Russians will go out of their way to send our prisoners westwards at once or to deal with them in any special manner.
>
> In any case, the dilemma is so difficult that for my part I should like a Cabinet ruling as to its solution. If we hand the Russian prisoners back to their death it will be the military authorities who will do so on my instructions, and I am entitled to have behind me in this very unpleasant business the considered view of the Government.[6]

Anthony Eden was asked to prepare a Cabinet Paper and this was ready on September 3.[7] The number of Soviet prisoners in Britain was now 3,750, he wrote, and an urgent decision was required about their future. He recognised the force of Grigg's and Selborne's concern that 'if we do as the Soviet Government want and return all these prisoners to the Soviet Union, whether they are willing to return to the Soviet Union or not, we shall be sending some of them to their death.' But he had in no way modified his view that such an act was necessary.

Eden's paper mentioned the humanitarian aspect of the case only in passing. Many of the men had joined the German army only 'under great duress', he wrote, and it was possible that 'harsh measures would be taken against them back in Russia'. But he balanced this faint concern by repeating his statement that all the prisoners had been captured while serving in German formations, whose behaviour 'has often been revolting'.

Here Eden was not being quite accurate. Some of the captured Russians had served in no military formation of any sort. In particular, a growing number of Russian women was being brought to England, and they had done no more than work in cookhouses or as servants. And while it was true that the behaviour of *some* of the Russians had been revolting, it was equally true that other Russians behaved well and decently. Eden was trying to make the Russians collectively responsible, to make them pay the price for the brutalities of a few of their number, men who in any case operated under orders and threats. He was being unjust towards those Russians who had done nothing wrong.

Eden repeated his fear that 'we may be saddled with them [the prisoners] permanently, to our great embarrassment'. And it was true that they were already proving a thorough nuisance. They were consuming British food, which was scarce and rationed. British accommodation had been provided to house them and British soldiers to guard them. If large numbers stayed, then Britain would have to find some country to take them in as refugees after the war, or else give them asylum herself. It was true that this would cause great inconvenience and that it would be much simpler to hand them all over to Stalin.

It was true also that there were severe dangers if Britain were to refuse to meet Soviet wishes. The Soviet government was bound to take a suspicious view of any attempt to protect 'traitors' from Soviet justice. Ever since the Russian Civil War, when Britain more than any other country had supported anti-Bolshevik forces, the Soviet leaders had reserved a special brand of dislike for the 'English interventionists'. Only too easily would they suspect that Britain was planning to harbour enemies of the Soviet Union, to build up a nucleus of collaborators with fascism, anti-Soviet fanatics, who would one day be armed with British or American weapons and launched against the Motherland. Were any such idea to take root in their minds, the Grand Alliance would be under the most severe strain. As a first step, the Red Army might be ordered to halt its advances along the eastern front, and this at a time when the British and Americans needed constant pressure from their Allies to help them build up their bridgeheads in France and consolidate their invasion.

It was part of the atmosphere of the time, this reluctance to discriminate between the Soviet Union and the other Allies. It had become British and American policy to minimise or ignore altogether the unacceptable features of the Soviet government, its injustices and massive repressions. The discussions which followed the discovery of the Katyn Forest massacre in April 1943 had shown that in any such dispute the western Allies could be relied upon to take the Soviet side. It was not a matter of justice but of military reality. In the autumn of 1944, as in the spring of 1943, the Red Army was bearing the brunt of the war. It was unthinkable to offend the Soviet government by accusing it of inhumanity.

This was what led Eden to write that Britain had 'no legal or moral right' to interfere in how Stalin treated the men who had gone against him. He was asking the government to break the British tradition of affording political asylum to the oppressed and persecuted, to hand thousands of people over to punishment which, he freely acknowledged, would probably be a death sentence, and this without distinction between the innocent and the criminal. He must have known too, for he had many learned advisers, what sort of justice there was in Russia under Stalin, that there would be the merest travesty of a trial, after which the innocent as well as the guilty would be condemned either to death or to years of killing imprisonment. It was to meet precisely such situations that civilised countries conceived the idea of political asylum.

When asked about the affair in 1973 Eden replied that 'he really could not remember the details surrounding this matter.' He was unwilling either to answer questions or, when sent a copy of his Cabinet Paper, to comment upon it. But there can be no doubt that in 1944 he was the one who, in the face of Selborne's strong protest and Churchill's initial reluctance, pushed the policy of forcible repatriation through the British

Cabinet. On September 4, a War Cabinet of seven approved Eden's proposals 'after a short discussion'.

The decision came not a moment too soon for the people whose job it was to look after the prisoners. A few days earlier, 550 Russians captured in France in civilian clothes were sent to Butterwick camp in Yorkshire to join 2,400 Russians who had been taken in German uniform. These 550 had probably assisted the Germans in one way or another, but they had not joined the German army, and they were horrified at the idea of being lumped together with people who had. Only when they were issued with prisoner-of-war clothing did they realise the full implications— that these clothes might be the death of them.

They therefore took off their trousers. The astonished British guards were at first inclined to see this as a mark of general protest, an idle gesture. There was a shortage of interpreters and it was hard for Englishmen in Yorkshire to appreciate the nuances of the Soviet internal security system. But eventually the truth emerged and the Director of Prisoners-of-War was told that 'the strikers are afraid that, being in prisoner-of-war clothing, they will be confused with other prisoners whose loyalty to the Soviet may be in doubt.'

On August 30 they wrote a letter to the Commandant, 'demanding' the return of their civilian clothes and vowing never again to put on their 'insulting' uniforms: 'If our lawful demands are not complied with before September 1st of this year we will consider ourselves justified in protecting ourselves from the cold by any means we deem fit.'[8] The Commandant, amazed by such an attitude, ordered them on September 1 to parade and to dress themselves. Only 100 of the 550 obeyed the order. He then awarded the remaining 450 a collective sentence of 28 days' detention. The compound was declared a detention barracks, their tents were struck and they were all put on a bread-and-water diet.

That night it rained heavily and the next day, when the local Commander-in-Chief wrote to the War Office, it was still raining. In spite of the weather, said the General, the Russian prisoners showed no sign of giving in. He was worried because he saw no solution to the situation. The camp had only a skeleton guard. Men were scarce and he would not be able to deal with massive outbreaks of unrest. The strikers wanted someone from the

Soviet Embassy to visit them, and they would regard no reply as satisfactory unless it came from this source. He went on: 'The prisoners are being and will continue to be given as rigorous treatment as is practicable. They have however become so enured to hard treatment in concentration camps on the Continent that it is considered very doubtful whether they will weaken.'

It would take more than bread and water or a few nights in the rain to make an impression on these men. Not only had they endured years of harsh treatment under the Nazis, but they were also terrified of what would happen to them in Russia when they had to account for whatever acts of collaboration they might have committed. Any punishment the British might impose would be a pin-prick in comparison with this. But from the British point of view the situation was a wretched one. Only two months after the invasion of Normandy they had more important things to bother about than the Soviet Union's internal problems. The Russian prisoners were consuming precious manpower as well as the time of busy men, generals and government ministers.

The prisoners were also a possible source of Anglo-Soviet discord, and this danger grew when some of the strikers began to suffer from exposure. Viscount Bridgeman, the Deputy Adjutant-General, wrote on September 3, 'They are still without tents and there is the risk of further serious illness.' His conclusion came close to panic: 'I do not think we can go on much longer without someone visiting these men.' From the army's point of view this was the obvious solution. The problem and the prisoners must be handed over to the Soviet Union. This was where it and they belonged. The prisoners wanted to see someone from the Embassy. The Embassy was clamouring for access to the prisoners. All that was holding up this most desirable meeting was the Cabinet's decision on the political issue. When the decision came, the day after Bridgeman's note, that all prisoners were to be sent home whether they wanted to go or not, deep sighs of relief were breathed by the senior officers of Northern Command.

The problem was that there were strikers of a different sort. At a camp near Cooden in Sussex, 42 prisoners rebelled for reasons exactly opposite to those of the men at Butterwick. They were strongly anti-Soviet and wanted to be taken under the protection of the British government. George Youmatoff, a Canadian officer of Russian origin then attached to the British

War Office, was sent to interview them. They told him, 'Whether we live or die does not matter, but at least we shall do so together and unpolluted by the rest of the camp.' They had isolated themselves from the loyal Soviet prisoners and announced that any Soviet official who came near them did so at his peril.

The 42 told Youmatoff that they had joined the German army as a group to fight the communists, but that as soon as they were transferred to the western front they gave themselves up. Their quarrel was with the present regime in Russia, not with the British or the Americans. Youmatoff advised them to restrain their tongues. Such remarks 'would only put additional black marks against their names'. But they continued in the same vein: 'They were perfectly willing to work for us or do anything, but they did not recognise the Soviet authorities, and when such authorities approach them they do so at their own risk. They declared that as they had spent their lives fighting the communist "beast", they would gladly die for the chance of sending some of them to their graves.'[9]

When this note was communicated to the Soviet desk at the Foreign Office, the reaction was one of alarm. Christopher Warner, later British Ambassador in Brussels, pointed out that the strikers had voluntarily joined the enemy to fight against Britain's ally, and there was no proof of their having given themselves up without trouble in the West. (By the same token, of course, there was no proof that they had done otherwise.) Warner advised that the men's appeal to be allowed to stay in Britain must of course be rejected. They were Soviet nationals and would therefore be sent back to the Soviet Union whether they wanted to go or not. What their fate would be in Russia might be guessed at, but it was none of Britain's business. The Foreign Office's official letter to the War Office on this matter, signed by John Galsworthy, contained the following harsh sentence: 'They seem to us to deserve no sympathy, and we think our principal aim where they are concerned should be to ensure that they cause no trouble between us and the Soviet authorities over here.'

One might have thought that the Soviet government would be glad at being granted such a concession, such an important departure from tradition, but it was not to be. On September 11, the Soviet Ambassador, Gousev, called to see Eden, and the two men had what Eden described as 'a somewhat acrimonious wrangle'. Gousev had received a letter of protest from a group of Russian prisoners:

> Here we have been interned in a prisoner-of-war camp together with Germans, 'Russian Liberation Army' men and other bitter enemies and traitors. Our civilian clothing has been forcibly taken from us and we have been dressed in degrading uniforms bearing a diamond-shaped patch on the back and trousers. We are treated worse than the Germans and kept under a strong guard as criminals. Our position has become much worse. The food is bad, we are not given any tobacco. We are not listened to, are not told any war news. We beg you, Comrade Ambassador, to clarify our position and to take steps to expedite our departure to our country, the Soviet Union.[10]

Major A. G. Burrows, Camp Commandant of Butterwick, wrote, 'The agitation for return to Russia may be due more from fear of what might happen to them if they do not by agitation proclaim their position.' This was probably correct, although there were doubtless many among the prisoners who genuinely wanted to go home and were totally loyal to the Soviet Union. What the Ambassador would not admit was that there were also many prisoners who felt they owed their country's government no loyalty at all and who were resolved never to set foot on Soviet soil again, except as members of an invading army.

Eden was therefore not inclined to sympathise with Gousev's demands that Britain no longer treat captured Russians as prisoners-of-war. He told him, 'These Russians and indeed other foreigners that had been captured fighting in the ranks of the German army against our troops had created considerable problems for us ... The least the Soviet government could do would be to help us in handling this problem and not to bring complaints that we were not treating the men well.'[11]

Gousev replied—a complaint which was to recur many times in future months—that the Russians in British camps were being subjected to anti-Soviet propaganda. If there was any unrest among the prisoners, it was because the British were allowing it to be fomented. Some of the Russians 'seemed terrified as a result of the things that had been said to them.' Eden writes:

I managed not to retort that they were probably more terrified as to what awaited them in Russia, but I did say that our sole desire was to return these men to the Soviet Government as soon as possible. It was not our fault that they had been found fighting in the ranks of our enemies and no reproaches could or should be levelled against us. Our parting was distinctly cold.

But at least the problem was now a joint one, and it was with relief that the British army arranged visits to the Russian camps for senior officers of the Red Army then attached to the London Embassy. At Kempton Park Camp in Surrey the prisoners were addressed by Colonel Gorsky in terms that the British found entirely agreeable: 'Whilst you are in England you must of course do as the English authorities tell you to do. You are on their soil, you must be thankful to them for your liberation from German hands.' He gave them a summary of the war situation which was generally optimistic and paid due regard to the American and British achievements in the West. They would soon be issued with new brown suits, without the objectionable 'ace of diamonds' markings carried by prisoners-of-war. 'You are now considered by us as true Soviet citizens, regardless of the fact that you were forced to join the German Army,' he told them. He was at pains to hide from them the terrible fate that awaited them in Russia. If he could reassure them, they would be more likely to go home without trouble.

The visit of General Vasiliev, a military attaché at the Soviet Union's London Embassy, to camps in Yorkshire did not go so smoothly. At Butterwick he had an angry exchange of words with a group of former Red Army soldiers whom he was trying to pacify. 'There is enough room in the Soviet Fatherland for everyone,' he said, to which a prisoner replied, 'We know what sort of room there will be for us.' The General told them not to worry because they had been forced to bear arms for the Germans: 'The Soviets never treat people in bulk. We shall find out who among you are guilty and who not. And these German uniforms you are wearing—we shall throw them in the incinerator.' A prisoner retorted, 'Yes, we know, and us inside them too.'[12]

The General also spoke much of Anglo-Soviet friendship, perhaps to make it clear to the prisoners that it was no good trying to woo the British and that they could expect no asylum. The friendly relations between British and Soviet officers seems to have made itself apparent, since some of the prisoners who, on the first day of the visit, behaved defiantly towards the General, refusing to salute him and sporting their anti-Soviet 'Russian Liberation Army' badges, had by the second day taken off the badges and were duly respectful.

At Stadium Camp near Catterick the commandant, Lieutenant-Colonel Harbord, took Vasiliev to the recreation room and proudly showed him a mass of Russian-language literature. He was puzzled by the General's shout of anguish and distressed when told that the books were all virulently anti-Soviet, having been sent from London for the prisoners' benefit by a Russian émigré priest. They were removed at once. Humble apologies were offered and the General agreed not to mention the matter in his report.

But by and large the visits were a success. The prisoners were made aware that they would not gain by continued protests. Many had decided that their best course lay in declaring their loyalty to the Soviet Union. Vasiliev had given them promises, and these might not be entirely empty, since the country needed able-bodied men for post-war reconstruction. Vasiliev also told them that by good behaviour in England they could earn their passage home and their freedom. Many prisoners were optimistic enough to believe him, which from the British point of view was good because it meant that they ceased their rebellion and became obedient. But despair grew among those prisoners who knew what fate awaited them and were determined not to go home.

Czeslaw Jesman, a British officer of Polish origin, who was an interpreter in one of the camps, reported that after the visits 'more soldiers than usual told me that they would commit suicide if returned to Russia.' Until then the men had maintained a certain solidarity in the face of the British, whose habits and language few of them in any way understood. But after the visits they became suspicious and began to divide up into groups. They realised that there were only two ways by which they could save themselves, by showing such loyalty to the Soviet Union that they would be forgiven or by showing such hatred of the Soviet Union that the British would take pity on them and not force them to go.

In September General Vasiliev told General E. C. Gepp, the Director of Prisoners-of-War, that he wanted the British to treat all Soviet citizens as Allied nationals. This was on the face of it strange, since many of them had been captured in enemy uniform, but Vasiliev's request was well received, for it would relieve Britain of the embarrassment of having to sort the prisoners out and both sides of the embarrassing admission that thousands of Russians had fought for Germany. On September 18 Gepp told a meeting that there were 12,000 Soviet citizens in Britain and that they were arriving at a rate of 2,000 a week. Vasiliev wanted them all to be held in special camps under their own officers and undertook to supply such officers, since the ones the British had captured would hardly be suitable.

At the same meeting it was agreed that an order would be made under the Allied Forces Act of 1940 to enable Soviet officers to administer these camps and hold the men under Soviet military discipline. They would be asked not to execute the death sentence without consultation with the British authorities, but 'no consultation was required in relation to other punishments, provided the Russian military code was applied.' The British would supply the Soviet officers with detention facilities. Similar arrangements were in force for the administration of Polish, American, Czech and French forces in the United Kingdom. The Russians could thus be discharged from prisoner-of-war status, but still kept in suitable conditions of confinement.

The problem about this seemingly excellent arrangement was that the Allied Forces Act would catch in its net only those Soviet citizens who had once been members of the Soviet army. But what about the others, the women and the young men who had been conscripted by the Germans and put into uniform without ever having served in the Soviet forces? Legally, there was no way of holding them except as prisoners-of-war. But to do this was unacceptable to the Soviet Union. It was therefore decided to hold all the Russians brought from France under this Act, even the people who had never been Soviet soldiers. Officials realised that this was illegal, but there seemed to be no other way.

British officials were still anxious to obtain some more formal agreement on the matter. 'The status of Soviet nationals in this country is rapidly becoming a serious bone of contention,' one such memorandum reads.[13] It was estimated that two-thirds of the British and Commonwealth prisoners-of-war held in Germany were in camps which would be liberated by the Red Army. Britain was worried by the situation, by the dangers it posed to her own prisoners in Russian hands, as well as by the trouble the Russians seemed likely to cause in Britain if they were not quickly removed.

On September 25, Eden received a letter from M. Gousev claiming that 'the attitude of some Allied authorities towards liberated Soviet citizens involves a whole range of irregularities.' Gousev listed a number of complaints: that Soviet citizens were being treated as prisoners-of-war, that their accommodation was unsatisfactory, that they were being sent in large numbers to America without Soviet permission, that propaganda hostile to the Soviet Union was being conducted in the camps and attempts made to enlist prisoners in foreign armies. All this, wrote Gousev, was 'neither in accordance with the principles of international law nor all the more with the spirit of the Allied agreements.' He expressed his 'expectation' that instructions would be issued to the British forces 'to prevent such things taking place in future'. It was, as Eden rightly remarked, a 'rude note', and especially upsetting in the context of the 'acrimonious wrangle' he had had with Gousev only two weeks earlier.

The rudeness was in marked contrast to the friendly tone of a telegram from Stalin to Churchill, dated September 30, which warmly welcomed Churchill's and Eden's plan to visit Moscow in October. The two British leaders reached Moscow on October 9 and at ten o'clock that same evening they were received by Molotov and Stalin in the Kremlin. It was the famous meeting when Churchill scribbled on a piece of paper the 'percentages of influence' to be enjoyed by Russia and the West in various Balkan countries—90/10 in Britain's favour in Greece, 90/10 in Russia's favour in Rumania, 75/25 in Russia's favour in Bulgaria. Stalin just ticked the paper with a blue pencil and handed it back to Churchill. 'It was all settled in no more time than it takes to set down,' Churchill writes in his memoirs. On October 11 he reported to President Roosevelt, 'We have found an extraordinary atmosphere of good will here.' Stalin had accepted an invitation to dine at the British Embassy that very evening, to the delight of British officials. The nagging problem of the Soviet prisoners and the rudeness of M. Gousev seemed petty and remote.

Eden decided nevertheless to raise the matter. On October 12 he telegraphed from Moscow:

> At dinner last night my conversation with Marshal Stalin turned for a moment on the Russian troops whom we had in England. The Marshal said he would be extremely grateful if any arrangements could be made to get them back here. I said we should be glad to do anything we could to help and that I knew that though shipping difficulties were very considerable we were now re-examining the possibility ... The Marshal repeated that he would be deeply in our debt if we could arrange the matter for him about this. I replied that he could be sure that we would do all we could to help, and I felt sure that in return his Government would give all the help in their power in respect of British prisoners in Germany as and when the Red Army reached the German prison camps in which they were located. The Marshal said at once that certainly this would be done. He would make this his personal charge and he gave me his personal word that every care and attention would be given to our men.

Eden was strangely impressed by this brief, unofficial conversation. He was now all the more convinced that there was no need to 'buy' the British prisoners or to 'swap' them for the Russians in Britain. Nor was there any need now to reply to Gousev's rude note. One gathers from the tone of Eden's telegram that in his opinion the matter was now settled and the controversy resolved. It would be enough in future dealings with Soviet officials on the issue to 'remind' them of what Stalin had said to Eden at dinner. It did not occur to Eden that Stalin might be trying to deceive him, that he might have given less helpful instructions to his subordinates. He considered that 'in view of Marshal Stalin's satisfactory assurance' the matter could safely be left. As Harold Nicolson noted in his diary two months later, 'He [Eden] has a real liking for Stalin.' He told Nicolson over a drink, 'Stalin has never broken his word once given.'[14] This belief in the Soviet dictator's honesty was to lead Eden and other Allied leaders into error many times in the next few months.

On October 17, Eden again discussed the matter, this time with Molotov, who raised it in more direct terms. For the first time reference was made to the possibility that Britain might be called upon to repatriate prisoners by force. Eden writes:

Mr Molotov said that the Soviet Government particularly wished to learn as a matter of principle, on which they had so far received no indication of our views, whether His Majesty's Government agreed that all Soviet citizens without exception should be returned to the USSR as soon as possible. He insisted that the problem was not merely one of shipping (earlier in the talk he had expressed gratitude at my assurance that it would prove possible to repatriate 11,000 persons in the immediate future) but of His Majesty's Government consenting to the repatriation to the USSR of *all* Soviet citizens, without reference to the wishes of the individuals concerned, who in some cases might not wish to return because they had collaborated with the Germans. The Soviet Government demanded this as their right.[15]

Eden told Molotov that he agreed with him and that Britain 'merely wanted these men, within the limitations of British law, to be placed under Soviet administration and discipline until they could be repatriated.' Molotov was satisfied by this, although only, he emphasised again, 'on the understanding that the Soviet government were permitted to demand the return of all their citizens.' He then mentioned one or two of the old Soviet complaints, but politely, not in the hectoring language of Gousev's note. Eden told him he would look into these complaints, assuring him again that 'it was our wish that the Soviet authorities should exercise control over administration and discipline of their nationals, subject to the overriding requirements of British law.'

The matter was then passed to junior officials for implementation. Neither Churchill nor Eden had pointed out the basic imbalance in the understanding, which was that Britain was requesting merely the safe return of her men who had fallen into enemy hands in combat and who wished to come home, where they would of course be received with honour, whereas many of the Soviet prisoners were unwilling to go home, fearing rightly that they would be humiliated and ill-treated for the 'crime' of having been taken prisoner. But this most embarrassing fact, that large numbers of Soviet citizens wanted to stay in the West, whether because they had fought for the Germans or simply because they disliked the Soviet government, was glossed over in all high-level British-Soviet discussions on the prisoner-of-war issue.

Arrangements went ahead towards fulfilling the agreement and, as Eden had indicated to Molotov, some 10,000 prisoners left British ports on October 31 for Murmansk in northern Russia. This was the shortest sea route between Britain and the Soviet Union, involving a total of three or four weeks of travel, but it was not a popular run because of the danger of air attack from German bases in Norway. This first batch consisted of men who had no violent objection to returning, their fear of punishment not yet being acute enough to drive them to acts of desperation. Many of them believed the assurances which Soviet officers had given them in Britain that no harm would befall them. Only twelve showed any resistance and it was a simple matter to put them on board by force.

On November 7, Major S. J. Cregeen, a British officer stationed in Murmansk, saw the prisoners just after they had been disembarked from their ship, the 'Scythia'. He noticed that they were all dressed in British battledress and that most carried small parcels of personal belongings. But there was no welcoming reception for them and no 'comforts' were provided. Instead, they were formed into ranks and marched under armed guard to a camp outside town. An American diplomat called Melby also reported the scene, that the prisoners 'were first welcomed at the docks with a brass band and then marched off under heavy guard to an unknown destination.'[16] Cregeen was puzzled by the need for such a strict escort, one soldier for every ten or fifteen prisoners. True, some had been captured in German uniform, but others had remained loyal to the Soviet Union throughout the war in the face of great hardship. For them a hero's welcome would have been more appropriate than an armed guard.

But members of the Foreign Office in London saw nothing strange in Cregeen's report. Geoffrey Wilson pointed out that the lack of welcome was quite usual in Russia. 'Nor is the armed guard in the least surprising,' he added.[17] He presumably did not know that the march to the nearby camp and the subsequent checking process were mere preludes to the years of forced labour which all those repatriated were about to endure, those who had stayed loyal as well as those who had helped the Germans, in camps where intense cold and hunger made life an unending horror and survival an achievement to which only the most physically fit and mentally astute were able to aspire.

Until the end of 1944, the problem was mainly a British one because it was to Britain that the Russian prisoners were taken after capture or liberation. But the Americans had their own camps, where they kept their own prisoners, and within four months of D-Day they had collected 28,000 Russians in German uniform. Some of these they kept in Britain or France, others they shipped to America. The Soviet authorities were especially angry to find that some of their citizens were being sent across the Atlantic, and this was one of the complaints listed in a letter which the Soviet Ambassador in Washington, Andrei Gromyko, sent to the Secretary of State, Edward Stettinius, on September 23, a similar letter to the 'rude note' which Gousev had sent Eden.

The Americans had an early indication that the problem was going to be a difficult one. General Eisenhower had asked his Soviet liaison officers to advise him on what should be done about Soviet citizens caught in German uniform. Their reply was 'that the question would not arise, since there were no Russians so serving.' It was a ludicrous statement, but not one which required any immediate action, and for several months America just held the prisoners and treated them like Germans.

Britain kept the United States informed about their talks on the subject with Stalin and Molotov in Moscow, but apparently said nothing about the earlier dispute in Cabinet and the decision to repatriate Soviet citizens by force. In October, Bernard Gufler, the State Department official assigned to the matter, wrote of 'the new policy towards Soviet nationals', indicating that the United States would follow the British lead. 'The adoption of this new policy towards the Soviets will result in the delivery to the Soviet authorities of persons hitherto withheld from them because they were unwilling to return to the Soviet Union,'[18] noted Gufler.

On November 2, Admiral Leahy, Roosevelt's Chief of Staff, wrote to Stettinius: 'Since the British War Office with Foreign Office concurrence has agreed that all captured Soviet citizens should be returned to the Soviet authorities without exception . . . it is not advisable for the United States Government to proceed otherwise vis-à-vis the Soviet Government with respect to persons in this category.'[19] On December 20, Stettinius telegraphed: 'The policy adopted by the United States in this connection is that all claimants to Soviet nationality will be released to the

Soviet Government irrespective of whether they wish to be so released.'[20]

On the surface British and American policy was the same, but in fact there was an important difference, which any lawyer would have spotted by the continual reference in American papers to 'claimants to Soviet nationality'. This emerged in correspondence between General B. M. Bryan, the Assistant Provost Master General, and Major J. S. Thorp, of the British army staff in Washington.[21] Thorp advised Bryan, who was acting for the American War Department, that the British 'have been governed by the fact that Russia is our ally and that as these are the ally's nationals they should be allowed to deal with them as they wish.' Thorp referred to the recent meeting in London between Gepp and Vasiliev, quoting Vasiliev's statement: 'The USSR wished to repatriate all Soviet citizens regardless of what they had or had not done . . . All would be returned to the Soviet Union without exception.'

There was an obvious conflict between the two terms 'all Soviet citizens' and 'claimants to Soviet nationality'. The difference was that the Americans accepted as German citizens any soldier whom they captured in German uniform unless he claimed to belong to some other country. This was their interpretation of the Geneva Convention. Men who were obviously Russians were asked their nationality. If they said it was the Soviet Union they were moved to one of three special camps at Fort Dix (New Jersey), Winchester (Virginia) or Rupert (Idaho). It was thus accepted at an early stage by the State Department, though not yet by the War Department, that such 'claimants to Soviet citizenship' would be transferred to the Soviet Union, whether they wanted to go or not.

But if a Soviet citizen captured in German uniform maintained that he was a German, the Americans treated him as such and gave him the protection of the Geneva Convention. It had always been American policy, they pointed out to the British, who did not share this view, not to look further than the uniform in determining a prisoner's nationality. But officers in the camps found it strange to be asked to treat as Germans men who had clearly come from the Soviet Union and did not speak the German language. They put the matter to General Bryan, but on December 21 he ordered them: 'Ask them first, do they claim Russian citizenship? If they claim Russian citizenship then they have to go back. If they do not claim Russian citizenship, they do not go back . . . In other words, if a fellow is smart he will say, "No, I'm a German." He's a German then.'

The reason for this strange policy was that there were many non-citizens fighting in the American forces and some of these had fallen into German hands. The United States wanted all of these to be protected as prisoners-of-war, the aliens as well as the Americans. She was frightened at the idea of repatriating by force men taken in German uniform who claimed to be Germans. If she did this, it was thought, Germany might take sanctions against non-Americans taken in American uniform. But the British saw this line as illogical and unworkable, pointing out in an official letter to Washington: 'If this view were accepted, all traitors could evade responsibility and could claim to be treated as prisoners-of-war merely by putting on enemy uniform and fighting actively against their own country.'[22]

On November 8, Stettinius replied to Gromyko's note. He could not yet say, he wrote, how many of the American-held prisoners were 'claimants to Soviet citizenship'. There were after all 300,000 prisoners of war in American hands and it had not yet been possible to sort them all out. But as soon as this was done they would be turned over to the Soviet authorities at a West-coast port for shipment to Russia. Meanwhile they would be employed on the land and paid 80 cents per day. The problem of the Soviet citizens who did not 'claim' such citizenship was at this stage avoided.

The State Department and Bryan's section of the War Department agreed that, while firearms must not be used to control this group, 'the necessary restraint should be employed to prevent escapes and the necessary force employed to ensure the delivery of these individuals to the Soviet authorities.' They should be isolated from the other 1,000 prisoners at Camp Rupert and special guards sent to deal with them. A week later attempts were made to clear the camp and send the inmates back to Russia. E. Tomlin Bailey, of the Special War Problems Division, reported: 'Among the 1,100 men sent to the ship about 70 did not want to go. These 70 men had however previously claimed Soviet nationality, obviously in ignorance of the consequences. Three of them attempted suicide, one by hanging, one by stabbing himself, and one by hitting his head against a beam in one of the barracks. In the end the three men have departed for the port.'[23] On December 29 1,179 Russians, including these three, left San Francisco for home on the ss 'Ural'.

Secretary of War Henry Stimson expressed his misgivings about the policy in a hand-written memorandum: 'I think we are unnecessarily running into danger by turning over German prisoners of Russian origin to the Russians. First thing you know, we will be responsible for a big killing by the Russians. This will ensure that no more such prisoners surrender to us. Let the Russians catch their own Russians.' Stimson's worries were increased by a letter he received on January 5, 1945, from Robert H. Jackson, the Attorney-General. Jackson wrote that he had heard of the forced repatriations and was disturbed:

> The individuals involved are being removed from the United States without fulfilling the requirements of either the deportation provisions of the immigration laws or the provisions of extradition treaties. I gravely question the legal basis or authority for surrendering the objecting individuals to representatives of the Soviet Government. The question might also arise whether this Government's obligations under the Geneva Prisoners-of-War Convention are fulfilled by transfer of these individuals to a co-belligerent which is not bound by that convention.

Stimson forwarded this letter to the State Department. He wrote that he was inclined to think that the Attorney-General was right: 'Before we deliver any to the Soviets, I think we should be sure that we are not delivering them to execution or punishment.' Surprisingly, both he and Jackson, two members of Roosevelt's cabinet, were unaware of the agreements on the matter already concluded by the British and acceded to by the United States. Stimson was informed only as a result of his January 5 letter that 'claimants to Soviet citizenship' were being repatriated by force and that a letter agreeing to do this had been sent to the Soviet Ambassador on November 8.

Stimson could therefore do little more than pass this information on to Jackson. On January 11, he wrote to him of the situation and explaining the Soviet insistence that Soviet prisoners be treated on a similar basis to Americans liberated by the Red Army in Europe. The illogicality of treating the two groups in the same way had been pointed out to the Russians, Stimson wrote, but they had shown no sign of changing their attitude. And at the back of this Soviet attitude lay a concealed threat: 'To refuse to return those claiming Soviet citizenship to the Soviet Government, even against their express desires, might result in the retention of our released prisoners-of-war in Russian custody.' The State Department had assured him, Stimson concluded, that before this agreement was made, 'all questions of applicable international law were thoroughly considered as well as the practicalities involved.'

Although in theory America was pledged to return by force only those Russians who, in their ignorance, claimed Soviet citizenship, it was soon apparent that this policy would not satisfy the Soviet Union and that it would have to be broadened to coincide with the British line, which covered all Soviet citizens without exception. On November 11, George Kennan, the American *chargé d'affaires* in Moscow, reported that demands seemed to be growing in the Soviet press and among officials for immediate and total repatriation. There seemed to be a fear, he wrote, that such prisoners would become a source of trouble if they were not brought home at once and that, more importantly, 'prestige of Soviet Union will suffer if it becomes generally known that some Soviet citizens are not accepting with enthusiasm offers of repatriation.'[24] On January 10, 1945, the United States Ambassador, Averill Harriman, reported from Moscow: 'Extreme touchiness was shown over reported reluctance of many of these people to return and over alleged encouragement being given to such sentiments by foreign authorities.'[25] Harriman knew that the Soviet press was full of stories of Soviet citizens abroad pining for home, and of their delight and happiness when finally they set foot on their native soil. But he knew too from reports of the arrival of the British ship in Murmansk early in November that this was a distortion. Such articles, Harriman wrote, 'apparently reflected the desire to disarm the suspicions of those still abroad.'

It seemed nevertheless to the American authorities, as it had to the British, that there was no way out and that a formal agreement would have to be concluded giving the Russians what they wanted. The matter had become one of Soviet *amour propre*. It was impossible for the Kremlin leaders to admit that millions of their people had voluntarily deserted from the Red Army and fought for the Germans. To admit this would be to admit failure on a grand scale, and there was no more chance of this than there was of Stalin's resignation from power. Molotov had told Eden categorically just before D-Day that the number of Russians fighting on the enemy side was 'very insignificant'. Eden wrote on the letter a few days later in the Foreign Office, 'I don't think it is.' But even at that early stage in the affair he felt obliged to add, 'I should have thought it pretty useless to return to the charge. The Soviet government will never admit the truth of this.'[26]

The British and American governments therefore found themselves, not for the first time in the war, obliged to accept as the truth something which the Soviet authorities had told them and which was false, and which all three sides knew to be false. Yet again the realities of world politics and military might triumphed over the need to tell the truth rather than to lie. Britain had been at war for more than five years. The turn of the years 1944-45 saw victory in sight, but by no means yet within the Allies' grasp. After the successes which followed D-Day, there were optimists in Britain and America who thought the war would be over by Christmas, but this had not happened. Disappointment was widespread, and there was a lurking fear lest some devilish miracle save Hitler from defeat.

On December 16, the worries of the western Allies were sharpened by Rundstedt's famous offensive in the Ardennes, the 'Battle of the Bulge'. For a month the Americans and British were actually forced into retreat along a wide sector of the front in southern Belgium. By the end of January the attack had been beaten off and the Germans were back behind their frontier, but the whole episode shocked the West, making people realise that the Nazi beast, though cornered and out-matched, was still very dangerous and not to be under-estimated as a source of violence and death.

By contrast, the month of January was for the Red Army one of triumphal progress through Poland and pre-war eastern Germany. After finally forcing the Vistula and capturing Warsaw on January 17, the Russians poured across the indefensible Polish plain, north to the Baltic and west towards the river Oder. By the end of the month they controlled all Poland and all East Prussia, apart from the fortress of Königsberg, and were well on their way towards forcing the Oder. Never were the courage and achievement of the Red Army described more glowingly in the western press, and on this occasion the contrast between progress in the East and setback in the West was clear for all to see. American and British admiration for Russia's fighting men was a genuine, valid emotion which could only too easily lead people towards admiration for the Soviet government and Stalin. Surely the men who led such a noble force must be admirable too? True, anti-communists and émigrés had levelled serious charges against them, accusing them of the most bestial cruelty. But surely these charges must be untrue, or at least exaggerated? And as for these wretched prisoners, it was not suggested that Stalin would punish them *en masse*, by the million? Such an idea seemed absurd.

THE FIRST UNPLEASANTNESS

THE THREE great powers, having agreed to exchange prisoners through a succession of letters and private conversations, now resolved to formalise the matter in a written agreement, and the obvious time for this was during the Conference at Yalta in the Crimea, which began on February 5. That same day Eden wrote to Stettinius, his American opposite number: 'The Soviet forces are overrunning the sites of British and United States prisoner-of-war camps very fast and we know that a number of British prisoners-of-war (though not exactly how many) are in Soviet hands, and no doubt some United States prisoners-of-war also.'[1] There were nine camps holding British prisoners-of-war which, Eden thought, would now be overrun by the Red Army. These held an estimated 50,000 prisoners. Churchill put this point to Stalin in a private talk on February 9. They agreed to put discussions underway among experts from the three countries and to seek a text which all could sign.

The first problem was to decide the scope of the agreement. Would the Americans be able to maintain their policy of repatriating only 'claimants to Soviet citizenship'? Eden was advised by the Foreign Office: 'We fear that such an amendment would inevitably lead to prolonged discussions with the Soviet Government and that all chance of early conclusion of agreement would disappear.'[2] The Americans then accepted the British formula and the proposal to include in the agreement displaced civilians as well as prisoners-of-war. Once this hurdle was over the discussion went quite well. Eddie Page and John Deane for the Americans, Patrick Dean and Henry Phillimore for the British, and Kiril Novikov for the Soviet Union spent many hours discussing such details as the standard of food to be provided for liberated Allies and the rates of pay they would receive while working for their liberators. It was assumed that Russians would be put to work in

Britain and the United States, but there was great difficulty when it came to accepting the logical consequence of this—that British and American prisoners could be forced to work for the Russians. Still, this was smoothed over, and the most controversial aspect of the agreement, the undertaking to send large numbers of Russians home by force, was hardly discussed.

On February 10, the matter came up in a talk between Stalin and Churchill at the Yusupov Villa, the only other people present being Molotov, Eden and the two interpreters, Pavlov and Birse. The record reads:

> The Prime Minister spoke of the embarrassment caused by the large number of Russian prisoners in the West. We had about 100,000 of them. 11,000 had already been transported home, and 7,000 more would leave this month. He wanted to know the Marshal's wishes about the rest. Marshal Stalin hoped they could be sent to Russia as quickly as possible . . . those who had agreed to fight for the Germans could be dealt with on their return to Russia.[3]

One must assume that Churchill and Eden knew full well what Stalin meant when he said he would 'deal with' these people, but they had already committed themselves to giving them to him and at this stage they did not argue. The next day, two bilateral agreements were signed, the British one by Eden and Molotov, the American one by Major-General John Deane, military attaché at the United States Embassy in Moscow, and Soviet Lieutenant-General Gryzlov. The two agreements were, apart from a few details, similar. The British text began:

> All Soviet citizens liberated by Allied armies will, without delay after their liberation, be separated from German prisoners-of-war and shall be maintained separately from them . . . These Soviet citizens will be concentrated in definite places and camps to which Soviet repatriation representatives will immediately be admitted . . . For purposes of internal administration and discipline these Soviet citizens shall be organised into formations and groups which shall be subject to Soviet laws . . . Liberated Soviet citizens may, until their repatriation, be employed in the management, maintenance and administration of the camps or billets in which they are situated . . .[4]

The last paragraph of the agreement was the one which was to cause the greatest trouble:

> The competent British authorities will co-operate with the corresponding Soviet authorities in the United Kingdom in identifying as such liberated Soviet citizens who may reach the United Kingdom. They will provide such liberated Soviet citizens with transport until they are handed to Soviet authorities in places reached by agreement between the competent Soviet and British authorities. The competent British authorities will give such assistance as is practicable, having regard to the available resources, in providing means of transport for the early conveyance of these Soviet citizens to the Soviet Union.

There was nothing in either text specifically indicating that Soviet citizens were to be repatriated irrespective of their own wishes and by force if necessary, but this was taken to be the legal meaning of the agreement, especially in the light of the October meeting in Moscow and other previous undertakings. Still, in spite of the 'toning down' of the text's more unsavoury implications, all three parties thought it wiser to keep it secret. Stalin said that 'this matter had formed no part of the Conference and he thought that it should not be included in their report.'[5] The White House revealed that there was an agreement, but made it seem to be about prisoners' welfare, nothing more.[6] In London, the Foreign Office was asked whether the agreement should be publicised and registered with the United Nations, like all the others, an innocent question to which a junior official, Thomas Brimelow, minuted on February 19, 'STRONG objection. This agreement must remain secret.'[7]

Recent criticism of the whole Yalta Agreement, especially the agreement on Poland, has tended to obscure the delight with which the western world greeted it at the time. Many people in Britain and America had noticed the brilliant Red Army advances of January and were worried at the idea that the West was negotiating from a position of weakness. The announced agreement, even the Polish part, seemed on the face of things quite favourable to the West. King George VI telegraphed to Churchill on February 13, 'I send my warmest congratulations to you and Anthony on your achievements.' Churchill's friend Brendan Bracken, then Minister of Information, was more effusive:

'The whole British press acclaims the results of Argonaut ('The Yalta Conference). *The Times* in its first leader uses such glowing language about you that I might have written the article myself.' The American press was similarly enthusiastic, the *Washington Post* referring on March 1 to 'the hearty response already given by the American people to the Yalta Agreement'.

The western leaders were naturally anxious to present a front of Allied unity and to paper over the cracks of discord. 'I felt bound to proclaim my confidence in Soviet good faith in the hope of procuring it,' wrote Churchill in his memoirs. The record shows, though, that even in their thoughts and inner councils they were ready to trust Stalin and place reliance on his word. For instance, Churchill told the British cabinet on February 19: 'He [Churchill] had a very great feeling that the Russians were anxious to work harmoniously with the two English-speaking democracies. Premier Stalin was a person of great power in whom he had every confidence.' On February 17, he wired to Stalin: 'I pray that you may long be spared to preside over the destinies of your country, which has shown its full greatness under your leadership.'[9]

Alexander Cadogan, Permanent Under-Secretary at the British Foreign Office, wrote an even more adulatory letter to his wife Thelma on February 11:

> I have never known the Russians so easy and accommodating. In particular Joe [Stalin] has been extremely good. He is a great man, and shows up very impressively against the background of the other two ageing statesmen . . . I think the Conference has been quite successful. We have got an agreement on Poland . . . and we have got a number of other things settled, including an important agreement with the Russians about the treatment of our prisoners whom they liberate.[10]

Edward Bridges, Secretary to the British cabinet, minuted on February 12: 'I am sure that the main impression which most of us will carry away from the Crimea will be of the outstanding friendliness of our Russian allies and of the obvious sincerity of their desire to do us well and their wish to be on good relations with us and to co-operate with us after the war.'[11]

But in little more than a month the British found themselves taking a less euphoric view. On March 21, Eden telegraphed

Molotov: 'I am surprised to hear that the agreement which we reached about our prisoners at Yalta is not being carried out.' He pointed out that no news of British prisoners liberated by the Red Army in Poland was being released to British authorities, and that no American or British officers were being allowed into Poland to look after prisoners or arrange for their repatriation. 'I must ask you to give immediate permission for visits by our officers (including medical officers) to the forward areas in Poland,' wrote Eden—a naive request, since the Red Army was then busily engaged in suppressing all resistance to communist authority in Poland and had no intention of allowing westerners to watch them do it.

The point was that at the Yusupov Villa on February 10 Stalin had agreed to allow British liaison officers into the liberated areas and there had been a formal agreement to this effect. This was why the wording of Eden's note was unusually firm. He concluded by reminding Molotov: 'I know you will realise that the people of this country are closely following the fortunes of our prisoners-of-war and the effect on them of the Crimea Agreement.'[12]

On February 15, three British ships—'Duchess of Richmond', 'Moreton Bay' and 'Highland Princess'—left Liverpool for Odessa with a total of 7,000 Soviet prisoners. Charles Rayner, who was a carpenter on the 'Highland Princess', remembers that 'the Russians were a very dejected crowd as they had been compelled to fight for the Germans and they were not looking forward to going ashore.' It was on this journey that some of the Russians tried to jump ship, literally, by leaping into the water whenever they were close to land.

'They were plopping into the sea all the way along the route,' recalls C. H. Tamplin, a colonel on the Russian Liaison Staff. Several did this while passing through the Straits of Gibraltar and several more while passing through the Dardanelles. In Odessa, the Russians were disembarked, the ships searched by Soviet troops to make sure that no one escaped back to England, and 1,847 British prisoners already in a reception camp near Odessa brought on board in their place. By the end of the voyage some of them had been 'debriefed' and their stories formed the basis for specific complaints.

Averell Harriman, American Ambassador in Moscow, writes that 'the Soviets did not live up to their agreement to let our

teams go to where the prisoners were being liberated in Poland.'
The areas newly occupied by the Red Army were in total chaos.
Placards were posted on buildings in English and French inviting
Allied prisoners to report to various repatriation centres. Some
did this and eventually, after many adventures, were taken to
Odessa, where the ships awaited. Others hid in the homes of
Poles and waited for the end of the fighting, when repatriation
would be possible across the Allied lines. Some brave souls
actually tried to make their own way to Moscow, the only acces-
sible place where there were American or British representatives.
The fact that one or two actually arrived, without documents and
without speaking a word of Russian, is a measure of the disorder
that prevailed along the route.

It emerged that there was no malice in Soviet treatment of
Allied prisoners. A British report says, 'There have been cases
of ill-treatment and robbery, but these seem to have been
exceptional, and as a general rule the treatment by the Soviet
forces seems to have been friendly.'[13] There were complaints
about the British soldiers being held up at gunpoint and relieved
of their watches. There were two cases of British women being
raped. But investigation revealed that these things had happened
when the Soviet soldier in question was drunk and unable to
distinguish an Englishman from a German. One must remember
that during these weeks of Soviet victory looting was permitted
and even encouraged by the Red Army command, as was the rape
of German or Austrian women. A British army 'padre', newly-
liberated in Poland, reported to his superiors when he finally
reached London that 'in occupied territory rape to the Russians
was as necessary as religion to the righteous.'[14]

Western authorities complained of the bad food and appalling
accommodation provided for their men. 'Their medical condition
is very bad. The Russians are doing nothing for them,' wrote
Cadogan in a personal note to Churchill.[15] But it emerged that
conditions were no worse than those endured by members of
the Red Army. All in all, the British concluded, the treatment was
'good by Russian standards, indifferent by British, barbaric by
American'. Once they reached Odessa the prisoners found themselves confined to a transit camp and not allowed out except on
organised route marches, or for the occasional trip to the opera
or the circus. Rayner noticed that 'the town and docks were in

a terrible state, having been pounded by both sides,' and there could be little doubt that the lack of comfort enjoyed by American and British prisoners was caused by the prevailing chaos rather than ill-will.

Stalin and Molotov naturally rejected the western complaints. Stalin wired to Churchill; 'So far as concerns British prisoners-of-war, you have no grounds for anxiety. They are living in better conditions than was the case with Soviet prisoners-of-war in British camps, when the latter in a number of cases suffered persecution and even blows.'[16] Stalin told Roosevelt on March 25 that, speaking for himself, he would be glad to let American observers into Poland, but 'he felt bound to consult with his generals in the field and they were unwilling to saddle themselves with liabilities and anxieties or caring for foreign officers in the midst of their own urgent military preoccupations.'[17] Eden was advised by the War Office 'that we shall do more harm than good by taking a strong line with the Russians until we get more definite evidence that they are in a position to do more than they are now doing.' By the end of April, 3,639 British prisoners had been repatriated through Odessa,[18] as well as several thousand more belonging to the United States and the other allies, and it seemed on the evidence that the Soviet Union was making reasonable efforts.

However, the Soviet prisoners in Britain were causing great trouble. By the spring of 1945 they had found out the true situation—that once they were proved to be Soviet citizens they would be sent home whether they wished to go or not. If, therefore, they feared retribution and wished to stay in the West their only hope was somehow to convince the British that they were not Soviet citizens. In achieving this difficult task they had some room for manoeuvre, since there was an important difference of view between the Soviet Union and the others on what a Soviet citizen actually was. Britain and the United States had not yet recognised the Soviet acquisition of territory seized in 1939 and 1940: the Western Ukraine, Western Byelorussia and the Baltic States of Lithuania, Latvia and Estonia. They did not therefore recognise anyone who came from these areas as a Soviet citizen. Those who feared repatriation soon learnt that they could avoid it if they could show, whether correctly or falsely, that they had been living outside the Soviet Union in 1939.

A British-Soviet commission therefore had to be set up to deal with such claims, under the joint chairmanship of General Ratov, head of the Soviet Military Mission in Britain, and Brigadier R. Firebrace, the liaison officer between the Mission and the War Office. Ratov and Firebrace spent many distressing hours sitting in judgment over 'disputed cases', men who refused to acknowledge their citizenship. Both officers had subordinates who spoke the various languages of the area, so usually it was enough to subject the men to a simple test of speech. It was no good, for instance, for a man to claim that he came from the Western Ukraine if he spoke only Russian. He would have to show a native knowledge of Ukrainian and some knowledge of Polish, since it was to Poland that the area had belonged before the war. Neither could a man claim to be a Balt unless he spoke the relevant Baltic language, and Firebrace knew enough of these languages to be able to tell if the man was lying. The test could be applied even to old émigrés, people who had spent the between-the-wars years in western Europe, for the language had changed during twenty-seven years of Soviet rule. A subtle ear could detect a difference between the Russian language of 1917 and that of 1945.

On April 12, the first such meeting took place. In eight hours of strenuous work Firebrace and Ratov dealt with fifty cases. Ratov was accompanied by four other Soviet officers, the Soviet Consul Krotov and a shorthand writer, who took down every word said by the men being interviewed. Firebrace had only one task, to decide whether or not the man in question was a Soviet citizen in 1939. If he thought he was, the man was moved to the new Soviet camp at Newlands Corner, near Guildford. If he thought not and Ratov disagreed, which he usually did, the man was placed on the 'disputed list' and kept in a separate camp to await a final decision.

On April 14, Firebrace wrote a plaintive letter to Christopher Warner at the Foreign Office:

> You have given me a most unpleasant task as, with few exceptions, the men, whether claiming Soviet or Polish nationality, protest violently at being sent back to the Soviet Union or even to their homes in Poland. A large number insisted on giving reasons for their not wishing to go back and related with wealth of detail their experiences in the Soviet Union or in Poland after the entry

of the Red Army. It was one long story of shootings, arrest, ill-treatment and deportation of families. They stated that they did not want to return to a land where these things were allowed and where a man had no rights. There were cases of kulaks' [private farmers'] sons who had been chased from pillar to post and one young man stated that he had been in prison from the age of twelve until released to join the Red Army. Most of them said that they preferred death to returning to the Soviet Union and some even invited the British to shoot them in preference to handing them over. I have never in my life seen such human misery or such despair.[19]

Firebrace attached to his letter some details of a few of the individual cases. There was the man who told Ratov openly that he did not want to go home because he was ashamed to call himself Soviet. He said that his father had been a priest who had first had his tongue cut out to prevent him from preaching and had then been shot by the Soviet authorities. He himself had spent some years in prison, then escaped and lived for months in the woods like a hunted animal until war broke out, when he surrendered to the Germans. There were dozens of stories like this one, flung defiantly and desperately into the teeth of the Soviet general and his officers, presumably to make it morally more difficult for the British to send them back to Russia.

Ratov sat through these tirades, making no attempt to stop them but looking very uncomfortable. 'He obviously did not enjoy their revelations as to Soviet methods being made in the presence of British officers,' Firebrace noted. But every word was being taken down by the Soviet shorthand writer, and Ratov could console himself with the thought that, once inside the Soviet Union, the prisoner would pay dearly for his abusive tone. Firebrace found it 'very unpleasant and painful' every time he had to agree with Ratov that such a man was undoubtedly a Soviet citizen and therefore due for repatriation. But whatever his sympathies, his orders were clear, he had no right to save anyone who could not lay some reasonable claim to a nationality other than Soviet.

Only once, Firebrace says, did he let emotion intervene and save an individual. This was when a prisoner pointed an accusing finger at Ratov and shouted, 'You killed my father, you killed my mother, you killed my brothers, and I ask the English general to shoot me here and now before he sends me back to the Soviet Union.' Firebrace could not find it in his heart to condemn the man after such an outburst. Although there was no evidence to support such an idea, he told Ratov he thought the man must be a Pole, thereby keeping him on the 'disputed list' and temporarily safe.

But this was the only time Firebrace saved a man by a deliberate lie. 'I wish I could have saved more, but it wasn't possible, my orders were so clear,' he says. He knew that if he consistently bent the rules he would bring down upon his head the wrath not only of Ratov, but also of his superiors and especially of the Foreign Office. True, the prisoners were in Britain and under Britain's control, but Ratov lost no time in making clear what would happen if he did not get his way and obtain the custody of all undoubted Soviet citizens. During lunch at Newlands Corner Camp on April 11 he had an argument with Firebrace, during which he said that if Britain acted in this way the Soviet authorities would have to retain fifty British prisoners-of-war in Odessa. 'And how would you like that?' he snapped. Cool as a cucumber, Firebrace replied, 'Unless your remark is a very poor joke I will report it to higher authority.' But though he did his best to sound unconcerned, in his heart Firebrace knew that the Soviet authorities were quite capable of doing such a thing, and that if they did so he personally would be blamed for the consequent suffering inflicted on British soldiers.

Firebrace was one of the first officers to be put into this horrifying moral situation, to be called upon to do something which personally revolted him in order to fulfil the demands of higher policy. He was told that there were sound reasons why the Agreement had been signed and why it had to be observed. Whether he thought it right or not, it was not his job to challenge it and it would have been absurd for him to try to do so. He had only a small part of the information which had been available to the diplomats who negotiated it. He could not take the broad view. All he knew was that it was forcing him to do work which he found morally repugnant.

There was one individual case, concerning Ivan Sidorov and his wife Nataliya, which illustrates particularly well the dilemma and the moral burden which the Agreement imposed on officers and diplomats. Sidorov was born in 1914 in southern Russia and studied as an engineer. Suspect politically because of his family background, by the time war broke out in 1941 he had been arrested more than once by the Soviet police and imprisoned for short periods. In 1942 he was captured by the Germans and put in a prisoner-of-war camp. Several times he was asked to work for the Germans, but he refused. Then a major in General Vlasov's 'Russian Liberation Army' came to the camp and offered him work in a labour battalion.

Sidorov's British interrogator explains in a report why he accepted this work: 'He was told that if he did not accept the work he would stay in the camp and starve. He knew he would be asked to fight against the Russians sooner or later if he went to work and was not keen to go for that reason. But the food in the camp was very bad. When he worked with the labour battalion, he had quite good food and pay.' He was put to work building roads in the southern Ukraine and in 1943 he married a local seventeen-year-old girl, named Nataliya. He worked on the railways and on bridge-building until March 1944, when he was transferred to the west coast of France to help defend the Atlantic Wall against the forthcoming invasion.

Nataliya was able to accompany him to France. For three months he worked near Cherbourg, digging trenches, while she worked in the battalion cookhouse. But after a few weeks the men were given military uniform and rifles. They were now no longer a labour battalion but a military unit. Any Russian who resisted this change was shot. Ivan therefore found himself wearing the uniform of his country's enemy and helping to defend the coast which was about to be invaded by his country's allies. He was suddenly in a dangerous position. There could be no doubt that under Soviet law he was committing treason, but it was a predicament which he could only have avoided by staying in the prisoner-of-war camp where the food was not adequate to support life. On June 6 the D-Day invasion began and on June 26 Ivan's unit fell into American hands.

Ivan and Nataliya were then separated. Both were shipped to England, but he was sent to a prisoner-of-war camp at Kempton Park in Surrey, she to a Ministry of Health hostel at Retford in Yorkshire. He and his friends soon learnt that it was British and American policy to send home all Soviet citizens irrespective of their wishes. He realised that he would be tried for treason if ever he entered Russia and that his only way out was to convince the British that he was not a Soviet citizen. So he pretended to be a Pole. His problem was that he then had to appear before the Anglo-Soviet commission on repatriation. Both Ratov and Firebrace had Polish-speaking officers with them specifically to deal with such claimants and they could tell at once that his Polish was almost non-existent, while his Russian was perfect. During the interview he started shouting abuse at Ratov and the Soviet officers. As a result his name was noted and the Soviet side became insistent that he be handed over.

Up to this point Sidorov's story was not an unusual one. Many of the Russian prisoners brought to England were resisting repatriation just as frantically. Many of them had wives in England too. But Ivan and Nataliya had two vital pieces of luck. The first was that Nataliya had been expecting a child when she was captured by the Americans, and this child was born in January 1945 in Retford. By being born in England the little boy was automatically a British subject. As parents of a British subject the Sidorovs now had a stronger claim than the rest to be allowed to remain in the United Kingdom.

Their second piece of luck was in obtaining an introduction to Ethel Christie, a British Quaker who had done enthusiastic relief work in Russia during the famines of the 1920s. She began to agitate on the Sidorovs' behalf. Her efforts made it clear to the authorities that they would not be able to dispose of the family quietly. If they sent the Sidorovs home, with or without their British baby, there would undoubtedly be a scandal.

Had it not been for their son and for the help of Ethel Christie the Sidorovs would have quickly been transferred to the camp for Soviet citizens at Newlands Corner in Surrey. And once there they would only have had a short time to wait before a boat was available to take them to Russia. In Foreign Office memoranda various officials outlined the case against the family. Enquiries had been made with Polish groups in Britain, but they knew nothing of Sidorov. On the basis of this and of his interview before the mixed commission, Firebrace said that he was ninety per cent certain that Sidorov was Russian. Poles had told him that they found it impossible to believe that a man could have lived for more than twenty years between the wars in the Tarnopol area, as Sidorov claimed, without learning to speak adequate

Polish. His language deficiency seemed to have condemned him.

Geoffrey Wilson of the Foreign Office recommended that Sidorov and his wife be handed over to the Soviet authorities forthwith. It was a difficult decision, Wilson admitted, but one which had to be taken without sentimentality and on the basis of practical politics and diplomacy:

> This decision should be taken irrespective of the consequences as regards the wife, who is undoubtedly a Soviet citizen, or the child, who has British nationality as well as Soviet or Polish citizenship. We shall only get into the most hopeless muddle and Brigadier Firebrace's job will be made absolutely impossible if we decide cases of this nature on humanitarian grounds and not on the facts as we know them.

Patrick Dean wrote that Sidorov could well be lying about his nationality, 'because he knows that, having served in Vlasov's army, he will certainly be executed if he is sent back to the Soviet Union.' In fact he was likely to be selected for especially severe treatment, thought Dean, because 'presumably all the harsh things he has said against the Soviet Union in the course of his examination before General Ratov will be remembered.' But all this was irrelevant from the legal point of view. John Galsworthy, another official, wrote that the only important point was that Sidorov was, almost without a doubt, a Soviet citizen and that 'there is therefore nothing we can do to keep him from the Russians, to whom under the terms of the Yalta Agreement he now belongs.' The same applied to Nataliya, who was as Soviet as her husband. Galsworthy concluded: 'There is thus no legal difficulty about handing over these two to the Russians though I shall be greatly surprised if they do not commit suicide.'

There was however, he thought, a difficulty in the case of the child. The baby had dual British-Soviet nationality, but so long as he was in Britain his British nationality predominated. On the one hand, it would be both wrong and difficult to separate the baby from his parents. On the other, it would be illegal to send the child to Russia if his parents wanted him to stay in England. One cannot deport a British subject from Britain. The Sidorovs themselves were of course ignorant of these legal niceties, but Galsworthy thought it would be dangerous simply to bundle the baby out with the parents. The problem was that 'if it leaked out in any way at Retford (which is by no means improbable) it would surely arouse the most serious criticism and provoke enquiry into our general interpretation of the Yalta Agreement.' This agreement was still secret and 'the less said about it the better'.

This was the element in the case which from then on dominated the officials' thinking. What was the best way of avoiding a scandal? Which decision would cause less embarrassment to the Foreign Office and the authorities generally? Either course of action was fraught with difficulty. Then a compromise was considered. Might it be possible to deport Sidorov himself, but to keep Nataliya and the baby? It was he that the Soviet authorities really wanted. If they got him, surely they would not make too much fuss about the woman and the child? On this basis an approach was made to the Home Office, the department responsible for immigration, to see whether permission might be obtained for Nataliya to remain with her baby. The Home Office's initial reaction was 'that they do not want to have her here at any price . . . They fear that if she is allowed to stay here and her husband is sent back there will be endless trouble with her, since she will be always enquiring about her husband.'

Throughout the first half of 1945 Ivan and Nataliya lived in agony, believing that they would most probably be executed and that, if not, they would almost certainly be separated for an indefinite period. For Nataliya it was perhaps even worse, for she was only nineteen, nursing her five-month-old baby and totally devoted to her husband. If the decision went against them she would leave her child in England. She would probably never see him again either. It would be hard to imagine greater torment than those months which she lived through in terror of separation from the two people she loved. On one occasion an emissary from the Soviet Embassy called to see her in Retford and spoke to her in such a bullying way that she had to be taken to hospital. She was on the verge of nervous collapse.

By June almost all the Soviet prisoners in Britain had been sent home. Those that remained were the few disputed cases like the Sidorovs and a few others who were too ill to travel. Nataliya knew that her British baby was no guarantee that they would be allowed to stay, for there had been other pregnant women among the Russians taken prisoner in France. She knew that, baby or no baby, they had all been sent back and that only she remained. The difference in her case was that she had a worthy champion in Ethel Christie who, the British authorities feared, would make trouble unless the case was properly considered.

On June 19, Ethel Christie brought Nataliya from Retford to London for an interview at the Foreign Office. 'I was terrified, I can hardly remember that day at all,' Nataliya says now. Crushed by the months of waiting, speaking no English, quite unaware of the problems she had aroused in international politics and of the Yalta Agreement, she was overwhelmed by the corridors of Whitehall. The two women were shown into the office of Thomas Brimelow, then a junior official on the Soviet desk. Brimelow writes: 'She [Nataliya] fell on her knees, placed her forehead on the ground in the traditional Russian manner and implored my assistance in saving her and her husband from deportation. I told her that I could not give her any explicit assurances as no decision regarding the fate of herself and her child had yet been taken.'

Foreign Office officials are not used to such scenes. Ethel Christie says: 'Poor Mr Brimelow, she knelt there on the floor and grabbed him round the knees so that he couldn't move. He just had to stand there. I felt so sorry for them both.' Nataliya told Brimelow through her tears of the efforts she had made to stay with her husband, how she had followed him across Nazi-occupied Europe, and of her distress at being separated from him while she was bearing and nursing his child. She said that she would die without him, and Brimelow could see that probably she was not exaggerating. They had been through so much together and their love was unusually strong.

Nataliya had brought a petition with her addressed to Churchill. Ethel Christie remembers what happened when they were shown out of the Foreign Office: 'She wanted to deliver her petition, so I took her to 10 Downing Street, just next door to the Foreign Office. The street was full of tourists and I remember them gawping at us as we walked up to the door of Number Ten, with Nataliya in floods of tears, and pushed her petition through the letter box.' She then took her back to Retford and advised her to wait as patiently as possible while her fate was decided.

The Prime Minister and the Foreign Office were both given English translations of Nataliya's petition. This remarkable document began: 'I implore you to take pity on an unhappy woman and a poor unfortunate child. All our hopes are centred on you. My husband and I will work all our life for the English people, and my son who was born in England will always be indebted to the British Government and to the kind English people for saving his unhappy parents.' It continued with a summary of the family's sufferings after war broke out in 1941, admitting that 'cold, hunger and terrible conditions forced my husband to put on German uniform.' They suffered terribly during the war, she wrote, 'but our mutual love sustained us.'

Nataliya described how her requests to visit her husband at the camp at Kempton Park were refused. He had never seen his son. She ended her letter:

> I beg you to help a poor unfortunate woman. Return to our country is impossible either for me or for my beloved husband. There they will never understand the sufferings we have both endured and never will they forgive that he put on German uniform. My little boy is five months old. They will take him away from me. I know that only too well. Take pity on us, take pity on my unhappy husband, send us if possible to the most distant, hard and lonely colony. We shall work with all our strength for the good of the British Government and for the kind, sympathetic English people.

Meanwhile, Ivan was interrogated by Robert Hodgson, a former British *chargé d'affaires* in Moscow who spoke good Russian. Hodgson reported very much in Ivan's favour: 'I could detect no trace of hesitation or of a tendency to prevaricate. He impressed me as being honest and truthful.' Hodgson was shocked to hear of Nataliya's intimidation by a Soviet agent, as a result of which 'she has been reduced to a grave state of nervous terror.' His view was that 'incidents of this kind render it extremely difficult for us to carry out the terms of our agreements' and that 'we should be fully justified in refusing to surrender Sidorov, the activities of the NKVD being intolerable.' He understood the need to maintain friendly contact with the Soviet Union and the problems that would arise if Britain blatantly flaunted the terms of the Yalta Agreement on prisoners-of-war. Nevertheless, he concluded, 'it is surely incumbent on us to do what we reasonably can to avoid being willing accomplices in acts of gross injustice.'

But the diplomats were still inclined to consider the matter in terms of Britain's foreign policy. It seemed to them that to refuse the Soviet request and to keep the Sidorovs in England was unthinkable. They were Soviet citizens and under an agreement freely entered into by Britain and the Soviet Union they were to be repatriated, by force if necessary. Some British officials felt sorry for the Sidorovs and understood the reasons which compelled him to bear arms on the German side, but they were reluctant to save him since this meant breaking a solemn treaty.

They remembered launching Britain into war six years earlier in order to preserve precisely this principle, respect for treaties and international law. Millions had died in order to demonstrate to budding Hitlers that disputes must be settled by negotiation, not by unilateral action. Four months earlier a most important agreement between the Soviet Union and the western Allies had been reached at Yalta, and part of it was the agreement on forcible repatriation. It seemed in the summer of 1945 that Stalin was observing this agreement. He had not intervened on the communist side in the Greek civil war and he had induced the communists who ran Poland to admit non-communists into their government. The Sidorov case might be a small matter, but the legal position was quite clear, and the Foreign Office was aghast at the prospect of being the first to violate the Yalta Agreement in order to help two individuals.

What led them to give special attention to this case was not sympathy for the Sidorovs, but fear of unpleasantness and publicity. In June the matter was discussed with Moley Sargent, one of the Foreign Office's most senior men, and Patrick Dean wrote, 'It seems that the disposal of Sidorov and his wife is now settled and that they will have to go back to the Soviet Union.' This decision was made in full awareness of the fact that they 'will receive very rough treatment when they get home and will probably be executed.' The British-born baby, he thought, 'will no doubt be brought up by the state and has nothing to fear.' One point that worried him was how the couple should be told of this decision and whether or not they should be asked to decide either to take their baby with them or to leave him in England. Dean thought that in many ways it might be better not to consult the parents on this point. But, he went on, 'I am afraid that if nothing is said to the mother about the baby and they are both taken to an airfield or port suddenly in order to be sent back to the Soviet Union, the mother may create a scene by trying to press her baby onto the guards.' If this happened it would 'put them [the guards] in a most difficult position and also cause trouble if it becomes known.'

It was then decided to submit the case to the highest authority. On July 9 John Galsworthy prepared a long memorandum which represented the general view of the junior men on the Soviet desk. Both Ivan and Nataliya must be told, he advised, that they were being sent back to the Soviet Union. In his view, this was 'the only action possible in view of the binding commitments of the Yalta Agreement'. There were still a few British prisoners-of-war in Soviet hands and these could well be kept as hostages if there was any delay over the Sidorovs. Also, General Ratov had been given an assurance, after Sidorov's claim to Polish nationality was shown to be untrue, that the family would be delivered soon. The Soviet General was bound to react violently if this promise was not fulfilled.

On the other hand, Galsworthy advised, there were several Russian émigrés in London known to be following the case with interest. He thought that 'a decision which is unpalatable to them may lead to a general leakage of the facts and provoke undesirable criticism in Parliament.' Also, there was Ethel Christie, a woman highly respected in the influential Quaker movement. She would hardly remain silent while the family was bundled away. He had read Captain Youmatoff's report of his voyage to Odessa. There was, he pointed out, 'strong evidence that certain persons sent back to the Soviet Union by us in accordance with the Yalta Agreement, after begging to be allowed to remain in the United Kingdom, have been shot on arrival at their destination.' If this terrible fact leaked out as well the publicity would be even worse.

Galsworthy thought that the question was one of principle: 'It would be dangerous to become "soft" about any individual case of this sort . . . If once we start to modify the application of the [Yalta] Agreement on humanitarian grounds there would be a very long list of candidates for lenient treatment.' Their duty was therefore clear: the family would have to go, but Galsworthy at the end of his long note still felt bound to express his worries about the plan:

In carrying it through we can expect trouble from three quarters: the Soviet authorities, the sympathisers and the victims themselves. The first two factors have already been mentioned. As regards the third, there is every likelihood, given the strong attachment between the husband and wife, that the latter's reaction to our notification will be to try then and there to kill herself and her baby; or to hand the baby over to us and kill herself; or to pretend to accept her fate and agree to return with her husband and baby, only to attempt suicide in more dramatic circumstances when the time for embarkation comes . . . Obviously either suicide or escape will be liable to provoke undesirable publicity.

Ethel Christie received a distraught letter from Nataliya. She wrote to Thomas Brimelow at the Foreign Office to say that she had answered the letter, 'giving her [Nataliya] the assurance that everyone concerned is doing their best for her and her husband.' She had introduced Nataliya to some of her friends, she went on, in particular a naval captain called W. T. Haydon and his wife. They liked Nataliya so much that they invited her to stay with them in Richmond, Surrey. The Foreign Office could see that support for the family was growing. Mrs Christie continued her letter: 'The suspense is worse for her than for him, because his mind is more or less at rest about her future and the baby's, while she has no illusions about his if he gets back to Russia. As a matter of fact, he does not intend to cross the frontier alive.'

At this point the decision was delicately balanced. Who would cause more trouble, the Soviet authorities if the family was kept in England or their sympathisers if they were deported? The poor Sidorovs had quite unwittingly become people of importance, for their case seemed bound to cause either severe damage to Anglo-Soviet relations or else grave embarrassment to the British government. It is here that a new argument can be detected in the diplomats' memoranda, that since there seemed no way of avoiding trouble of one sort or another they might just as well do the humane thing and keep all three Sidorovs. Patrick Dean wrote, 'It is for consideration whether we should not in the special circumstances of this case keep the father as well, since we are bound to have a serious row with the Soviet government in any event.' Thomas Brimelow agreed: 'Since we are proposing to break the [Yalta] Agreement in respect of the mother, we might as well break it in

respect of the father too.' Nataliya had touched their hearts during
her distressing visit to the Foreign Office, and for the first time
they were allowing considerations of humanity and morality
to enter the argument. 'It would be entirely contrary to English
notions of justice that mother and child should be parted,'
noted Dean, while Brimelow wrote: 'If we repatriate him he will
probably be shot out of hand and we shall have been a party to
sending a man whom we believe to be innocent, though admittedly
anti-Soviet, to his death.'

A few days later Patrick Dean and Christopher Warner, the
head of the Soviet desk, discussed the problem with Alexander
Cadogan. They decided that the matter must be put before a
minister as soon as possible. Cadogan addressed a note to Alec
Douglas-Home (then Lord Dunglass), who had just been appointed
an Under-Secretary in Churchill's 'caretaker' government, and
to Anthony Eden, the Foreign Secretary:

> This is an unpleasant case arising out of our obligation under the
> Yalta Agreement to return all 'liberated' or captured Soviet citizens
> to Russia . . . This is an exceptional case in that the baby technically
> has British nationality and I should like to resist the demand to hand
> the family over. That will produce a pretty good row with the
> Russians. On the other hand you will see that the family have
> obtained a certain amount of publicity and support here, and to
> hand them over will, or may, cause some excitement in England. I
> hope you might be willing to face a row with the Russians in this case.

On July 13 Anthony Eden gave the decision which meant life
for the Sidorovs. The Foreign Secretary wrote: 'All right, keep the
family. But delay our answer as long as we can so that we can get
as many people out as we can. I have some fear of reprisals.'
It was one of his last decisions in office, for two weeks later it
emerged that the Conservative Party had lost the general election
and the government had to resign. Even then, the Sidorovs could
not be told of the decision which would put them out of their
misery, since permission for them to remain had to be obtained
formally from the Home Office. This consent arrived on August
27, and shortly afterwards the family, though given no information
about the high level on which their case had been considered,
were given to understand that they would not be sent back to the
Soviet Union.

In the event, the promised row with the Soviet Embassy did not take place—a fact remarked upon with amazement by several officials during the months that followed. Probably the Russians too feared an open discussion of the case, with consequent disclosure of details of the secret agreement. Maybe they appreciated the problems involved in separating a mother from her child, if not for the family themselves, for whom they had scant sympathy, at least for the British government which would have to do the deed. They may have realised that, were they to attack Britain publicly on this matter, the only possible defence would be to pillory the Soviet Union as inhumane. Or they may have decided that Sidorov was a small fish, not worth a serious row. The change in government may have helped here, for there was a brief honeymoon period during which the Soviet government thought it would find the new Prime Minister Attlee and his Social Democrats more amenable and helpful than the Conservatives under Churchill. There were still many bitter enemies of the Soviet Union on whom Stalin wished to lay his hands. Sidorov had slipped through their fingers, but only by a fluke, and it was hardly worth while making a fuss about him which might damage the chance of getting hold of the other thousands of 'traitors' who remained in British and American hands.

Nataliya and her baby moved from Retford in December 1945 to live with the Haydons in Richmond. But Ivan still could not be released. He was moved from Kempton Park to prisoner-of-war camps at Bury and Kirkham. He had by now been told that he was not to be repatriated, but he was still worried about what the British would eventually do with him, for he had heard stories about Soviet citizens being sent home by force even after being assured that they would be allowed to stay. For the rest of 1945 and during 1946 Soviet officials still wandered around the prisoner-of-war camps looking for Russians who were masquerading as subjects of other nations. As the months passed he began to complain a little. He wanted to get to work, so why could he not be released? Officers told him to think himself lucky that he was in a camp and safely under British military protection.

Sidorov was in a unique position, for he was the only man recognised by both sides as a Soviet citizen who was able to stay in England. The months passed and the other Russians left the camps, to be shipped home if they were revealed as Soviet, to be released if they were able to maintain otherwise, but Sidorov remained, until by the end of 1946 he was the only Russian in a camp of Germans. Then in December he was given a railway warrant and told to go to Tunbridge Wells to rejoin his family. He had to go to Liverpool to change trains, and this worried him, since it was from Liverpool that many of the ships bearing his unfortunate fellow-countrymen had departed for Soviet ports. But there was no basis for his fears. A British officer even gave him five shillings to buy refreshments on the train. 'I just wish I'd taken his name and address. I'd have liked to have sent him that five shillings back out of my first pay packet,' says Sidorov.

And so, just before Christmas 1946, the family was reunited after two and a half years of tortured separation. From then on things began to go well for the family. Sidorov soon obtained work in England and by 1974 he had become a successful engineering executive. Like most of the men who managed to avoid forced repatriation, he is effusively and touchingly grateful to the country which gave him sanctuary. 'I've done my best to be a good citizen. We've always paid our taxes and done what was expected of us. Everything's so gentle here and we feel so safe,' he says. They live in their own house near London.

Their son, without whom they would certainly have been sent back to Russia and probably shot, went to a British university and is well embarked on a professional career. The memory of what happened in 1945 is still very painful to them, which is why they asked the author not to reveal their identities. Their names have therefore been changed in writing this account, though all other names and facts are correct. The 'Sidorovs' have always appreciated how lucky they were and that their story was one of very few with a happy ending. But it was only after living in England for thirty years that they learnt of the unique nature of their particular salvation, that it was only through a blatant breach by Britain of the Yalta Agreement and through a personal decision by Anthony Eden that they were able to escape the wrath of Stalin and build themselves a life.

DEATH ON THE QUAYSIDE

THOSE less lucky than 'Sidorov', once the Raiov-Firebrace commission had declared them to be Soviet citizens, were sent to Newlands Corner, a camp centred round a weekend hotel near Guildford in Surrey. Letitia Fairfield, a well-known lawyer and the sister of the famous writer on treason, Rebecca West, used to visit the camp often during the spring of 1945, staying next door to it with her friends the Stracheys. The son of the house was John Strachey, a former communist who in 1950 was to become Britain's Minister of War. She recalls: 'John Strachey was quite merciless. He said that they were quislings because they had been found in German uniform and that they deserved everything that was coming to them. As usual, he was excusing the Soviet Russians for everything they did.'

Miss Fairfield took a more sympathetic view of the inmates, as did the British commandant, a Russian scholar who appreciated what the men under his charge had been through in recent years. 'His compassion and kindness towards them and his human sympathy was one of the most moving things I ever saw,' she says. She and John Strachey's mother used to save pieces of chocolate for the prisoners out of their rations and occasionally invite them to tea. Although forbidden to leave the camp without permission, they were not surrounded by barbed wire. There was little likelihood of escape attempts. They had no money, ration books or identity cards, little knowledge of English and no one to whom they could turn for help. Anyone who did escape would not get very far.

The prisoners never numbered more than a few hundred and they were housed in huts hastily constructed in the hotel garden. The commandant arranged concerts for them and provided them with radio sets. Such consideration reassured the prisoners, leading them to believe that they would not in fact be sent home to Russia. Having appeared before the commission they were of course marked men and could expect the worst if ever the

Soviet authorities got hold of them. Miss Fairfield says, 'They told us how they dreaded going back to Russia and they were quite terrified. But they were convinced the British would never send them back. I remember walking down to the bottom of the garden and talking to some lad who came from a very remote part of Russia, and that's what he said: "The British will never send us home. The British are kind." It just sent my heart into my boots.'

Eventually the time came for the prisoners to depart and the Commandant escorted a party from the camp to Hull, where a boat was waiting to take them to Russia. They spent the night in a warehouse on the quayside and were told they would go on board the next morning. During the night the Commandant was sent for by a sergeant and taken to the warehouse where the body of one of the prisoners dangled from a beam.

A few days later the Commandant came to see Mrs Strachey and Miss Fairfield. 'I remember that he burst into tears while he was talking to us. He said he felt like a murderer when he saw the dangling body,' Miss Fairfield recalls. It was a moment of anguish to be endured by many British and American officers during the weeks that followed. Hardened men who had suffered years of cruel fighting without flinching became unusually emotional when confronted by such unwarlike situations, where they were expected to deceive people who trusted them, to lull them into a sense of false security before handing them over to probable execution.

An equally distasteful incident occurred at the end of March. The United States army obtained permission to move 6,000 Russian prisoners, captured in German uniform, across England to Liverpool, where a ship was waiting to take them home. The British authorities were against the idea. A grave security risk was involved in the movement of so many desperate men. There were also legal difficulties since, according to the agreement with the Soviet Union, these were not prisoners-of-war but friendly nationals and there was no legal way in which they could be held under guard by British or American soldiers. Still, the practical need to ship these men home outweighed such considerations and the scheme was allowed to proceed. It was agreed that Firebrace would send 150 British-held Russians to join the ship also, all men who had declared in no uncertain terms their unwillingness to go home.

On March 28 Colonel Tamplin, Firebrace's deputy, telephoned Patrick Dean with disturbing news: 'Unfortunately one of the Russians whom we wanted to send back hanged himself at Scarsbrook Camp [Yorkshire] before the party set off for Liverpool, and another cut his throat on the quayside at Liverpool and will shortly be dead.'[1]

Colonel Tamplin remembers boarding the ship and finding the dying man, crudely patched up, lying in the ship's cells. He wanted to have him taken to a hospital on shore, but the Soviet authorities insisted that he sail with the ship. The news moved Patrick Dean to write: 'It is extremely distasteful that we have to send back to the Soviet Union persons who, whatever faults they may have committed in collaborating with the Germans, prefer to commit suicide here rather than go back to their own country.' Nevertheless, he went on, the men had undoubtedly been Soviet citizens. Britain was bound by international agreement to send them back and would have to carry on doing it.

But a man had died and there would have to be an inquest—something which filled Dean with alarm, for it meant press coverage and possible revelations about the Yalta Agreement. There had now been four or five suicides at least, Dean wrote, and there was the possibility of political trouble. It would not be possible to have the inquest held *in camera*, because even under wartime legislation this could only be done if the court was satisfied that secrecy was essential to the public safety or defence of the realm. This did not apply in such a case. 'I wish it had been possible to hush this up under 18B or some other wartime regulation,' noted Moley Sargent. What happened in the end was that the press were 'advised' at the inquest not to report the matter. Journalists are receptive to such advice in wartime and they did what they were told.

The voyage to Odessa was a disagreeable one, with much tension between the Soviet liaison officers and the British. Czeslaw Jesman, a British interpreter, reported that regular talks were given to the Soviet prisoners on board the 'Almanzora' to prepare them for their return to Soviet reality. It was only under the strongest pressure, they were told, that the British had released them and allowed them to go home. To prisoners who enquired innocently about the high standard of food on board, the lecturers replied that the 'Almanzora' was the showpiece of the British merchant navy and that on other ships conditions were quite appalling.

At Istanbul the ship stopped to pick up four Soviet citizens who had leapt into the Dardanelles during a previous voyage and who had in the meantime been held by Turkish police. When they reached their destination Major Shershun, the senior Soviet officer, spoke frankly to the British and admitted that the prisoners would probably all be sent to 'educational labour camps'.[2] The problem was, he explained, that no one would be able to tell for certain who the prisoners had been in contact with, and who had or had not collaborated with the Germans.

The 'Almanzora' reached Odessa on April 18 and that very day, while the Russians were actually being disembarked, Jesman heard two salvoes of machine-gun fire coming from behind a large shack on the pier. A little later he had the chance to speak to one of the Soviet guards, who told him that two men had just been executed on the spot because they had been working for the British police and 'had sold out to the capitalists'. He reported the matter to the ship's Master, Captain Bannister, and to the senior British officer on board, Colonel Boyle, but no official protest was made. The prisoners were now Soviet citizens on Soviet territory and their fate was no longer any of Britain's business.

But the most terrible incidents of all occurred on the British ship 'Empire Pride', which left Liverpool on May 23. It was clear from the beginning that this was going to be a difficult voyage. Many of the Russians were ill because of the bad treatment they had received in Germany. A few were advanced cases of tuberculosis and not expected to survive the voyage. There were so many sick people that one whole deck had to be converted into a hospital ward. There were also several women in the group, most of them pregnant.

On board the ship there were two officers from Firebrace's team, James Martin and George Youmatoff, the latter a Canadian of Russian origin whose family had emigrated in 1920. There was also a Colonel Miroshnichenko, from the Soviet Military Mission, and two of his officers. Trouble began as the 3,000 Russians were being embarked. Most of them were marched to the quayside in platoon formation. A few were stretcher cases and had to be carried on board. But there was also a group of about a dozen which was under heavy guard, two escorts for every prisoner. As this group was being marched towards the gangplank, one of the prisoners bent down, smashed against the ground his china tea-mug which they all still carried and proceeded to slash his throat with the jagged remains.

Martin and Youmatoff made arrangements to have the man rushed to hospital in Liverpool, but the Soviet officers intervened and insisted he be carried on board. His name was on the manifest, they said, and there could be no excuse for leaving him behind, especially as there was a fully-equipped medical team on the ship. A British doctor attended to the bleeding man and actually sewed up his throat then and there on the quayside. He was then taken on board and locked up in the ship's cells, even though these had just been painted bright green. Youmatoff writes:

> The man was stripped of all his clothes and his hands were tied to a bunk. In spite of this he managed twice to break open the stitching and it was not until the medical officer had sedated him that we were able to bring him under control. The sight of that man and his cell, both heavily mottled with green paint and red blood, is one that I have never been able to forget.

On May 30, as the 'Empire Pride' was passing Gibraltar, a man called Dachenko leapt into the sea and was spotted swimming steadily towards the African shore. The alarm was given and a search instituted, but without success. After a few minutes the captain said he thought there was no hope of finding the man in the darkness and the ship went on its way. The Straits of Gibraltar are nowhere less than eight miles wide and Youmatoff remembers that the shore seemed many miles away when the man jumped. He could see the twinkling lights, but not the shore itself. It was thought unlikely that Dachenko would make it to Africa and more probable that he would drown. A few days later in the Dardanelles a few other Russians leapt overboard. They were picked up by Turkish patrol boats, and one of them was returned on board, only to attempt suicide by slashing his arteries with a razor blade. He was then arrested and put in the cells.

The most disagreeable feature of the voyage was the behaviour of the senior prisoner-of-war officer, Major Polyachenko, who every day came to Miroshnichenko and the other Military Mission officers with the names of fellow-prisoners who, he said, had collaborated with the Germans or committed other acts of disloyalty. A few of these, thirty-one in all, were immediately arrested and transferred to the cells, but Polyachenko was denouncing fifteen or twenty a day and there was not room for all his victims. The rest, who Youmatoff thinks numbered between 200 and 300, were left at liberty unaware that their names were on the black list. The British officers watched this process with growing alarm and fear of what was going to happen when they reached Odessa.

The ship arrived on June 10 and at 6.30 that evening disembarkation began. Most of the prisoners walked off unescorted and without incident, but Youmatoff and Martin were shocked to see what little care was taken of the sick Russians. Youmatoff wrote in his report:

> The Soviet authorities refused to accept any of the stretcher cases as such and even the patients who were dying were made to walk off the ship carrying their own baggage. Two people only were carried off, one man with his right leg amputated and left one broken, the other unconscious. The prisoner who had attempted suicide was very roughly handled and his wound opened up and allowed to bleed. He was taken off the ship and marched behind a packing case on the docks. A shot was heard but nothing more was seen.[3]

When the rest had been disembarked, between ten and eleven o'clock, Youmatoff saw the thirty-one prisoners who were under close arrest being dragged off the ship and into a warehouse some fifty yards away. Youmatoff and Martin stayed on deck together watching. Fifteen minutes later they heard machine-gun fire coming from the warehouse. Youmatoff says, 'We looked at each other and one of us said, "Well, that's the end of that lot." ' Twenty minutes later a covered lorry drove out of the warehouse and headed towards the town. Having seen the way in which the thirty-one men had been pulled off the ship, the two officers were not surprised by the shooting. They were however intrigued to note that Polyachenko, the informer and main contributor to the black list, had been taken and presumably killed with his victims. It was a classic technique, but a surprising twist of events which, in Youmatoff's words, 'brightened an otherwise dark day'.

It was now nearly midnight. The British officers and crew

retired to bed. The next morning some of them were allowed to go ashore. After much discussion about passports and landing permits, Youmatoff and two of the Soviet officers got into a jeep on the quayside and set off to have breakfast at Odessa's London Hotel. A few yards from the ship the jeep had to stop, the road being completely blocked by a heavy lorry which in spite of everybody's entreaties the driver refused to move. At this point Youmatoff realised that he was alongside the warehouse into which the thirty-one prisoners had been dragged the previous evening and from which he had heard the shooting:

> I left the jeep and made my way to the nearest window which was about six feet from the ground. But thanks to all the mess there was no difficulty in finding a box light enough to move and large enough to give me the extra few inches required for a good look. I saw a long shed with concrete up to the level of the windows and at one end some large sliding doors. On the right side and near a smaller metal sliding door the concrete was badly chipped and pitted. The floor and indeed portions of the wall were stained with dark blotches.

After this, Youmatoff says, there remained no doubt in his mind that the thirty-one prisoners had been shot the previous evening. It was true that he had not actually seen the shooting, but the weight of evidence—the manhandling of the prisoners off the ship, the sound of machine-gun fire, the emergence of the covered lorry, the chipped and stained state of the walls and floor—convinced the British officers that there had indeed been a massacre. For the Captain of the 'Empire Pride' this was the last straw. He declared that he would not accept the Soviet Military Mission officers for the return trip. The British officers had to repeat the old arguments many times, that there was an agreement on repatriation and that Soviet internal affairs were none of Britain's concern, before he finally agreed to allow them on board.

Several thousand French and Belgian prisoners-of-war came on board in the Russian prisoners' place. They had been liberated by the Red Army in eastern Europe and, Youmatoff writes, were in a terrible state, having been forced to march hundreds of miles in their weakened state in order to reach Odessa. The ship's Captain and crew boycotted the Soviet officers during the voyage, but no such small satisfaction was possible for Martin and Youmatoff. 'Correct relations had to be kept. We couldn't have any incident which would create any diplomatic rift,' Youmatoff explains. In talks with the Russians they avoided all reference to the prisoners' fate, and for some days indeed they saw little of the officers, such were the problems of administration caused by the French and Belgian prisoners who were disembarked in Marseilles. The British and Soviet officers got off there also and flew together back to England. There was plenty more repatriation work to be done and the two groups of men would somehow have to work together in harmony, whatever their personal feelings about one another.

Youmatoff, who is now an Anglican parish priest near Ontario in Canada, was deeply upset by what happened in Odessa:

> Most of us on the staff of the Russian Liaison Group were born Russians and had fled in the arms of our parents at the time of the Revolution. We were dealing with men who might well have been our cousins, and who most certainly were our allies, and yet who treated their own kin worse than cattle . . . There was a callous disregard of human dignity and Stalin's hard line—a prisoner-of-war is a traitor and to be considered a dead man—came through loud and clear.

Youmatoff felt too that he had been put personally in a false position. For nearly a year it had been his job to soothe the fears of the Russians in Britain, to dissuade them from trying to avoid repatriation and to convince them that all would be well for them so long as they agreed to go home quietly. Then suddenly in Odessa he was presented with facts which convinced him that all was not well. He does not believe that all 3,000 of the Russians on the 'Empire Pride' were executed, though like other repatriates they presumably all went into the labour camps and suffered the deadly cold and hunger of those terrible places. He is convinced, though, that some of them were killed, certainly the thirty-one in the warehouse and probably the 200-300 whom Polyachenko contributed to the Soviet colonel's list.

Youmatoff's report caused some consternation in Whitehall. Firebrace was able to check the names of the thirty-one victims against his own records and conclude that they had all either refused to return to the Soviet Union or else tried to evade repatriation by enlisting in the Polish army. It made him all the more alarmed about the ultimate fate of men who had appeared before his joint commission and been placed on the disputed list: 'This report has impressed upon me the necessity for the most thorough screening of all doubtful cases, and I can only hope that no man on the disputed list will ever be sent back to the Soviet Union.' He reminded the Foreign Office that from the Soviet point of view pre-war residents of the Baltic states and of the western Ukraine were Soviet citizens as much as any of the others, and that it was only because of British non-recognition of Soviet claims to these areas that the men were being temporarily allowed to remain. 'Such men will be shot on arrival without the slightest doubt,' concluded Firebrace, for they had all been vocal in their descriptions of Red Army behaviour during the invasions of 1939 and 1940 and every word they said had been recorded on paper.

It was now the end of June. In six months 32,044 Soviet citizens had been transported home by ship from Britain, some via the northern route to Murmansk, others through the Mediterranean to Odessa.[4] The problem of the Russians in Britain was nearing its end. All that remained now were the disputed cases, the unique 'Sidorov' family and a few who were ill or had successfully concealed their identity. Several weeks earlier the practice of bringing prisoners-of-war to Britain had ceased. It was simpler to hold them on the Continent. And as the collapse of Nazi Germany drew near, with huge armies converging from east and west, it became clear that within a short time repatriation would be possible overland.

After Hitler committed suicide on April 30, the reins of Nazi authority slackened and millions of people were released from confinement to wander in all directions. By the time Germany formally surrendered a week later the Allies could see that these 'displaced persons' constituted a huge problem, greater even than the problem of disarming and controlling their former enemies. Prisoners-of-war and conscript workers from all the Nazi-controlled countries were taking to the roads, inhibiting Allied military traffic and threatening law and order.

On May 5, a special message from General Eisenhower was broadcast to Europe in many languages with instructions for displaced persons: 'Do not move out of your district. Wait for orders. Form small groups of your own nationality and choose

leaders who will deal for you with the Allied military authorities.'
Obviously the problem was not so acute with western Europeans
and Americans. For them it was only a question of waiting for
transport. They had homes to go to, friends and relatives to
welcome them. But in the East there had been a disruption of
society. National frontiers had been moved hundreds of miles,
with death and destruction on a huge scale. Under Red Army
influence left-wing governments were being set up. Many of the
refugees viewed the situation with such alarm that they were
resolved not to go home.

Poland was one such country, and Eisenhower's message
recognised the fact that automatic repatriation of Poles would not
always be possible. He therefore announced: 'Liberated Poles
in the area of Germany controlled by the Supreme Commander
will have an opportunity to indicate their wishes whether they
wish to return to Poland or not. Each case will be dealt with
individually.' But his message to the Russians was quite different.
It ran simply: 'All Russians liberated within the area controlled
by the Supreme Commander will be transferred to the Russian
authorities as soon as possible.'[5]

This was enough to alert the astute journalists and on May 24
the *New York Times* wrote with surprising accuracy: 'At the
Yalta Conference it was apparently decided that all pre-1939
Russians should accordingly be sent back to Russia. Now they
are being repatriated despite the unwillingness of many.' The
London *Daily Herald* too announced on May 30 that 'all Russian
subjects will be compulsorily returned, whether they wish it or
not.' The secret agreement was by now known to many Allied
officers. Inevitably it was leaked to the press, but not in a way which
made any impact on the western public. Few Britons or Americans
knew that force was being used to ensure repatriation and that
some Russians were killing themselves rather than go home.

The repatriation of Russians from the field in Germany was
done in a rough-and-ready way, without the discussion and
documentation that accompanied the transports from Britain.
As one American officer put it, 'Some of them were being pushed
into trains without our asking many questions.'[6] British and
American officers were simply ordered to hand Russians over
to Red Army officers, to direct or transport them to exchange
points on the frontier line between the occupied zones. On June

2, the *Daily Herald* reported that 10,000 Russians, most of them women, were passing through the lines every day. A pontoon bridge had been built across the river Elbe to carry them. The Soviet side was decorated with red flags and slogans of welcome, said the *Daily Herald*, and 'recordings of Russian songs play all day long as interminable columns of uprooted humanity trudge back into Russian territory.'

A reporter from the *Chicago Daily News* watched Russian conscript workers being shipped home from Austria:

> They are not a good sight to see, simple peasants without imagination, awkward and poorly clothed, and with eyes that see with a dull emptiness. They are rounded up and brought to Linz, bathed and deloused and hauled to a train. They clamber aboard and the train grinds slowly away. They will get off a few miles behind the Russian lines, facing several hundred miles of travel to homes that probably have been burned or bombed. The children have German fathers. Hundreds of pregnant women will rear more children by German fathers. The amazing bundles which they insist on carrying hold their worldly possessions. It is heartbreaking to see them clinging desperately to clothing we would refuse to wear and carrying sacks of wheat, sewing machines, saws, tools, kettles and beans.[7]

American and British officers were anxious to speed up the process of repatriation. The Russians were a source of difficulty in many ways. For years they had been appallingly fed and many of them were ill. They were consuming scarce food and medicines, all of which was badly needed for the German population. The Americans and British accepted that Germany would endure many months of hardship and they felt it only right that their Allies should have better treatment. Indeed, there were Russian liaison officers only too eager to protest if they thought that Soviet citizens were not obtaining appropriate rations. The Russian displaced persons were a constant annoyance and a possible source of conflict between the Allies.

It was the Russians who had suffered the most as prisoners-of-war or forced labourers in Germany, and once the German administration of their camps collapsed their behaviour was quite uncontrolled. Almost everybody who was in Germany during the extraordinary days that followed the end of the war remembers the wild behaviour of the Russians. For instance

John Stanton, who was a prisoner in a camp for British officers near Munich, recalls how the Russians from a camp nearby descended on the local village as soon as they were free: 'They just made mayhem. They broke into all the houses, raped all the women and drank the place dry. The Germans were quite docile and just tried to hide. The Russians weren't organised. They were just individuals on the rampage. They'd been quite brutalised by what they'd gone through as prisoners.'

The British officers too, though their sufferings were small compared to those of the Russians, had lost some sense of proportion. Stanton remembers that he and his friends were entirely on the Russians' side during these days of chaos and horror. They were delighted to see the Russians giving their captors 'a taste of their own medicine'. But the members of the British and American occupying armies found it a gruelling and almost impossible task to control so many crazed men. The report written for Senator Wiley explains: 'The desire for revenge on their German masters was perhaps strongest of all in the Soviet displaced persons. They are reported also to have shown a disregard for authority and for the property of others.'

Most of the incidents were hushed up in the interest of Allied unity, but there was one which did appear in the press. A few days after the German surrender the inhabitants of a Russian prisoner-of-war camp, 1,600 officers and 8,000 others, went on the rampage and looted a German freight train near their camp in the Nuremberg area. They found a number of cars loaded with 50-gallon drums of methyl alcohol. For the Russians, newly released after years of confinement, the temptation was too great. They mixed it with water and drank it, and within a few days 400 of them were dead.[8] The Americans declared that alcohol poisoning was second only to typhus as a health problem among displaced persons.

One may be sure that it was only because of the particular horror of this incident and the large number of the fatalities that any public mention was made. The Russians were desperate, and though this was only understandable after all they had endured, it was equally understandable that the Allied authorities were anxious to be rid of so many difficult and dangerous men. Their orders were to prepare for an influx of more than a million Allied nationals, one third of them prisoners-of-war, the rest displaced persons. Although in the event only 450,000 came from East to West, the problem was acute in those early days of peace. At the end of May, so many people were pouring into American territory that bridges had to be blown up in order to halt the flow temporarily. Vincent Paravicini, an American colonel in charge of refugee matters, explained to journalists on May 29 that as well as the Allies who were expected to come West and were welcome—Frenchmen, Belgian, Dutch, British and American —there were hundreds of thousands of Germans also pouring into the western zones. They feared the Red Army, often with good reason, and they thought the western Allies might be more sympathetic.

On May 22, Soviet and American representatives met at Leipzig and worked out a 'Plan for the Delivery through the Army lines of Former Prisoners-of-War and Civilians Liberated by the Red Army and Allied Forces'. Red Army authorities held 2,200 American and British prisoners near the demarcation line and these were handed over at Luckenwalde as soon as the Leipzig Agreement came into effect. A number of exchange points were set up and arrangements made obliging both parties to convey prisoners-of-war in suitable transport to within marching distance of the line. The Leipzig Agreement was of course subsidiary to the Yalta Agreement on Repatriation. The British and Americans were encouraged by this early delivery of their prisoners and by Soviet observance of decent standards of treatment. By the end of May 28,662 American prisoners had been recovered from Soviet control, 2,858 of them by sea from Odessa, the rest overland.[9]

The Times reported the smooth process of mass repatriation and that 'all had but one goal—to get home.'[10] The *Daily Herald* also gave the impression of millions of Russians all longing to return to the Soviet Union. Their reporter had heard 'rumours of the Russians not wanting their displaced people back, rumours even of shootings'. She therefore went to watch a trainload of 1,600 Russians crossing into Soviet-occupied territory at Weddendorf. She found wagons chalked with slogans in Russian—'Long live our Motherland' and 'Glory to the Father of our Victories, the Great Stalin'. She found nothing at all to disturb her: 'No one seems reluctant to be going back to Russia. They have spent the whole night travelling, but they are smiling, singing in harmony, laughing and gesticulating. They sing to the accompaniment of an accordion. A mandoline is twanging too.'[11]

One can hardly be surprised that this mood of accordions and twanging mandolines was the one that prevailed. It was only a few days after the end of the war, and there was an almost physical revulsion in Britain and the United States against anyone who suggested that there was disunity among the Allies. The very idea of further battles was unacceptable to men who had endured so many years of bloodshed, of separation from their homes and families. Had the various conflicts between the Soviet Union and the West become acute it would have been necessary to delay demobilisation, perhaps to explain to the soldiers that there might be more fighting. There can be no doubt which side would have been more demoralised by any such suggestion, more inclined to insubordination or even mutiny. True, the Red Army was in a state of temporary disarray, literally drunk with victory, but cruel battles had instilled into the soldiers a sense of discipline which they would not violate. They had endured the greater hardships, the more numerous casualties, and they were less likely than American or British soldiers to grumble to their superiors or question unpopular orders. There was none of that in the Red Army, for the penalties were draconian.

Though relations between East and West during 1945 never became so bad that armed conflict was possible, the British and American leaders could not avoid an uncomfortable awareness of how weak they would be if relations were to deteriorate seriously. It was a question not only of army morale, but also of public opinion at home. Wives and mothers wanted their menfolk home. They would be horrified at any suggestion of another war and another period of separation. They would protest most vigorously if they thought their leaders were even contemplating such an idea.

In a democracy it can take years to persuade the people that war is necessary. This had been Britain's and America's problem when faced with the need to destroy Nazi Germany. Could they count on the full support of the nation? Against the Nazis they could, though it was a struggle. Against the Soviet Union they would have far greater difficulty. For years pro-Soviet feeling had been officially encouraged. It would take more than a few months to undo it.

In Russia, on the other hand, affection for the western Allies, while proclaimed on formal occasions and in the press, had been rigidly controlled among ordinary people. Allies or no allies, they were still the class enemy, and any Soviet citizen who came too close to them was likely to find himself under arrest. It would be less of a surprise, less of a wrench for the Soviet people to be informed that America and Britain were now their enemies. In any case, the Soviet people would do what they were told.

Such thoughts were a constant worry to western leaders, making it difficult for them even to contemplate any breach of the Yalta Agreement. At the end of the war there were a little more than two million Soviet citizens in western Germany, and so quickly did repatriation proceed that within two months 1,393,902 of these had been delivered to Soviet forces. Records of this chaotic period are sparse and one cannot tell how many of these put up any resistance. Interviews with local commanding officers make it clear that a majority went home willingly, apprehensive perhaps about the welcome they would receive, for they had surrendered in the face of Stalin's stern warning, but not anticipating such a punishment as ten years in a labour camp. Others resisted at first. Several officers have told the author that individual Russians tried to break away from east-bound transports, some even inviting their captors to shoot them in preference to their delivery to the Soviet authorities. But most of these, once they realised that the British and Americans had orders to send them back by force and were resolved to carry out these orders, accepted the inevitable and obeyed. It was then, of course, in their interest to pretend to be delighted at the prospect of repatriation, to protest their loyalty as often as possible in the hope that it would be believed.

Of the two million Soviet citizens in western Germany, not many could claim total innocence of any charge of collaboration with the enemy. Only a few had resisted all German threats and passed those years of captivity without helping the enemy's war effort at all. With most the collaboration had been mild, the fulfilment of menial or dangerous tasks in exchange for slightly better food and conditions. But with others it had been gross. Hundreds of thousands of Soviet citizens had fought willingly and enthusiastically on the German side. In the chaos of May and June 1945, many of these tried to mingle with groups of displaced persons. With luck they would be able to go home and no one would ever know what they had done. Throughout these weeks agonising choices had to be made. What should they do? Go home and hope for the best? Run away and try to stay in Germany? Whatever they did the chances of survival seemed slim.

A *New York Times* report showed how little public sympathy there was for the Russians who had chosen the wrong side. It referred to '100,000 to 150,000 Russians traitors who are being held as prisoners-of-war and presumably will ultimately face Soviet justice'.[12] At a press conference on June 8, General Omar Bradley was asked about Soviet suggestions that their citizens were being ill-treated in American camps. His reply was one of puzzlement: 'We do have some Russians but I don't believe Russia would complain on anything we did to them. We captured 100,000 to 150,000 of them fighting on the side of the Germans. I don't believe those people have much future.'

On June 9, Colonel Robert J. Gill, an American officer responsible for enemy prisoners-of-war, announced in Paris that his men had delivered into Red Army custody 50,000 Soviet citizens who had fought in the German army. Many of these had been forced to do what they did, said Gill, but they were nevertheless 'under somewhat of a pall back in Russia'[13] and were scared to go home.

The men the Soviet authorities were most anxious to get their hands on were the followers of Andrey Andreyevich Vlasov, a Soviet general who fought most bravely defending Moscow and Leningrad during the first year of the war, but who fell into German hands on June 12, 1942. In his early weeks of captivity he came to believe that all Russia's ills, including the sufferings of war, were brought about by the Soviet system. His biographer, V. Osokin, described the thought which came to dominate Vlasov's mind: 'If Bolshevism dies, then the Russian people will live. If Bolshevism survives, then the Russian people will die out, will cease to exist. Either—or. There is no third choice.'[14]

It was a typically Russian single-minded approach. Vlasov did not feel it necessary to analyse the character and aims of Nazi Germany, its murderous racism and its determination to subject all 'inferior peoples', including the Russians, to slavery and ultimate extinction. All he saw was that the German invasion of the Soviet Union provided the one chance of a lifetime to overthrow the communist system. On September 10, two months after his capture, he published a leaflet accusing Stalin of ruining the Red Army by his purges and the farmland of Russia by his policy of collectivisation. He called on all Russians 'to strive with all their strength to overthrow the hated Stalin regime'. By the end of 1942 the Germans had put him at the head of a 'Russian National Committee'.[15]

Vlasov's idea was for this Committee to form its own army and political groups, for his soldiers to fight side-by-side with the Germans who had already penetrated deep into Russia, for his supporters to take over the government of Russia after the Soviet Union had collapsed. In this he was being more than a little naive, for Hitler had other plans. On July 16, 1941, he had said:

> It must never be permitted that anyone but the Germans bear arms. This is particularly important. Even if in immediate terms it appears easier to call on some other conquered nations for armed assistance, this is wrong; one day it will hit out against us, inevitably and unavoidably. Only the Germans may bear arms, not the Slav, not the Czech, not the Cossack or Ukrainian.[16]

Nevertheless, large numbers of Slavs were armed and sent into battle alongside the German army, but not in the way Vlasov hoped or expected. The 'Russian Liberation Army' was created not as a unified force under the command of Vlasov and other Russian officers, but as a large number of separate battalions scattered among the German army and officered by Germans. No one knows exactly how many there were, but most sources estimate that between 1943 and 1945 the number of Russians so serving was more than 500,000 and perhaps as many as a million.[17]

Clearly the Nazis were anxious to exploit Vlasov for propaganda purposes, to build him up in the eyes of the world and especially of Red Army soldiers, who were to be encouraged to desert. They also wanted to use him to drive a wedge into the Grand Alliance, to make the British and American leaders suspicious of Russia's loyalty to the war effort. In an 'Open Letter' Vlasov declared that 'England has always been the enemy of the Russian people'. He accused Stalin of using Britain and the United States to further his own aim of world domination and of 'tying the fate of the Russian people to the future of England'. In several documents he expressed his dislike of 'capitalists' and 'imperialists' as well as Bolsheviks.

At the end of 1942 Vlasov was allowed to set up a 'propaganda centre' at Dabendorf just outside Berlin, where his supporters published two newspapers, called *Zarya* (Dawn) and *Dobrovolyets* (Volunteer), and trained Russians to recruit their fellow-country-men from prisoner-of-war camps. Those familiar with the teaching at Dabendorf bear witness to the independent spirit of the Russian instructors and to the lack of overt Nazi propaganda. But it is clear that the centre was regarded as suspect by Gestapo and other extreme forces in Germany and that continual efforts were made to discredit it with Hitler. Inevitably, the Russian instructors at Dabendorf mixed some Nazi propaganda with their Russian nationalistic message. They had to ingratiate themselves with the Nazis in order to make any progress at all.

Vlasov could not escape from the fact that, in the eyes of doctrinaire Nazis, he was a sub-human (*Untermensch*) and there-fore quite unfit to command men in German uniform. In vain did more practical German commanders plead for a realistic approach, for a better use to be made of this valuable man-power. They were faced with the cruel closed minds of men like Heinrich Himmler, who said in an address to ss generals on October 4, 1943: 'What happens to a Russian or to a Czech does not interest me in the least . . . Whether 10,000 Russian females fall down from exhaustion while digging an anti-tank ditch interests me only insofar as the anti-tank ditch for Germany is finished.'[18]

Ironically it was Himmler, the man who in this same speech described Vlasov as a 'swine', who was the first Nazi leader to take a more positive attitude to the Russian Liberation Movement. On September 16, 1944, Himmler and Vlasov met at Rastenburg in East Prussia and agreed on the creation of a new committee and army to unite Russians against Stalin. When Russia was reconquered this committee would become a provisional govern-ment. On November 14 the committee was founded at a ceremony in Prague and a manifesto issued which, in theory, offered Russians many of the freedoms hitherto denied them: the return of farmland to private ownership, liquidation of forced labour, freedom of religion and speech.

But November 1944 was hardly the moment for the launching

of such a grand enterprise. Four days later American troops entered German territory. By now the aims of Himmler and Vlasov were quite different. Himmler hoped not only to gain more men for the defence of the Reich, but also to undermine the alliance between the Soviet Union and the West. Only if this happened could the war be won. Vlasov, after all the rebuffs he had received, was concerned less with helping the Nazis, more with building up a force which would become a political unit. It was his plan, however the war ended, to negotiate with the winning side and enlist its aid in the march against Stalin. He was convinced that if the Allies won, as seemed probable, it would only be a matter of time before the Red Army came to blows with Britain and the United States. In that case Vlasov and his men would join the West wholeheartedly and throw themselves against the Soviet Union.

The Vlasov movement had one brief moment of glory. On May 5 one of his generals, Sergei Bunyachenko, flung a whole division of Russians into battle against ss troops in Prague, thus tipping the scale in favour of the resistance fighters and ensuring the city's liberation. The American journalist, Ivan Peterman, wrote: 'Prague really was liberated by foreign troops after all. Not by the Allies, who did not arrive until the shooting was all over, but by 22,000 Russian outlaws wearing German uniforms.' But the Czech resistance, much of it communist, was not inclined to feel gratitude towards such uninvited liberators. They invited the Vlasovites to surrender to the Red Army. Within two or three days Bunyachenko and his men had evacuated the city. Their only hope now was to come to some arrangement with the Americans, who were not far away.

By now Vlasov himself was a broken man. Wilfried Strik-Strikfeldt, a Russian-speaking Balt and Vlasov's main liaison officer with the German army, writes that he began to suffer periods of depression and heavy drinking, so that towards the end he quite lost control of the situation. Envoys were sent to the United States army, but no assurances could be given to them. By now it was as much as the Vlasovites could do to make their way into American-occupied territory and surrender. At first the Americans treated them friendlily. Ordinary officers in the field did not know about the Yalta Agreement on repatriation. Strikfeldt writes: 'When an American asked me whether Vlasov was a traitor, I put a counter-question—were Washington and Franklin also traitors?'

During May, some Vlasovites were overrun by the Red Army and either liquidated on the spot or sent to the labour camps. Some who surrendered to the Americans were delivered across the Soviet lines during the chaotic first days of peace. Others were confined in prisoner-of-war camps to await a decision about their fate. Vlasov himself fell into Soviet hands while under American escort on May 12 near Schlüsselburg, west of Hanover. On August 2, 1946, *Pravda* announced that he and nine of his officers had been condemned to death and hanged.

Supporters of Vlasov now in the West still feel that their cause was a just one, that their decision to take up arms on Hitler's side against Stalin was correct. Strikfeldt writes: 'The belief that the alliance of convenience between the Anglo-Saxons and the Kremlin could not endure was no empty dream. It was the conviction of all who knew what Bolshevism meant. What happened later proved us right. It was our timing that was wrong. We had of course no knowledge of what had been agreed at Yalta.'[19] He concludes his book with the following panegyric: 'The Russian Liberation Movement was smashed and Vlasov and his friends were executed, just as Stauffenberg and the men on July 20th [the 1944 bomb plot against Hitler] were executed. But because they gave their lives for freedom and justice, they have become a power that endures everywhere where freedom and justice are honoured.'[20]

Opponents of Vlasov point out that, however hard he tried to be independent, in effect he collaborated fully with the Nazis, the men who invaded his country brutally and treated Russians like animals, and that after the evils of Hitlerism became clear the Soviet people rallied behind Stalin and fought most bravely to drive the invader from their soil. Perhaps if Hitler's policies had been less diabolical there would have been more support for the German occupation, more desertions from the Red Army and more men ready to serve Vlasov. But as it turned out, Stalin did by the end of the war obtain the co-operation of almost all the Soviet people.

Still, it would have been strange if this had been otherwise. Countries do not like being invaded by foreigners, especially by foreigners as inhuman as the Nazis, and it is a measure of the social unrest that prevailed in the Soviet Union at the outbreak of war that so many of their citizens—perhaps as many as a million—were ready to take up arms on the enemy's side. As Alexander Solzhenitsyn writes in *The Gulag Archipelago*, 'They would never have joined the Vlasovite ranks of the Wehrmacht had they not been driven to the final extreme, beyond the bounds of despair, and had they not nursed an unquenchable hatred towards the Soviet regime.'[21]

The most furiously anti-Soviet group of them all was the Cossacks. These were allowed to form semi-independent units of the German army much earlier than the Vlasovites and had earned for themselves more of a reputation in battle. On May 17, Field-Marshal Alexander telegraphed his Chief of Staff in London to ask for instructions on how to deal with 50,000 Cossacks and 25,000 Croats who were in his territory. A quick decision, he wrote, would 'assist us in clearing congestion in Southern Austria'. He did however have one worry, that 'in each of the above cases to return them to their country of origin immediately might be fatal to their health.'

The next day Andrew Cunningham, Britain's Chief of Naval Staff, noted that the Cossacks would in any case have to go back to Russia, because they came under the Yalta Agreement. The case of the Croats, though, was more complicated. They were Yugoslav, not Soviet, and no agreement covered them. Cedric Price, a colonel who worked for the War Cabinet and later became Britain's Director of Military Intelligence, was ordered to consult the Foreign Office.

The Foreign Office was in favour of repatriating both the Cossacks and the Croats. In a letter signed by Geoffrey McDermott they replied to Price:

> The Croat troops are in effect regular forces of a quisling Government operating under German direction . . . We would therefore be in favour of handing the Croat troops in Southern Austria over to Tito's forces. Such a move would certainly please Tito and would show him that in some matters at any rate we are ready to treat him as a regular and responsible ally.[22]

On May 20, Churchill expressed some concern about the problem in a note to General Ismay, his personal Chief of Staff:

What is known about the number of Russians taken prisoner by the Germans and liberated by us? Can you discriminate between those who were merely workers and those who actually fought against us? Could I have a further report on the 45,000 Cossacks of whom General Eisenhower speaks? How did they come into their present plight? Did they fight against us?

Churchill did not follow up his worried questions, the replies to which were extremely vague and arrived only after the operations were well under way. On May 29, the Chiefs of Staff ordered Alexander to hand over both the Cossacks and the Croats to Stalin and Tito respectively. Repatriation had in fact already begun without waiting for the order, presumably on the authority of the Yalta Agreement, and some extremely bloody operations took place. As the following chapters show, it was for many British soldiers the most disagreeable episode of the whole war.

4

THE CROATS AND THE COSSACKS

DURING the Russian Civil War of 1918-20 some of the keenest fighters on the White side were Cossacks, members of that strange estate, half way between a nation and a community, which for centuries inhabited southern Russia, at times preserving a certain independence from the Tsar, at other times serving the Tsar loyally and receiving privileges from him. A frontier people whose settlements stretched from the southern Ukraine to the northern Caucasus and into Siberia, the Cossacks had a continual need for effective self-defence and military skill. They became renowned for their horsemanship and physical strength. The Tsar needed them to defend his southern borders and was anxious to keep them loyal, but he usually found it hard to keep firm discipline among a people so far from the centres of power, so militarily strong and so temperamentally prone to rebellion. In the seventeenth and eighteenth centuries two Cossacks, Stenka Razin and Emilyan Pugachov, launched bloody rebellions which were only put down with great difficulty.

The later Tsars came to terms with the Cossacks and an agreement was reached whereby every male was eligible for military service for twenty years from the age of eighteen. In return, they enjoyed some independence and, since many of them were close to the Tsar's court, great influence. At the beginning of this century there were five million of them in Russia, divided into 'armies' and administered by a sort of military self-government. The main armies lived north of the Caucasus and five of them—named Don, Kuban, Ural, Orenburg and Terek—contained about 85 per cent of the whole Cossack nation. Each army was ruled by an 'ataman' or headman. Vyacheslav Naumenko, ataman of the Kuban Cossacks from 1920 to 1958, remembers those pre-revolutionary days with nostalgia and longing. 'We had the status of a separate nationality within the Empire, just like the Poles or the Latvians or any other minority,' he recalls. But while some Russians admired the Cossacks for their bravery and martial artistry, others feared them as the 'praetorian guard' of the Tsarist authorities. In times of civil unrest they could be relied upon to disperse street demonstrations with some severity.

When Russia was gripped by revolution and civil war, most of the Cossacks fought against the new Bolshevik authority and the Red Army. When it was all over and the Reds had won, many thousands of Cossacks fled to the West. These old émigrés, former White Army men, watched in fury as the Cossack way of life was eroded and land redistributed. They plotted and schemed against the still fragile Bolshevik authority. For years there was little they could do, for the country was held in the iron grip of Stalin. Pathetic little invasions were mounted in the belief that the Russian people would rise up and overthrow the communists at the first sign of a White liberator. Things were not so simple. In most cases the invaders were quickly caught and massacred.

So it was among Cossacks most of all perhaps that hearts leapt when Hitler invaded the Soviet Union and for a time seemed likely to conquer it. For them the war seemed little more than a heaven-sent chance to overthrow the communists and restore their nation to the privileged position it had once enjoyed. Cossack leaders like Naumenko (who in 1920 had been a Major-General in the White forces) and the ataman of the Don Cossacks, Pyotr Krasnov, were quick to offer the Nazis their services. For a time such offers were rebuffed. The German army was doing well enough on its own and did not need the assistance of Slav *Untermenschen*. But after the Battle of Stalingrad and the defeats which followed, the Nazis felt inclined to take a more liberal view if this would help them to win allies. In November 1943, they promised to give the Cossacks back their traditional lands. Four months later they appointed Krasnov and Naumenko members of a directorate of Cossack forces within the German army. Another member was T. I. Domanov, a recently promoted general, who differed from the others in that he was one of the 'new emigration', a former Soviet officer who had joined the invading Germans and was now retreating with them.

The Cossacks had surrounded themselves with the trappings

of Imperial Russia. Although their basic uniform was German, they wore tall Persian-lamb fur hats, knee-length boots, flowing capes and generous beards or moustaches. The men carried long, curved swords on parade while the officers wore ornate, jewel-encrusted daggers, family heirlooms which had often belonged to many generations of each warrior clan. When they began to retreat, refugees attached themselves to many units—women and children who were afraid to remain in territory which was being reoccupied by the Red Army—until sometimes there were as many camp followers as fighting men. Many of the senior officers, veterans of the Civil War, were in their sixties, and would normally have been too old for active service.

In spite of their unwieldy and old-fashioned appearance, the Cossacks fought furiously, with a growing sense of desperation as they were forced to retreat farther and farther from their own territory. Towards the end of the war, Cossack units under Helmut von Pannwitz, a Russian-speaking Balt, were sent into northern Yugoslavia to fight Tito's communist partisans. With their horses and skill in the saddle they were able to police these mountainous areas most effectively, more so than the motorised German units which they replaced. In Yugoslavia it was a cruel war with no quarter given on either side. Soon the Cossacks had acquired a reputation for brutality. They had a habit, it was said, of charging into a village suspected of harbouring partisans and levelling it with fire and the sword.

Some Cossacks have claimed that these dubious activities began only after they were forced to retreat from their own territory. It was then that Nazi German pressure upon them intensified and their tenuous autonomy practically ceased to exist. Many trace the decline in standards from the time of the death of Ataman Pavlov on June 17, 1944. Pyotr Donskow, a former member of Pavlov's staff, has written to the author accusing Krasnov of conniving at Pavlov's murder in order to ingratiate himself with the Germans and gain the position of ataman. It is true that during the last year of the war many Cossack units came under direct ss control.

Cossacks do not deny that terrible incidents took place, but they blame this on the baleful influence of the Nazi German ss, members of which were attached to their General Staff, as well as on certain unworthy men from the Cossack lands who joined the German band-wagon when it appeared that Hitler was going to win the war. Nikolay Krasnov, grandson of the Cossack general Pyotr Krasnov, has written of these bad elements in his book *The Unforgettable:* 'They robbed like bandits. They raped women and set fire to settlements. Their disgraceful behaviour cast a stain on those who came to fight against communism and carried out their duty in an honourable and soldierly manner.'[1]

Another concession made by Alfred Rosenberg's *Ostministerium* during these dying months of the war was the gift of an area around Tolmezzo in the Italian Alps, a few miles from the Austrian border, which the Cossack nation was to occupy and use as a base for its military activities. It was a strange site to choose for the new 'Cossackia', but for nearly eight months it grew, until by the spring of 1945 it contained 35,000 Cossacks, half soldiers and half refugees. But they could never feel safe because of the bands of Italian partisans operating in the area, most of whom, as in nearby Yugoslavia, were communist and bitterly hostile.

Then they had to face the problem of the British and American armies, which were fighting their way up through Italy. In April 1945, the British were approaching Tolmezzo and the Italian-Austrian frontier. The Cossacks were in German uniform and nominally at least bound to fight, but they had decided that they would not do this. Their quarrel was with the Soviet Union, not with Britain or America. This left them with the choice of surrendering or withdrawing. At the end of April, a total evacuation of the community was ordered by T. I. Domanov, who had replaced Krasnov as ataman in February. On April 30 they loaded everything into their horse-drawn carts and set out for the Plöckenpass a few miles away. The next morning the advance guard was in Austria and within two days the whole community was camped near the first two Austrian villages, Mauthen and Kötschach. In Mauthen there was a German commandant, an elderly man with half a company of elderly soldiers. One can imagine their amazement at being descended upon by this extraordinary horde. The carts were put together out of crudely hacked planks of wood and roofed with canvas canopies. They held arms, ammunition, food, wives, children, babies—everything needed for family life as well as for battle. The commandant ordered them to halt, but his forces were puny and his authority was that of a dying regime. The Cossacks were not inclined to take notice of him.

Dmitri Frolov, a member of Domanov's General Staff, remembers their first contact with the British. On May 4, an advance guard of an officer and a few men came upon the Cossack camp near Mauthen. 'Who are you?' the British asked. The Cossacks did their best to explain. Apparently satisfied the British said 'O.K.', turned their motorcycles round and departed.

The British were indeed worried about how the Cossacks would react. Earlier in May, Lieutenant-Colonel Alec Malcolm, commanding officer of the 8th Battalion, Argyll and Sutherland Highlanders, received orders to move to Lorenzago, twenty miles west of Tolmezzo, and 'use the place as a starting off point for operations against a Cossack division'. His Brigadier, Geoffrey Musson, was unaware that the Cossacks had already left for Austria. Jack Bates, who wrote the diaries of the 36th Infantry Brigade, recalls that their advance towards the Austrian frontier met no opposition, that it was 'more like a peacetime drive through very beautiful scenery'.[2] They were agreeably surprised by the Cossack decision not to resist.

The British brigade also had reports that several thousand Georgians from the Caucasus were camped near Forni Avoitra, right on the border. Bates writes that the Georgians were on the best of terms with the local Italian population, but that there had been bloody battles between them and the Cossacks. Like every other Englishman, Bates was amazed at the sight presented by these old warriors:

> These Georgians were an aristocratic throwback to the days of Tsarist Russia. Their officers, ten of whom were princes, were arrayed in glittering uniforms and treated their soldiers like serfs. Many of them had been taxi-drivers in Paris before the war. Just before the arrival of the 6th Royal West Kents there was a sound of shots in the town and all the civilians ran for cover. It was discovered that one of the Georgian officers had shot another in a duel.

The Georgians surrendered willingly, explaining that they had no quarrel with the western Allies, only with the Soviet Union. It was, said Bates, 'an argument we were soon to learn by heart'. There was one tense moment when the Georgians' commanding officer emerged from the mountains some distance away and accused the officer-princes of surrendering without authority. Bates remembers: 'The commanding officer, unlike many others we have known, more's the pity, was a beautiful princess . . . Clad in buckskin trousers she presented a striking and commanding figure as she demanded to see the British general.' Another officer remembers her as 'very tough-looking and bristling with hand-grenades', as he showed her into Musson's caravan during the small hours of May 9. Musson recalls that she was a good-looking woman of about thirty, wearing a white high-necked sweater, breeches, boots and a bandolier of rifle bullets slung round her body. They agreed on surrender terms.

On May 7, Malcolm's battalion reached the outskirts of Tolmezzo, ready to do battle with the Cossacks who had lived there for nearly a year, and it was only then that they found that there had been an evacuation. They moved into the town and spent the day rounding up large numbers of stragglers. These had not only to be fed, but also to be protected from enthusiastic partisans, who would have killed them all if given their heads. At 5 pm they heard their best news of the war, that Germany had surrendered unconditionally. The record reads: 'Unfortunately the Battalion was not in a suitable position to celebrate, but an extra beer issue was authorised.'[3] The London Irish Rifles, a short distance away, were more adventurous. Their commanding officer, Lieutenant-Colonel H. E. N. Bredin, gave the men a victory speech, after which he set fire to a 15-foot-high bonfire of logs. The record reads: 'Rum-punch, vino, sandwiches, cakes and a calf roasted whole were provided for all ranks. An effigy of Hitler, escorted by pipers playing the slow march, was brought to the fire and duly burned.'[4] But most units were unable to indulge in such extravagances. Jack Bates remembers how little affected they all seemed by the news of victory. Events were moving too fast and there were too many problems.

On May 8, a Cossack delegation drove back over the pass to Tolmezzo to say that they were ready to surrender unconditionally. They spoke to the divisional commander, Robert Arbuthnott, who arranged that there would be a meeting the next morning at nine o'clock in the railway station at Oberdrauburg where Domanov would surrender unconditionally to Musson. Once this was agreed there was considerable relief in the British ranks. In spite of their strange appearance, the Cossacks were well-armed and seasoned soldiers. In Bates's words, 'they would still have been a force to be reckoned with if they had refused to capitulate, and until that capitulation was complete we could not feel secure.'

Bates's record continues: 'Harried on all sides, with all their hopes of conquest disappointed, they now faced the certainty of return to the Soviet Union as traitors.' It is here that he was gravely mistaken, for the one thing which the Cossacks did not contemplate was that the British would turn them over to the Red Army, their mortal enemies. According to Frolov, the delegates took an early opportunity to make this point with Musson and his staff: 'We told them we were Cossacks who had spent all our lives fighting against Soviet power. We had fought to the last man. But we had never fought against regular units of the western Allies, because we regarded the Americans and the British as our friends.' Indeed, so ill-informed were the Cossacks of the political and military realities of the time that they thought the British and American alliance with Stalin was a sham, that it would shortly collapse. They actually imagined the war was going to continue on a new basis—the West against the Soviet Union. In that case the Cossacks would be valuable allies on the western side. Had they suspected the truth, that the West was counting on Stalin's good-will and was about to make him a present of these people, his bitter enemies, they would certainly never have surrendered.

Musson ordered the Cossacks to proceed down the mountain and to cross the river Drau by the bridge at Oberdrauburg, ten miles from Mauthen. They were then to take the road which ran westwards parallel to the river as far as Lienz, twelve miles farther on, and pitch camp in the fields just east of the town. At Peggetz, a mile or so from Lienz, there were the barrack huts of an abandoned camp, and here the women and children were to live. They would receive rations from the British and be responsible for their own internal discipline. Officers would retain their side-arms and control enough rifles for a proper guard to be mounted.

Between Lienz and Oberdrauburg ran a river, a road and a railway, three parallel lines a few hundred yards from each other. It was a valley a few miles wide with steep rocks on either side. The Cossacks spent May 9 and 10 travelling. The British were irritated by the squadrons of horses that kept galloping hither and thither, impeding their advance. Bates wrote that it was useless to give them orders: 'Few spoke German or English and few who understood seemed inclined to obey.' But in spite of the apparent chaos, he noticed, they moved quickly and efficiently to their allotted areas and were soon concentrated.

For them it was a welcome change from life at Tolmezzo, where they had been short of supplies and in danger from the partisans. Zoe Polaneska, a seventeen-year-old Russian girl from a village near Odessa, not a Cossack, who had somehow joined the community, remembers the kindness with which they were treated by the British:

> After we crossed the mountains we got little beds to sleep on and blankets and I thought, 'This can't be so bad.' And then I always remember, they gave us three cream crackers at breakfast time and I thought, 'This is better still.' And then they gave us white bread, pure white, we hadn't seen it for years. I thought, 'This is heaven!'

By May 16, according to British figures, there were 22,009 of Domanov's Cossacks under British supervision in the Drau Valley—15,380 men, 4,193 women and 2,436 children. A few miles to the east of them near Oberdrauburg the 4,800 Georgians had set up camp. A little farther east British soldiers were also guarding the 15th Cossack Cavalry Corps, commanded by a German, Lieutenant-General Helmut von Pannwitz, which had surrendered with its full strength of 18,792.[5] But the confusion was such that figures as precise as these must be viewed with caution. For instance, Cossack historians claim that there were 35,000 in Domanov's community in Italy, 13,000 more than the British figure. This is because many Cossacks were left behind in Italy during the evacuation and others vanished in various directions during the march across the mountains. Every day people were coming and going in large numbers. Alec Malcolm remembers: 'I was told that there would be 25,000 Cossacks in my area and that we were to "look after them". But it was an impossible task.'

Confusion reigned in occupied Central Europe during those early days of peace, and in the Drau Valley, so close to the Italian and Yugoslav borders, it was worse than elsewhere. There were so many nationalities, so many political groups, so many semi-independent partisan groups owing only vague loyalty to the general Allied cause. Newly-liberated prisoners-of-war were wandering from place to place, most of them anxious to get home, but a few desperately resolved to stay put, all of them causing worry to the British and Americans, whose job it was not only to administer the conquered territories, but also to seek out war criminals and deal with Nazi fanatics who were not obeying the order to surrender.

The language problem was acute. British and American soldiers are not known for their linguistic ability and they had the greatest difficulty in dealing with all the Poles, Hungarians, Bulgarians, Italians, Russians and Yugoslavs who fell into their hands. By that time most people in central Europe had acquired a few words of German, so in many official talks two interpreters were used, one to translate from English into German, the other to translate from German into the language of the man being interviewed. American and British officers often held positions of great power and were required to make decisions involving life and death, often many times daily. They had little knowledge of central European politics, and little understanding of many of the complicated disputes they were being asked to resolve.

Brigadier T. P. Scott, commander of the 38th (Irish) Brigade, had one of the most horrible situations of all. Near Lavamund in Eastern Carinthia he came across a regiment of Cossacks, about 400 men, who were in imminent danger of being attacked by a division of Bulgarians. Scott says, 'I didn't even know which side the Bulgarians were on, whether they were friend or foe. Apparently they were on our side then, having started on the other side.' The Bulgarians were keen to attack the Cossacks, Scott thought, with an eye to booty rather than to military necessity. The war had been over several days and Scott saw no reason why there should be a pitched battle in his area.

He went to see the Cossack commander, Prince Carl zu Salm-Horstmar. The situation was simple, Salm said. The Cossacks would surrender to the British so long as they were sure that they would not be handed over to the Soviet Union. Scott told Salm that British prisoners were British prisoners, and on this understanding Salm surrendered. Scott had no forces to speak of in the area, but he was able to find about thirty men to watch the Cossacks while they laid down their arms. The next morning they marched through the Bulgarian lines, escorted by two Irish soldiers on mules.

The next day Scott's corps commander, Lieutenant-General Keightley, came into the area and was alarmed to hear that Scott had accepted the Cossacks' surrender and given then certain assurances. He told him of the Yalta Agreement. 'It was the first I'd heard of it,' says Scott. Under this agreement, Keightley said, the Cossacks would probably have to be handed over to the Russians. Scott says, 'I told him I thought it would be a damn bad show if they were. I'd accepted their surrender and given my word. I got very hot under the collar about it.' Keightley told him to move the Cossacks back into Austria and leave the solution of the problem to him. It was a compromise solution which Scott accepted only under the strongest protest. He told Keightley again that he did not think it right to accept the Cossacks' surrender under false pretences.

Scott says today that he found that week which followed the German surrender the most strenuous of the whole war: 'The long and the short of it was that nobody had the least idea what was going to happen next or where it was coming from. It was a complete pig's breakfast.' His next problem was even more massive. On May 14, he received reports that two groups of the Croatian army, numbering 200,000 in all, were moving towards the British line at Bleiburg on the Austrian-Yugoslav border. 'The Croats had apparently been fighting on the wrong side,' Scott noted. They were escorting an estimated 500,000 civilians and wished to enter British territory in order to surrender and place themselves under British protection.[6]

Scott knew little about Yugoslav politics, but he was convinced that there could be no question of allowing hundreds of thousands of Croats to advance into his area. Where would they go? Who would feed them? The problem was terrifying. His only communication with higher authority was a wireless set in his car, but this only worked spasmodically and it was not possible to place the matter before Field-Marshal Alexander, as the Croat general wished. Scott would have to deal with the matter himself.

To complicate things still further, an army of Tito's partisans was encamped only a short distance from the Croats, ready to attack them. A deadly hatred existed between the two groups. For four years the Croats had been governed independently of the rest of Yugoslavia by the fascist Ante Pavelić and his 'Ustaša' movement. All this time guerilla warfare had been widespread: Serb against Croat, communist against fascist, communist against royalist. No quarter had been given on either side, and it is the Cossack intervention on the side of the German occupying forces which marks the darkest episode in their career.

Unaware of recent history and of the personal risks he was running, Scott drove in his scout car straight into the space between the two armies and began to negotiate. At first they seemed inclined to ignore him and fight the matter out. Then, Scott says:

> By the luck of God an aeroplane happened to come over and I said, 'You see that aeroplane? I've just called that up on my wireless set. That's just a reconnaissance aircraft, but the next lot will be bombers. So if you don't bloody well shut up and go home, this is what is going to happen to you. You'll be bombed!' I made it quite clear to them that if they did start fighting I would go for the whole lot quite indiscriminately. The fact was that I only had two men and a boy to do it, but they didn't know that.

By this piece of imaginative bluff Scott was able to extract the two groups of generals from their hordes and drive them up to his headquarters at Bleiburg Castle. Having installed the Croats in one room and the Titoists in another, he invited them to see him separately in the hope of arranging a peaceful solution. First of all the Titoist commissar, a young man in his twenties, told him that he was resolved to attack the Croats without delay. Scott told him that the Croats would be liquidated far more quickly and with fewer Titoist casualties if they could be induced to lay down their arms. The commissar agreed to postpone the attack for half an hour. He then retired and was replaced by the Croat general.

The Croats told Scott that 'an emigration of the whole Croat nation' was taking place, for they had decided that it was impossible to live under the communists. They asked him to regard the problem as a political matter and to refer it to Field-Marshal Alexander. Scott asked them to which country they proposed to emigrate. They had no idea. He told them that there was nowhere in war-ravaged Europe where such a multitude could be housed and fed. Such a movement could only take place after careful preparation. They suggested that it might be possible to ship them to Africa or America, to which Scott replied that there was no means by which this could be done. They would undoubtedly starve if they insisted on coming to the West. They told him that starving was far preferable to surrendering and that they 'would rather die where they were, fighting to the last man, than surrender to any Bolsheviks'.

Meanwhile, the commissar had sent Scott a message that he would wait no longer and the battle must start. Scott describes what he did then:

> Quite concisely I gave them three alternatives and five minutes to make their choice. The alternatives were these. First: that they would surrender to the Yugoslavs, that I would use my influence— although unofficially—to try and ensure that they would be treated correctly. Secondly, that they stayed where they were and were attacked by the Yugoslavs. Third: that they endeavoured to advance into the British lines.

It was this third alternative that Scott was most anxious to avoid, for it would present him and his men with the most appalling problems, political as well as administrative. He therefore assured the Croats that if they came towards his lines 'they would not only be attacked by the Yugoslavs, but also by all the weight of the British and American air forces, land forces and anything else that I could get my hands on'. In such an event 'they would unquestionably be annihilated'. He thought that it would be difficult for the Titoists to murder such a large number of people and doubted whether they would want to. Large numbers would survive, he suggested, if they followed the 'obviously sensible first course'. The Croat general told him that he personally would without doubt be murdered by the Titoists, to which Scott replied, 'Well, I'm sorry, but better for one person to have his throat cut than for the whole lot to be slaughtered in battle.' Their choice was clear because, he told them bluntly, 'if they took any of the other alternatives they were bound to die, so what?'[7]

Such rough-and-ready approaches to great human problems were part of the cruelty of the time, part of the legacy of war. It did not mean that Scott had no sympathy for the Croat general. 'He seemed a decent man, very correct and German in his bearing. I felt sorry for him,' he recalls. But his orders were clear—the Croats were the enemy and the Titoists were allies. Realising finally that their position was hopeless, the Croats agreed to surrender. Scott brought the two sides together and the Croat surrendered then and there to the commissar.

The Titoists promised that the civilians would be returned to Croatia and the soldiers treated as prisoners-of-war, 'with the exception of political criminals, who would be dealt with by Allied courts established to deal with this matter.' In Scott's view 'the terms of the surrender were fair enough,' and so they were if there had been any question of their being observed. But it was clear that once they were away from British influence there would be no one to enforce the bargain or even to know whether it had been kept. Scott says: 'I got an assurance that they would all be repatriated and looked after, but whether it was observed or not I just don't know. I've no idea whether they were all murdered. I wouldn't be surprised if they were.'

No one knows exactly what happened to the Croats, but it is clear that the spirit of the agreement with Scott was not observed. One account of the aftermath of the agreement, admittedly taken from a violently anti-Titoist source, runs as follows:

> The most horrible aspects of the Bleiburg tragedy were the death marches organised by the Seventh Brigade of the 17th Partisan Assault Division and led through many cities, towns and villages of Slovenia, Croatia and Serbia. Tens of thousands of Croatians were grouped in a number of columns, their hands tied with wire in typical Russian fashion. Then starved, thirsty, emaciated, disfigured, suffering and agonizing, they were forced to run long distances alongside their 'liberators', who were riding on horses and in carts. Those who could not endure such a running 'march' were stabbed, beaten to death or shot, then left along the roadside or thrown into a ditch. Thus very few Croatians reached the final destination of their 'march'.[8]

As for the promised trials of 'political criminals', when these took place it was in Yugoslav courts, not Allied courts, and the justice meted out was rudimentary to say the least. It was true that Pavelić, the leader of the Croat 'Ustaši', had been a most brutal man. Many of his lieutenants doubtless deserved their fate. But many other ordinary Croats, uninvolved in politics and innocent of any crime, suffered horribly during the years when Tito was consolidating his communist authority in Yugoslavia.

It is these victims, and their relatives who managed to escape abroad, who blame Britain most bitterly for handing hundreds of thousands of Croats over to their Titoist enemies.

The Yugoslav problem was only one of many which threw the British and American officers then administering central Europe into utter bewilderment. As Scott noted at the end of his frank account of the amazing (but little known) Bleiburg incident, 'the long and short of it was that nobody had the least idea what was going to happen next or where it was coming from.' What did the ordinary officer know of the difference between the Titoists and the 'Ustaši'? How could he arbitrate between them? But this was his job, and any mistake was liable to cause severe diplomatic difficulty between Washington, London and Moscow, with consequent upsets in the delicate military equilibrium. Army officers naturally dread political situations and avoid them if they can, for they are not trained to cope with them, but at such moments they needed all the qualities of diplomats, historians, linguists and social workers. It was no wonder that sometimes they felt out of their depth.

As well as the fascist and the communist Yugoslavs, they had to deal with the royalists, the followers of Draža Mihajlović, who were known as 'četniki'. Such people might well be personally friendly to Britain and the United States, but this friendship could not be returned, for Tito was the 'official ally' and the 'četniki' were ready to die rather than accept Tito. Ronald Belcham, in charge of a brigade in Germany, wrote a worried letter: 'There are two sets of Yugoslav officers officially acting on behalf of Yugoslav displaced persons—one lot being Royalists, the other Titoist. These rival factions make frequent attempts to arrest one another. Which side are we supposed to take?'[9] The answer was that he was to support the Titoists, which on the face of it was absurd, since Tito was causing the Allies severe trouble, almost to the point of armed conflict. But as far as Washington and London were concerned, particularly the State Department and the Foreign Office, Tito was the ally and any Yugoslav who opposed him was the enemy.

The Allies also had problems with the Nazi ss, all members of which were liable to arrest. Instructions were issued to senior officers on how these men could be identified. Their uniforms were described—the black collar and shoulder straps, the special badges of rank, the death's-head cap badge. Most decisive of all was the blood-group tattoo near the left armpit. At the end of the war many ss men had tried to lose themselves in ordinary army units, and Allied officers were constantly watching for such concealment. There were even cases where the ss tattoo was removed surgically by German army medical officers. The Allied policy of rooting out suspected war criminals was bound to lead to friction with the ordinary German forces which had surrendered.

Then there were those few Germans so imbued with Nazi ideas that they would not give up the fight in spite of surrender. Major R. S. V. Howard of the Royal Irish Fusiliers remembers a battalion of Hitler Youth which caused his unit great trouble:

> These were fifteen- or sixteen-year-old boys who had sworn to take an Allied soldier with them before they went. They did surrender, but we had great difficulty in guarding them, because they were bent on mischief. It took one platoon all its time to look after a smallish battalion, and the men were on 'two hours on, four hours off' on a twenty-four-hour basis. We couldn't keep this up because a lot of the men were young national servicemen and they were falling asleep over their weapons. We didn't dare relax with these youngsters, because we searched them and found that quite a number of them were still armed. We collected quite a tidy pile of weapons. It was really more tiring than fighting a war.

The Cossacks were, therefore, by no means the only problem facing the victorious armies in Austria. In fact, they were less trouble than many other groups. They were almost self-sufficient, providing their own accommodation and keeping their own discipline. They obeyed British orders quickly and without question. There was a supply of German summer uniforms in a store neat Lienz and these were distributed, much to the delight of the Cossacks, whose heavy clothes were unsuitable for the hot weather and in bad condition after the winter in Tolmezzo. The British were full of admiration for the Cossacks' superb horsemanship, for their dignity and noble bearing. It was appreciated that they had until recently been fighting on the German side, but they had done no direct harm to the British and it was hard to look upon their train of caravans—horses, women, children, cows and even camels—as former enemy formations. They had surrendered so willingly and were clearly so eager to please. They seemed pathetic and harmless.

Major 'Rusty' Davies, one of Malcolm's company commanders, was made responsible for liaison between the Cossacks and the Argyll and Sutherland Highlanders. Within a few days he had come to like them and admire them. He remembers particularly his friendship with M. K. Butlerov, a young officer on Domanov's staff who spoke good English. Most days the two men would ride round the Cossack areas on horseback. Butlerov was a skilled horseman, Davies a beginner, and Davies remembers his friend's worry lest the 'English major' lose face with the Cossacks because of his indifferent riding. Within a few days Davies was a familiar figure. All the Cossacks knew his name, especially the children, who followed him everywhere, laughing and calling out to him. Every few minutes he would stop to distribute sweets. His brother officers were bullied to give him their chocolate ration and Davies spent time dividing each slab into very small pieces, so that no child would be disappointed. He felt like a Father Christmas.

Ironically, considering the tragic part he was to play in the events which followed, Davies was at first delighted to be offered the liaison job. He knew that as soon as the tidying-up process was finished, boredom and a longing for home would consume the British soldiers. The officers would then have to spend their time organising recreation—sports, lectures and entertainments. The prospect was not an alluring one. But with the Cossacks he had a job which was challenging and new. 'They were wonderful people, warmhearted and brave, but they were not very good at administration,' he remembers. So he spent hours trying to persuade them to arrange their camp in a fashion more in keeping with British standing orders. He made them dig more latrines, arrange regular sick parades, publish daily orders and eat more nourishing food. They found Davies, a Welshman and a Celt, more sympathetic to them temperamentally than the stolid Scotsmen who mostly manned the battalion. Russians, while naturally suspicious of strangers, tend to be generous with their friendship, and when they give their trust they give it entirely. Davies says, 'They had implicit faith in me. They believed every word I told them.'

Davies had at this stage no inkling of the decision already made by his superiors, that every one of the Cossacks—man, woman and child—was to be handed back to the Soviet authorities, irrespective of their individual wishes and by force if necessary. Lieutenant-General Charles Keightley, who commanded the British Fifth Corps, made it clear in an order dated May 24: 'It is of the utmost importance that all the officers and particularly senior commanders, are rounded up and that none are allowed to escape. The Soviet forces consider this as being of the highest importance and will probably regard the safe delivery of the officers as a test of British good faith.'[10] But Keightley was here ignoring one very important fact, that apart from Domanov the senior Cossack officers were old émigrés who had left Russia around 1920. Under the Yalta Agreement these men were not liable for forced repatriation. This was inconvenient for the British, because they knew how much the Soviet authorities wanted to get their hands on these men, and they wanted to be as obliging to their ally as possible.

Once he had the Cossacks in his grasp, it was thought, Stalin would be more inclined to place a restraining hand on Tito, who was then causing the West so much trouble with his claims on Austrian and Italian territory, to take a reasonable line during the conference on the future of Poland, which was to begin in Moscow on June 17, and to play a more active part in the war against Japan, which was not yet over. Conversely, Stalin could be expected to react aggressively if there was any noticeable British sympathy for the Cossacks, or if any efforts were made to harbour them, perhaps for use in some future attack on Russia. In London, and particularly in the Foreign Office, it seemed absurd to provoke Stalin by protecting people who had betrayed the Soviet Union and fought on Hitler's side.

There was little understanding of why the Cossacks had volunteered to fight with the German invader. Westerners were vaguely aware of the repressions and purges of the 1930s, but they had little idea of their extent, and there were many vocal 'fellow-travellers' ready to dismiss as right-wing propaganda any allegations that Stalin was treating his people cruelly. The mass deportations and famine of 1933 were almost unknown to the western public, but for years they dominated the lives of millions of Russians who fell victim to the terror. Such were the sufferings of these poor people, and so deeply did they come to hate the Soviet government that they had little sympathy to spare for the victims of the other arch-villain, Adolf Hitler. They had no access to western journals or other media, and if Hitler was denounced in the Soviet press as a fascist and a murderer, they were unlikely to pay much attention. They did not believe the wild stories that appeared in *Pravda* and *Izvestiya*. Their attacks on Hitler struck the isolated Soviet citizens as no different from the rest of the propaganda.

So it was that millions of Soviet citizens—Russians, Ukrainians, Kalmyks, Cossacks and others—came to believe that no man could be worse than the devil who governed them. To them Hitler was an unknown quantity. They were glad to help him and incautiously they threw themselves into battle on his side. Too late did they realise that by doing this they had placed themselves beyond the pale, not only with Stalin—this they accepted as natural and desirable—but also with the Americans and British, for whom they felt no ill-will. But to the decision-makers in Washington and London these were men in enemy uniform, traitors to the glorious Russian ally. There were many in the West who saw the matter in terms as simple as this.

General Keightley has written to the author: 'The repatriation of the Cossacks was of course an order from Army Group and certainly stemmed from Westminster, probably from Winston [Churchill] himself. Whether we were happy about the operation or not, therefore, really did not come into it. We had an enormous displaced person problem on our hands with many distressed communities to handle.' It was under Keightley's orders that the operation fell and even now he feels that the decision to send the Cossacks back by force was justified. But many of his subordinates felt quite differently. The junior men had several weeks of contact with the Cossacks and came to see them not as enemies but as people. At the same time, too, British officers were taking areas over from Soviet occupation. Having seen the rape and destruction which took place, they were less inclined to accept the idealised picture of the Red Army soldier which was still being put about. They were worried at what they were being asked to do.

The war had been over only a few days. Everyone was very glad that it had left them alive. Then suddenly there was this extraordinary order to deliver by force tens of thousands of apparently harmless people to an army which, quite clearly, had only a primitive idea of justice and discipline. Many British soldiers realised the horror of it, that they were being asked to act as jailors, or even as executioners. And apart from their moral scruples, the British faced a more practical difficulty. As soon as the Cossacks realised what was to happen to them they would fight. Some of them were still armed. They would resist the order with fury, for they had little to lose, and there would be British casualties. This was something very hard to accept in May 1945. The war was over. The Allies had won. The men expected celebration, then demobilisation, not dirty and dangerous jobs.

Such considerations persuaded senior officers that trickery and deceit would have to be used to minimise casualties and ensure success. British soldiers were treating their prisoners with kindness and friendship. The Cossacks were living quietly in the designated areas, not resisting and not trying to run away. But this was only because no one, prisoner or soldier, knew the terrible truth, that the decision to repatriate them all by force had already been taken. Very well, they must be kept in this state of false security right to the last moment. Only thus could the Cossacks be disarmed, loaded into vehicles and carried east without bloodshed and mass escapes.

The Cossacks were armed with an assortment of weapons. Most were German, of course, but others were of Italian, Yugoslavian or Soviet manufacture. The Germans had taken an ungenerous, suspicious attitude to their Cossack allies and had equipped them sparsely, leaving them to forage for themselves and gather weapons where they could. It was during the German retreat, after the Battle of Stalingrad, that they obtained Rumanian arms. The Rumanian soldiers, fighting on the German side, had little stomach for a war of such horror and were deserting in large numbers. Dmitri Frolov says: 'I remember the Rumanians selling us their rifles for a piece of gold or even a piece of bread. Then they ran away.' Later in the war, Cossacks fought against Red Army forces, against partisans in Italy and Yugoslavia, and when they won a fight, they took the weapons of the men they killed or captured. To avoid total confusion the weapons were then redistributed, so that at least each squadron was uniformly armed, but it was quite usual to find three or four different types of rifle being used in one regiment.

British officers began to drop hints that the Cossacks would be invited to join the British army as a sort of Foreign Legion. 'Our soldiers are tired, we are about to begin demobilisation and we don't have enough people to mount guards,' Frolov remembers one Englishman telling him. Alexander Shparengo, another Cossack officer, has written: 'We heard from reliable sources that the British had brought us to this out-of-the-way place to hide us from the Bolsheviks. We would remain here only until ships were available to take us to the 'black continent' [Africa], where we would be employed on garrison duty.'[11] Others gathered that they would be recruited to fight on the British side against Japan. Wishful thinking embroidered and reinforced such carefully placed hints. There were rumours that the American and British Embassy staffs were leaving Moscow and that a new war was about to begin. For the Cossacks this was the best thing that could possibly happen. They would be valuable allies of the West, worth their weight in gold, and when victory was won they would be given their traditional lands as a reward.

On May 26 Colonel Malcolm went to a Brigadiers' conference at Oberdrauburg and was given details of the unpleasant task which lay before him. He returned to Lienz and passed the information on to his company commanders, one of whom was Rusty Davies. 'I was shattered. It was a denial of everything we had ever said to the Cossacks. I couldn't believe it,' said Davies. He immediately asked to be relieved of his job as liaison officer. He had become too friendly with them, he told Malcolm. For weeks he had been their guide and adviser, answering their anxious questions and assuring them that there was no question of forcing them to return to Russia. If this was now to happen, it placed him in a false position and someone else should take over.

It was explained to Davies that precisely because of the confidence he enjoyed with the Cossacks he must continue to work with them and to pass on to them all British orders. Only if the prisoners were kept in a fool's paradise, in ignorance of what was to happen, could the operation be performed efficiently and quickly. And only if Davies kept reassuring them would they continue to believe that nothing was wrong. Up to this point he had been soothing their fears in all good faith. From now on he was to lie. These were his orders.

On the morning of May 27, British soldiers were read an order from Brigadier Musson calling for the total disarmament of all

Cossacks by 2 pm that day. It was written in a tone so menacing that it was clear that the relaxed approach to the prisoners was now to end. From now on they were enemies, Musson's words seemed to imply, and severe trouble was expected: 'You are faced with a problem that will demand great patience and tact, and I am sure that you will overcome the many difficulties with which you may be faced. Be firm. Remember that quick and determined action taken immediately may save many incidents and lives in the future. If it is necessary to open fire you will do so, and you will regard this duty as an operation of war.'

This was alarming language to use to describe such a normal operation as the disarmament of prisoners-of-war. After all, it was only to suit the British convenience that some of the Cossacks had retained their arms in the first place. Had there been enough room in the prisoner-of-war camps, they would all have been disarmed on surrender. Musson's order showed some apprehension: 'If a person or body of people attempts to escape, you will order them to halt by shouting at them. If they deliberately disregard your order and run away, you will open fire, aiming at the legs if you think that this will be enough to stop the attempted escape. If not, shoot to kill. If you are approached by an uncontrollable crowd, you must shoot to kill the apparent leader. You must not fire overhead or into the air. If you do this the bullet will kill or wound some innocent person a long way away.' Musson ordered his officers and men to carry arms at all times, and never go about alone. Furthermore, any prisoner found in possession of arms after 2 pm that day would be liable to the death penalty.

But no hint of these alarming words were being communicated to the Cossacks themselves. As far as they were concerned, everything was proceeding normally and plans were under way to find them a place to live and work outside the Soviet Union. It was here, Dmitri Frolov claims, that their lack of uniformity in weaponry was used as a pretext to explain the disarmament. He says, 'British officers told us that they had no ammunition for all our Russian, Rumanian and Italian weapons. If we wanted to serve them, we must hand in our rifles and revolvers. We would be given new ones in return, standard British models. We believed them and we did what they asked.' This story is confirmed by several émigré historians,[12] but whether or not deceit was used, few Cossacks saw anything unusual in the disarmament order.

After all, they *were* prisoners-of-war. The order was reasonable and they obeyed it. As Musson's records confirm, 'There is little doubt that the officers of both forces, Cossack and Caucasian, did all they could to ensure compliance with the disarmament orders issued to them.' British officers did their duty with such care and tact that no Cossack suspicions were aroused.

It was then time for 'stage two' of the operation. Shortly after the disarmament, Davies told the senior Cossack officers through his interpreter, Butlerov, that all officers were required to attend a conference which would decide the future of the Cossack units. This was a direct lie, and it was told by Davies under protest in the face of a straightforward order from his superiors. In fact, there was to be no conference at all. What was planned for the officers was not a discussion but an immediate transfer into the hands of the Soviet authorities. Colonel Malcolm told the author, 'We knew the Cossacks would not go home voluntarily if their officers ordered them not to.' The plan was, therefore, to behead the Cossack forces, to deprive them of leaders by trickery, so that they would be more amenable when the bad news was finally broken to them.

The announcement caused the Cossacks some consternation. At last their doubts were beginning to grow. A conference was all very well, but was it really necessary for *all* the officers to attend, all 1,500 of them? Davies explained that this was the order —every single officer without exception. He says, 'I remember Butlerov saying to me, "That's funny, why doesn't the British general come to us instead of all of us having to go to him?" He twigged it at once. Try to argue your way out of that one!' They told him that it was a crazy idea to have a conference with 1,500 people. Why could they not simply send their representatives? Frolov, too, remembers the argument: 'We were told that everyone would have to go. They told us that there were other units involved—Caucasians, Kalmyks, Ukrainians, as well as Russians who had fought in the German army. The British general would not have time to visit all these groups separately. 'Don't worry,' they said, 'it's only twenty kilometres to Oberdrauburg, you'll have dinner there and be back in Lienz by bedtime.' It was Davies's duty as a soldier to deceive, and today he is amazed at how successfully he did it: 'How the hell we lulled them into that, I just don't know. I look back on that moment with horror. It truly was a fiendish bloody scheme.' This attitude has provoked the following comment from Musson: 'Davies was a good officer but he got too involved. As for myself, I made sure that I had as little personal contact as possible with the Cossacks. Personal involvement can be very dangerous.'

Davies was told that the repatriation order came from the highest authority and had been agreed between Stalin and Churchill at Yalta. What he was not told was that the agreement applied only to people who were Soviet citizens on the outbreak of war in September 1939. Under the Agreement, many of the Cossacks gathered at Lienz, for instance the Krasnov family and his friend Butlerov, were not due for repatriation at all. Indeed, of the most senior officers, only Domanov had been a Soviet citizen in 1939. Under the Agreement British officers were obliged to sort the Cossacks, to separate the old émigrés from the new émigrés, repatriating only the latter.

What in fact happened was that an order was issued from General Keightley's headquarters which bore no resemblance to the terms laid down in the Yalta Agreement. In this order, whole groups and nationalities were earmarked for repatriation: the Cossacks under Domanov at Lienz, the 15th Cossack Cavalry Corps under General von Pannwitz, the units under General Andrey Shkuro and the Caucasians under General Klych Girey. All members of these units were assumed to be Soviet, said the order, and 'individual cases will not be considered unless particularly pressed.' In other words, there was a presumption of guilt. People were to be handed over to certain imprisonment and possible execution merely for failing to assert strongly enough that they were not Soviet citizens.

If any individual *did* press a claim for exemption, the order laid down the following guidelines:

> Any individual now in our hands who, at the time of joining the German forces or joining a formation fighting with the German forces, was living within the 1938 body of the USSR, will be treated as a Soviet national for the purposes of transfer. Any individual, although of Russian blood who, prior to joining the German forces, had not been in the USSR since 1930, will not until further orders be treated as a Soviet national. In all cases of doubt the individual will be treated as a Soviet national.

This was a further serious departure from the Yalta Agreement. The two definitions of Soviet and non-Soviet were not mutually exclusive. They did not cover those people who had left Russia between 1930 and 1938. One must presume that these were some of the 'cases of doubt' covered by the last sentence of the order which cut across three of the main principles of British justice: that a foreigner who has reason to fear persecution for political reasons is entitled to asylum; that an accused man is entitled to due process of law; and that he is innocent until proved guilty beyond reasonable doubt.

Seldom can a British authority have disposed of so many lives so haphazardly. Musson says: 'We were a small operational headquarters with no resources for interrogation or anything like that. My superiors knew that the interrogation of prisoners was never done at Brigade level. Even if they'd asked me to I couldn't have done it.' As far as the Cossack officers were concerned, there was no intention of sorting them out at all. Keightley's order not to repatriate Russians who had not been in the Soviet Union since 1930 was contradicted by his order of May 24, in which it was made clear that all officers without exception were to be sent back. It was this May 24 order which was the valid one.

During the evening of May 27, some of the senior Cossack officers—Domanov, Solomakhin (the new Chief of Staff), Vassiliev, Silkin and Frolov—held a meeting to decide whether or not to believe the British and attend the conference the next day. Frolov says:

> Everyone was for going. They thought everything was all right. But I give you my word, before God, that I was the only one who said he did not trust the English. I said I was worried about the way they had taken away our arms, and there were too many things left uncertain and unsaid. Domanov asked me, what did I suggest? The British were treating us so well, why was I suspicious? I said we should order our families, the wives and children, to leave Lienz and make for southern Germany or Switzerland. They weren't prisoners-of-war, the British had no right to hold them, so if they tried to stop them by force, it meant that they were our enemies. If they let them go, they were telling the truth. But Domanov would not listen to me. He became angry with me and we quarrelled. I left the meeting and never saw any of them again.

The Yalta Conference in the Crimea, February 1945, showing (seated) Winston Churchill, Franklin D. Roosevelt and Stalin and (standing) Anthony Eden, Edward Stettinius, Alexander Cadogan, Molotov and Averell Harriman

A Russian Orthodox priest blesses a recruit for the German army who has just taken the oath. The next recruit kisses the Bible in preparation for the benediction

Part of a volunteer Cossack unit

German army prisoners captured during the initial Allied landings in Northern France sit guarded by American soldiers, awaiting shipment to England. The armshield of the man in the right foreground indicates that he belongs to a Georgian unit. The white markings on the lapel of the man in the left foreground indicate that he is a member of Vlasov's Russian Liberation Army

Cossacks surrendering their arms to the British 8th Army near Klagenfurt in Austria

Lieutenant-General Andrey Vlasov, photographed in German uniform in 1943

Cossacks on parade near their camp in the Drau Valley, Austria, in May 1945

Russians and Cossacks gather at their cemetery in Lienz to commemorate those who died during 1945 repatriation operations, June 1974

HURT: Russian repatriate Constantine Gustonon grimaces with pain
after he slashed himself on the chest some 17 times in a suicide
attempt to avoid being returned to Russia. He is held by Capt. Kenny
Gardner, of the 66th Inf. Regt. Gustonon's was the first case of
attempted suicide among the deportees from Plattling to Russia as PWs.

A rare photograph, taken from the US Army newspaper *Stars and Stripes* of
March 6, 1946, showing a Russian who attempted suicide during operations
at Plattling

Field-Marshal Harold Alexander

Major-General Vyacheslav Naumenko, a veteran of the Russian Civil War, ataman of the Kuban Cossacks 1920-58

Lieutenant-General Charles Keightley at an observation post in Northern Italy, November 1944

A short distance to the east of the valley there was the other large group of Cossacks under General Helmut von Pannwitz, his 15th Cossack Cavalry Corps, which then numbered 18,792. Nearly half of the 452 officers were German and there were nearly as many horses as men. Here the British task was made easier by internal dissension within the Corps, the Cossacks trying to oust the Germans who still held key positions in the administration of the surrendered forces, the Germans trying to maintain their grip on the Corps as well as their separate identity as a body. The prisoners were so preoccupied with this conflict that they had little time to spare for worrying about the possiblity of being handed over to the Soviets. A British report, explaining these quarrels, mentions that von Pannwitz clearly wanted 'to disassociate his German officers and ultimately himself from the Cossacks who were traitors to their country'. He realised the potential danger he was in, but had no idea either that the hand-over of the Corps was already agreed, or that the blow could possibly fall so quickly, or that he himself and many other German officers were also to be sent to Russia.[13]

On May 25 there were shooting incidents within the Corps, German against Cossack, followed by loud protests to the British both by the Cossacks and by von Pannwitz. The British report reads: 'The position was very delicate, as it had been agreed with the Russians that the whole of the Cossack Corps would be handed over to them in the near future. It was clear that neither von Pannwitz or his staff suspected this, although it was equally clear that their suspicions were bound to be aroused when segregated nominal rolls were required.'

On May 26, the 139th Infantry Brigade took command of the area near Eberstein for the express purpose of administering the hand-over. That morning the senior Cossack officer from von Pannwitz's headquarters called on the British to tell them that the Cossacks wanted to be rid of their German officers. Von Pannwitz had already begun to separate the two groups, he said, but the Germans were taking all the best horses and equipment for themselves. It was here that the British officer saw his opportunity. He asked the Cossack to go and prepare nominal rolls that would show separate categories of Cossacks and Germans, divided into officers, non-commissioned officers and others. The report continues: 'In this respect the internal trouble in the

Corps proved an asset, as the nominal rolls were obtained without arousing any suspicion as to the hand-over to the Russians. It is certain that, had they known of this plan, there would have been wholesale attempts at desertion and suicide.'

On May 28, General von Pannwitz and some of the Germans from the Cossack Corps were driven to Judenburg, a small town 120 miles south-west of Vienna on the river Mur. The river runs through a gorge in the town and across the gorge is a bridge which was the frontier between the two Allied armies. Lieutenant V. B. English was in command of a Royal Artillery detachment guarding the bridge and he remembers Pannwitz arriving in a white scout car. As the car drove across the bridge English followed on foot, stopping where the neutral ground ended near the Soviet end.

He thus had a good view of the actual hand-over: 'Von Pannwitz was a very tall chap. He got out of his car and stretched himself and drew himself up to his full height and then looked. And this seemed to be the first moment he realised what was happening. Then he walked very slowly forward towards the Russians with everybody looking at him, and finally saluted them. He kept them waiting and stage-managed it very well.' The official British report gives a similar impression: 'The 139th Infantry Brigade succeeded in maintaining security and its success may be measured by the fact that, even when General von Pannwitz stepped out of the vehicle which had conveyed him across the Russian border, he was obviously surprised to see the Russians, throwing up his arms in the air and exclaiming, "Mein Gott!"'

P. C. Cockell was another young British officer who was at the border. His job was to stand on the sideline with two Russian interpreters, thinly disguised as drivers, and make reports on what the Soviet officers said to the men who were being handed over. He remembers the scene looking more like a genuine welcome committee than a mass arrest of dangerous criminals. Loud-speakers were playing Russian music, flags were flying and photographers were there to record the scene. He remembers too 'a large contingent of Soviet brass' arriving to greet their defeated enemies, doubtless curious to see the senior Cossack officers, whose names were well known in Russia. Soviet officers were checking the prisoners off against lists which the British had just given them. Cockell saw a Soviet officer approach a tall elegant

Cossack with what seemed to be a genuine greeting: 'Do you remember me? I used to be your stable boy!' He thought the Cossack officers 'rather magnificent-looking-men' and was impressed by the way in which, knowing full well that they were doomed, they treated the Soviets with disdain.

English asked a Soviet officer what would happen to the Cossacks and was told, 'The officers will be shot, but the ordinary soldiers will just be sent to Siberia.' But he remembers that the remark made little impression on him at the time. He says:

> The general feeling was that they couldn't do anything really bad to such a huge number of people, tens of thousands. We thought they'd just make an example of one or two, like we did to Lord Haw-Haw, and that would be it. The trouble was that we were very young and we were super-saturated with events. Enormous movements of population were taking place every day—refugees, prisoners-of-war, hundreds of thousands of them. But it didn't seem important. What *did* seem important was something like, 'Can I get off duty this afternoon for this game of tennis?' It sounds terribly callous, but that's the way we were, I'm afraid. And as for the Cossacks, we really didn't know who they were or what was happening. In some ways I'm glad, because if I had known, I don't know what I'd have done. And now I do know, I think it's a most terrible tragedy.

Cockell also asked what would happen to the Cossacks and was told that the officers would be shot. But the ordinary soldiers, he was told, would be 're-educated'. In fact it is hard to say how many of the officers were shot. The only death sentence actually announced was that of Pannwitz himself. (It appeared in *Pravda* on January 17, 1947.) But what is certain is that all the Cossacks spent ten years being 're-educated' in one of Stalin's labour camps in conditions so bad as to make survival very difficult. What is also certain is that many of the victims should never have been repatriated at all, even under the questionable Yalta Agreement. Neither Pannwitz nor the Germans attached to the corps nor the old Russian émigrés were Soviet citizens, and their hand-over was quite illegal.

Cockell now says, 'I went into the thing in complete innocence and came out disgusted. I suddenly realised I had been involved in something terrible.' He was shocked by the deception.

Along with the Cossacks the British also handed over most of the German officers and sergeants who had been seconded to Pannwitz's cavalry corps, more than a thousand of them. This was a further violation of the Agreement, because the Soviet authorities had no claim on these men. They had surrendered to the British and should have become British prisoners-of-war. Only the Soviet citizens were due for delivery.

In the corps's Sixth Regiment, the one commanded by Prince zu Salm, the German personnel did manage to escape. Leopold Goess, one of Salm's company commanders, says: 'Pannwitz had this crazy idea that the British would ship us all off to an island in the Pacific, so that the Cossacks could stay together. That is why he ordered his regimental commanders to keep everyone together. If he hadn't done this a lot of people would have been able to get away. It would have been quite easy, especially for the Germans who had somewhere to go.'

Salm and Goess did not share Pannwitz's dream of resettlement on a Pacific isle, especially after they were tipped off by a British officer that some new tough regiment was about to take over the guard and that 'this meant that something funny was going to happen'. Salm decided to take his 250 German subordinates to Mauterndorf, near Salzburg in the American zone, where their parent brigade was interned. He persuaded a local British commander to lend him some trucks and, though he abandoned his Cossacks, he got his Germans away in the nick of time, a few hours before the rest were taken to Judenburg.

A few other Cossacks and Germans trickled away, but throughout the Corps's other five regiments the deception was thoroughly successful, enabling the British forces to hand their prisoners over, nearly 20,000 of them, without violence or bloodshed. Those few hundred Germans who escaped were saved from a killing ten years in Soviet labour camps only because a British officer had disobeyed orders and told Salm what was going to happen.

THE CONFERENCE
THAT NEVER WAS

IT WAS BY no means certain that the delivery of the other 25,000 Cossacks, the ones attached to Domanov, would proceed so smoothly. At 11 am on May 28, Domanov addressed his officers and told them they must all attend the conference that afternoon. His words were met by a barrage of questions. How much baggage were they to take? Domanov told them there was no need to take anything, not even their greatcoats, as they would be back in Lienz that evening.[1] 'Why don't we make a break for it, take to the hills?' one officer asked. Domanov gave the man a direct order to stay with the rest.[2] He was convinced that no serious trickery was planned and that the worst that could happen to his officers, after the conference, was internment in a normal British prisoner-of-war camp. It would be disagreeable to be behind barbed wire, but it would be endurable. At best, of course, the officers would return to Lienz, the division would remain intact, and the struggle against the Soviet Union would proceed under American and British leadership.

In retrospect Cossacks who survived the affair find it hard to understand how they were taken in by the ruse. Their vigilance was dulled by the politeness of the British and by the conditions of internment which, after the rigours of winter in the Italian mountains, were little short of luxurious. They were confused by the sudden end of the war and anxious to believe that it did not mean the end of their crusade. Some of them blame Domanov for misleading them and for ordering them so firmly to obey British officers, even implying that he knew about the deportation in advance and played the British game in the hope of saving his own skin. One Cossack has written:

During interrogations in Soviet camps Domanov told the senior Soviet interrogator, Colonel Svinyev, in front of witnesses, that he

knew about the forthcoming deportations . . . Other officers who
had been handed over were present at this interrogation and were
so disturbed by Domanov's behaviour that it was necessary to
isolate him from them to prevent them doing him an injury.[3]

Ataman Pavlov's friend Pyotr Donskow has also, in a letter to
the author, denounced Domanov as a traitor and a Soviet agent.
The suggestion is that Domanov, who as an émigré from the year
1943 was due for repatriation anyway under the Agreement,
advised the British to hand over old émigrés as well, that he hoped
thus to gain favour with the Soviet authorities into whose hands
he was about to fall. General Naumenko has told the author:
'I did not trust Domanov or particularly like him. He got himself
promoted to general very quickly, by currying favour with the ss
and the worst elements of the German army. Some people think
he knew about the deportation, but there is no proof.' It is a
controversy which rages in the rarefied atmosphere of Cossack
émigré politics. In 1953, a group of victims of the deportation
published a letter in Domanov's defence.[4]

Most Cossacks feel that their gullibility must be explained by
the deviousness and treachery of the British, rather than by the
wickedness of Domanov. 'Russian officers, brought up in the noble
traditions of the Imperial Army, could not imagine such a lying
betrayal,' one Cossack has written. Naumenko writes, 'Russian
officers are accustomed to believing the word of an officer and they
could not imagine that the British would do such a thing.'
Nikolay Krasnov, grandson of the famous general P. N. Krasnov,
writes, 'No one realised that the British High Command was
capable of such deceit and such total evil.'[5] An old émigré told him:
'It won't be so bad being prisoners of the Anglo-Saxons. The
English are gentlemen. We're not dealing with that jumped-up
Hitler but with officers of His Majesty the King. A British officer
never gives his word on his own account, even if he is a field-
marshal. He speaks for the High Command, for the Throne
itself.'

Of course deceit and lying are part of modern warfare and there
is no reason to suppose that the Cossacks did not do their share
of it, for they fought the war more furiously than most. But
clearly, having been treated so well by the British, they came to
the conclusion that they could trust them. On the morning of

May 28, Butlerov had a quiet, man-to-man talk with Davies. He told him, 'You know, I have a wife and a child, and this afternoon I'm going to this conference of yours. And I want you to tell me, are we or are we not coming back?'

It is another moment which Davies remembers with horror. His position was impossible. Either he would have to betray Butlerov, whom he had made friends with and liked, or he would have to disobey his orders which said quite clearly that he was to keep the truth hidden. Davies says, 'I could have said to him, "Get your family and take them up to my house and all of you stay there for the rest of to-day." Maybe that's what I should have done.' He would thus have saved the life of his friend. But had he done this, what would Butlerov have done? Davies might tell him the bad news in strict confidence, but could Butlerov in all honour respect such a confidence? His loyalty to his fellow officers would surely compel him to tell them what he had learnt. It would be the act of a coward to save himself and his family, allowing the men he had fought with to walk on into the trap.

Dmitri Frolov was one of very few officers convinced that there would be no conference. After his quarrel with Domanov he returned to his family in the barrack block where the Cossack priests were living, a short distance from the main camp. He thus did not hear the order to prepare to move. Around midday a Cossack officer came to tell him the news and ordered him to come to the General Staff. Frolov said he would not go. The Cossacks tried to take him by force, but Frolov produced a revolver, which in spite of the disarmament order he had failed to surrender. The Cossacks departed, muttering dire threats. Frolov was by now in an emotional state, convinced of what was going to happen, resolved himself not to fall into the trap, and yet alone in his misery, rejected by his commanding general and, now that he had disobeyed a direct order, by his brother officers. The priests tried to reason with him. They told him his fears were groundless, and to think of his family, because if all went well and the Cossacks remained intact under British command he would need the goodwill of Domanov. He was a colonel and could expect work suitable to his position, but only if he maintained a proper military discipline and agreed to attend the conference with the others. The argument raged while the other officers were gathering themselves together for the journey.

A few other suspicious Cossacks took this final chance to take off into the hills. But desertion was not an inviting prospect. What future could there be for such a man, without identity papers or ration cards or money, able to speak nothing but Russian, alone in a newly conquered country bristling with armed men? He would have to steal to live, but for how long could he survive like that? The war was only a few days over. Fanatical Nazis were still about, so security patrols were tight and trigger fingers itchy. And where could they go? There was nowhere where they would be welcome or which they could call home. The life of a Cossack on his own in those mountains would be miserable and almost certainly short. Only in sheer desperation would he leave his unit, the only society which recognised him and to which he belonged. The Cossacks would stay together unless they had very good reason to believe that the British were about to betray them.

But by the same token one may be sure that, had they known the truth, they would have deserted *en masse*. At this same time John Greig was a lieutenant in the 46th Reconnaissance Regiment which was guarding about 1,000 Cossacks some distance away from Lienz, at Neumarkt, just north of Klagenfurt. He says,

> We looked after them for several weeks and we found them a very pleasant lot. They told us they were frightened of being sent back to Russia, but we said, 'Oh no, the British would never do such a thing.' Then we got this order that in three days they were all to be handed back. We were shattered. Our men kept coming to us and saying, 'Look, these Cossacks say they're going to be sent back and they'll all be shot.' But until we got the order we didn't believe it could happen. The feeling was that they'd be found somewhere to live. I'd never seen my blokes quite as shaken as they were over that particular incident. And they'd been with me for years. They were used to war. They'd come up all the way from Salerno. But they didn't like the idea of all these men being murdered in cold blood.

The difference between this case and others was that Greig discussed the matter with the other officers, and they agreed to tell the Cossacks what was to happen. He says: 'There was a general consensus of opinion. So I personally told this Cossack interpreter, who spoke French, that we had orders to send them all back. I make no bones about it, nor am I ashamed of it.' What he and the other British officers agreed to do was a clear breach of orders. But it was a small unit with only a handful of officers who trusted one another's discretion.

The Cossacks at Neumarkt were only loosely guarded, and as soon as they heard the news they began to melt away. Every morning the guards could see that the numbers had decreased. They did nothing to stop the flow. When the dreaded day came about half the Cossacks had gone. Many of those who stayed were officers, for they were more reluctant than the others to desert. This was doubly tragic, since the British order had emphasised the importance of sending all the officers back. The Soviet authorities wanted them more than the rest. Right at the end, when those who remained were being rounded up for loading, they refused to believe that the British were actually going to do this to them. Maybe they had been talking to the British soldiers, because some of them told Greig how disgusted they were and that they wanted no part of it. Greig says: 'I told them it was just one of those things and do it we will. And do it we did.'

But whereas at Neumarkt many managed to escape, in Lienz only a handful had the foresight and the good luck to make the break. Security in the area was tighter than at Neumarkt. As soon as the repatriation plan was known, British soldiers were ordered to carry arms and never to go about alone. Mass escapes would have presented the occupying forces with frightening problems. The Russians would assume there had been British connivance— as indeed there had been at Neumarkt. They would certainly protest and probably make trouble, suspecting that the West was planning to use these men, their bitterest enemies, in some future attack on the Soviet Union. Also the escaped prisoners would be roaming bands of desperate men, causing terror among the local Austrian population. The recapture of tens of thousands of such people would involve months of dangerous work by the already over-burdened and war-weary British army. Perhaps most importantly of all, from the point of view of those issuing the orders, the personal wrath of Churchill would descend on any general who allowed such a thing to happen. Such considerations may have convinced senior British officers that, if deception was the only way of avoiding such chaos and danger, deception there would have to be.

So when at 1 pm on May 28 the British trucks arrived in the
Lienz area, they found the Cossack officers formed up obediently,
ready for the conference which did not exist. Domanov and
Butlerov, who was still acting as the general's interpreter, were
taken in a staff car to a rendezvous nearby, where armed British
officers met them and escorted them to Spittal separately. Nikolay
Krasnov kissed his wife and mother goodbye. To cheer them up
he asked them to make sure they had six eggs ready to cook him
an omelette when he returned that evening. 'It was eleven years
before I got that omelette,' he writes.[6]

A few senior officers got into the cabs next to the British drivers,
the rest into the backs of the three-ton trucks. As yet there were no
guards. Dmitri Frolov, watching the scene from a wood a short
distance away, began to feel that maybe he had been wrong.
The British report reads, 'All officers, a total of 1,475, less one
duty officer per unit and a few who did not receive the order,
proceeded to the rendezvous in accordance with the plan.' This
was the same point a mile or two away where Domanov and
Butlerov had been met a few minutes earlier. Here two men armed
with Bren guns were placed on each truck, on the metal hood of
the driver's cabin so that they could see into the canvas-covered
body of the truck and cover the men inside. The trucks were
then dispatched to Spittal, each group escorted by a troop of
cars.

Frolov and a friend rode through the wood to this rendezvous
point:

> We stood there on the edge of the forest and watched. Someone
> gave a signal and the trucks moved slowly off. And at the same time,
> a lot of small armoured cars and motor-cycles, which had been lurk-
> ing just inside the wood like us, moved out of the wood and between
> the trucks that had our men in them. There was an armoured car
> between every two or three trucks. Aleksey and I thought to our-
> selves, 'Why the armed guard, and why such a strong one?' The
> British had been waiting there as an ambush. We stayed a little
> time in the woods and then went back to tell everyone what we'd
> seen.

It was about 1.30 pm. The Cossack officers had gone and now
was the moment, according to another of Brigadier Musson's
orders, to inform the ordinary soldiers serving in the Drau Valley

of what was to happen. Commanding officers were ordered to address their men in the following terms:

In accordance with an agreement made by the Allied governments, all Allied nationals are to be returned to their countries. This means that the Cossacks and Caucasians now in the Brigade area will be returned to Russia. Some of them will be willing to return—a considerable number of the Caucasians have already applied to do so —but on the whole it will be unpopular. In order to save trouble within unit areas the officers are being separated from the others today. Men, women and children will be moved as fast as available trains and motor transport will allow. We have as yet no detailed instructions about their horses and other animals. Carts cannot be taken on the trains so they must be left behind.

This will be an extremely difficult task. We do not speak their language, and even if they willingly comply with our instructions it is a tremendous undertaking. Particularly as there are so many women and children, some of you will feel sympathetic towards these people, but you must remember that they took up arms for the Germans, thus releasing more troops to fight against us in Italy and on the other fronts. There is no doubt that they sided with the Germans because they expected to regain power in Russia. When they saw that this was not possible they tried to excuse themselves in our eyes.

The Russians have said that they intend to put these people to work on the land and to educate them to be decent Soviet citizens. There is no indication whatever that there will be a massacre of these people. In fact the Russians need more people for their country. Remember what I said in my message yesterday. You have a very big task and a very unpleasant one. Let us try to carry it out firmly without bloodshed, but if it is necessary to resort to force do so promptly and without fear. I will support you in any reasonable action you take.

Today Musson says that the facts and instructions in this document were given to him by higher authority and that he merely promulgated them: 'I take responsibility for the order, but the thoughts in it weren't mine, I just passed them on.' But whatever its origin the order contains so many dubious assumptions that it cannot simply be allowed to pass. It ignored the fact, for instance, that many of the Cossacks and Caucasians were not Soviet nationals and therefore not liable to repatriation under the Agreement. It did not explain why the women and children should suffer because their menfolk had taken up arms for the Germans, or the simple fact that the men had joined Germany not out of any love of Hitler, but because he alone seemed to show a way out of Stalin's rule, of which they had had unpleasant personal experience.

One cannot of course know whether the British command really thought that the Cossacks were going home to be 'educated', but if they did they were being naive, to say the least. Their superiors in the government had no illusions, as is shown by Anthony Eden's reference in a Cabinet Paper dated September 3, 1944, to the 'probability that if we do what the Soviet Government want and return all these prisoners to the Soviet Union, whether they are willing to return or no, we shall be sending some of them to their death.' In the light of this and other British government papers it is hard to understand the view that there was no question of the prisoners being killed. Many British soldiers on the spot assumed that they would be and there was plenty of evidence to support this assumption.

Nor is it clear what was meant by the term 'decent Soviet citizens'. Perhaps those who initiated the order had in mind the ordinary people of the Soviet Union who had fought bravely and nobly for their country against the Nazi invader. But they probably also knew, and certainly their superiors in London knew, that by 1945 the Soviet authorities under Stalin had been responsible for the oppression and murder of innocent people on a scale so massive as to discredit the very word 'Soviet'. In 1945 the idea of 'Soviet decency' was, by any standard of human justice, a doubtful quantity indeed, and it was bizarre to find a British authority regarding the violation of this 'ideal' as proper grounds for what was to follow.

The talks were delivered and finally the British soldiers knew the facts, all except for the drivers, who were at that very moment making their way towards Spittal. It was vital to keep the truth hidden until the trucks with the officers were safely on their way. Archie Reid, one of the drivers, says, 'All we were told was that we were to take these officers to a conference, but then I was a private soldier, and privates are never told the full story. It was quite a peaceful journey. There were two Cossacks sitting in the cab with me, but they had no idea there was anything wrong, any more than I did. Afterwards we heard it was a trick, to get their leaders away.' Another driver, James Davidson, says, 'There were a Cossack colonel and his wife in the cab with me. He could speak quite good English. He asked me my name and I said it was Jimmy, and that's what they called me all the way along. I didn't see any escort or any armed men. They must have been out of sight. As far as I knew they were going to a conference.'

Other Cossacks saw the armoured cars and were worried by them, but they had not lost their seemingly inexhaustible capacity for optimism and self-delusion. 'It's only our escort. There must be partisans in the area,' a Cossack general told his subordinates.[7] 'There are ss groups in the area,' a British officer told Nikolay Krasnov.[8] Indeed there were fanatical communists and Nazis about, and both groups were a threat to the British forces. Alexander Shparengo, another officer, was disturbed by the strange need to summon everybody, instead of just a few spokesmen. As the trucks rolled towards Spittal he reassured himself thus: 'Maybe in western armies they decide questions in some new, democratic way that I don't understand. Maybe every officer, irrespective of his rank or position, has the right to speak his mind and assert his point of view. Maybe they decide controversial matters by voting.'[9] This would explain why every single one had to go.

Shparengo describes vividly how such thoughts raced through his mind, and how he tried to decide whether or not to jump out of the truck. If he did, would they shoot at him? Surely not. If the conference was genuine there would be no reason to shoot. If it was not, the machine-gunners would be afraid to open fire, because this would show that they were there to prevent the Cossacks' escape, not to protect them. There would be panic in the trucks. Shparengo thought this all out, convincing himself that he would be able to get clear. But then he had another worry: how would he feel if the British were telling the truth, if in a few hours his brother officers all returned to Lienz? They would take him for a fool. Worse, they would take him for a coward and a deserter. 'And what greater shame for an officer can there be than this? But then, a man who lets himself be taken he knows not where like a lamb to the slaughter is not much of an officer either.' Shparengo writes that suddenly 'my brain woke up.' He leapt out of the back of the truck and ran off into the trees. The convoy carried on without him. He writes, 'It is hard for me to describe how I spent the rest of that day. One minute I would feel I had done the right thing, the next I would be reproaching myself for cowardice and lack of spirit.'

The fact that Shparengo was only one of a handful who tried to escape from the convoy shows that even now the Cossacks would not accept that the worst was about to happen. The sudden appearance of a British armed guard convinced many of them that the conference was a trick, but this did not necessarily mean that they were to be handed over. Most probably they would become ordinary prisoners-of-war, in which case there might be enquiries and interrogations to determine who had committed acts of brutality and murder. These 'black sheep' from among the Cossacks—and by their own admission there were some—would then be tried and punished. The rest would be released. Those who had homes in western Europe where they had lived before the war would be allowed to return to them. The rest would somehow be resettled.

But by the time Domanov arrived at Spittal in the staff car at 2.30 pm the bad news had been broken. He was taken to an officers' mess and held under guard in a small room. At about 3 pm the Caucasian officers began to arrive and the Cossacks in a steady stream about half-an-hour later. Jimmy Davidson says, 'We drove them into an enclosure, which was a big cage, and as soon as we were in there was a guard put round us. The Cossack colonel sitting next to me said, "Why the armed guard?" I told him I had no idea.' The trucks were unloaded one by one. The officers were searched and many of them were found to possess knives or other dangerous objects. These were removed and the officers conducted to their huts inside the cage. Each man received a blanket, a mug and a spoon.

Captain G. A. Lavers, adjutant of the 1st Kensingtons, the unit responsible for maintaining the guard, issued the following orders to his men: 'Any attempt whatsoever at resistance will be dealt with firmly by shooting to kill. Any attempts by the officers to commit suicide will be prevented if there is no danger whatsoever to our troops. If there is the slightest danger to our troops the suicide will be allowed to proceed.'[10] One may assume therefore that he and his commanding officer, Lieutenant-Colonel B. L.

Bryar, were aware of the Cossacks' desperation and ready for any eventuality. Bryar went to see Domanov in the officers' mess and gave him various instructions. He told him that he (Domanov) was responsible for the discipline of his officers for as long as they remained in British hands. He was to appoint a senior officer to take charge of each hut, to make sure that supper that night and breakfast the next morning were collected from the cookhouse. At 7.30 pm Domanov would be allowed to address his men in batches of 500 for five minutes each. These talks were to be concluded by 8.20 pm and by 8.30 pm all Cossacks and Caucasians were to be locked up in their huts for the night. Reveille would be at 4.30 the next morning, breakfast at 5.00, stores to be handed in at 5.30, parade and roll call at 6.00. The loading of the trucks was to begin at 6.30 and be completed by 6.50. Ten minutes later the column of vehicles, with all the officers on board, would move off towards Judenburg for the hand-over to the Soviet authorities.

According to the British papers Domanov told Bryar, 'he would do his best to carry out these instructions'—a fact which, on the face of it, lends weight to the theory that Domanov was privy to the British plans and assisting them in the repatriation, perhaps hoping thereby to save his own skin when he found himself in Soviet custody. Anyway, the British papers note that he failed in his attempt to maintain discipline 'as a result of the effect his address had on his officers when he informed them that they were to be handed over to the Allied Russian Army the next day.' The Cossacks' suspicions had increased throughout the day. Incident after incident had seemed to confirm their worst fears. That morning they had been free, disarmed but intact as a fighting force and eager to serve the western cause. In a few hours they had been loaded, transported and caged. The record shows, though, that most of them were still unconvinced that they were to be handed over. Even behind the barbed wire they remained briefly hopeful. Domanov's four five-minute talks were like blows from an axe. Afterwards some of the officers were so shocked, so wounded in their souls, that they could do nothing but meekly accept the inevitable. But as the next few hours were to show, others had been roused to heights of despair and violence.

According to A. K. Leniwow, a Cossack officer who lived to tell the tale, almost all movable objects—tables, chairs, beds and other furniture—had been removed from the huts. This was to prevent their being used for self-mutilation or for resistance the next morning. Some of the officers, he writes, spent the night demanding the punishment of those leaders who were responsible for the situation.[11] But these were the 'hot-heads', and most were able to preserve some self-control. Old General Krasnov prepared a petition in French explaining why the Cossacks had taken up arms against the Soviet Union. According to his grandson, Krasnov asked to be held personally responsible for the behaviour of the Cossacks on the battle-field.[12] He demanded a fair trial both for himself and for any Cossack who was accused of crimes against humanity. Copies of the document, covered with many signatures, were addressed to King George VI, Churchill, the United Nations, the Archbishop of Canterbury and the International Red Cross—and these were handed in at dawn. They wanted Bryar to radio the texts immediately to London and Geneva, so that they could be considered and an answer received before the hand-over was due. That night the wire perimeter of the camp was closely guarded. Watch towers, searchlights and machine guns were in position. Escape was clearly out of the question.

One cannot tell exactly how many Cossack officers committed suicide that night. Leniwow claims that three killed themselves by cutting their arteries with pieces of glass from broken windows, that one of these was the commander of Domanov's First Infantry Division, Major-General Silkin, and that several others hanged themselves. This is confirmed in part at least by two British reports to which Leniwow did not have access. The first states: 'One officer carried out of the compound dead. Had cut his throat on previous night. One officer carried out unconscious. Had hung himself behind a door.' The second states: 'Two officers committed suicide during the night 28-29 May by hanging themselves on lavatory chains.' Several bodies were taken out of the huts and laid by their brother officers on blankets near the main gate of the compound, so that the British could see them when they arrived in the morning.[13]

By dawn the Cossack officers were outside their huts, desperately conferring in the hope of finding some way out of their predicament. The British guards and machine-gunners outside the wire also seemed to be nervous. Somehow the Cossacks were going to have to be got onto the vehicles and this was not going to be easy. At 5.30 am three Cossack priests asked Bryar for permission to hold a service. This was granted on condition that there was no delay in loading, which was due to begin an hour later. Bryar writes, 'The service they held was a most impressive affair and the singing was magnificent.'

Being a victim as well as an eye-witness, Leniwow has naturally described the scene much more emotionally:

> Thousands of Cossack generals and officers, due for forcible repatriation to the Soviet Union by the British, were kneeling on the ground, many of them in tears, as they offered up their prayers to God, while the barrels of the British guns bore down upon them . . . An improvised choir of thousands of Cossack officers, condemned by the British to death, knelt there, packed closely against the barbed-wire fence, as they sang the traditional prayers 'Our Father' and 'Save Thy people, O Lord'. The Cossack priest raised his hand high to scatter the congregation with holy water. Thus did he purify their humble and troubled souls.[14]

Punctually at 6.30 am the trucks arrived. One truck was backed up to the prison gate, blocking the opening. Bryar went to the hut where the generals and senior Cossack officers had spent the night and told them it was time to get on board the vehicles. Domanov told him that he refused to go and that he no longer had any jurisdiction over the other Cossack officers. It was now clear to the British that there could be no question of an orderly hand-over and that Domanov was no longer willing or able to help. Leniwow writes that the atmosphere was so emotional and the tension so acute that he felt the guards were on the verge of losing control and firing into the crowd. Bryar spoke to Domanov through the latter's staff officer (probably Butlerov) and told him 'that he would give the General ten minutes in which to alter his mind, and if the General still refused then methods would be employed to ensure that he and all his officers got onto the transport.'

Ten minutes later Bryar again asked Domanov to move. There was no response, so he ordered a platoon of the 1st Surreys to march into the cage. Their orders were to employ the classic tactic of crowd control—to go for the leaders. They went towards the senior officers' hut and proceeded to drag the men out one by one. A British report on the incident describes what happened next:

> Difficulties were considerable as they all sat on the ground with linked arms and legs. One Russian officer bit the wrist of a Company Sergeant-Major. This not unnaturally caused the CSM and the British troops around him to turn to sterner measures. Rifle butts, pick-helves and the points of bayonets were freely used with the result that some of the Russian officers were rendered semi-conscious.

Leniwow writes that the beating lasted for ten minutes, at the end of which senior officers—all of them unarmed and many of them elderly, well over sixty years of age—were dragged one by one to the truck. Domanov himself was one of the first to be loaded. Bryar writes, 'This display had the desired effect and from that moment the Cossack officers proceeded to get onto the vehicles.' And from this it seems clear that the beating and stabbing were done not in the heat of the moment or as retaliation for the Sergeant-Major's bitten hand, but as a deliberate act of violence designed to nip resistance in the bud. The idea was that the Cossacks, seeing the beating, would be finally convinced that the soldiers meant to get them on board the trucks by fair means or foul, and that if they did not move voluntarily they would be attacked in the same way. A British officer who was there has told the author that 'a minimum of violence' was employed, but this hardly concurs with the British report which mentions a 'free use' of rifle butts, pick-helves and bayonets. It would certainly have been possible to manhandle the senior officers on board without inflicting blows upon them. After all, they were elderly men whose recent lives had been far less active and who must have been physically weaker than the young British infantry-men. True, there would have been delay and inconvenience. But at least the job would have been done without the use of methods which, even taking into account the harshness of the time and the dulling of human sensitivity which war induces, must be described as brutal.

Many of the officers had some inkling of the Yalta Agreement and guessed that those among them who were Soviet citizens would have to go home. They thought there would be a personal check 'to separate the sheep from the goats'. While the loading was in progress, Leniwow writes, many Cossacks approached British officers waving Nansen passports and other identity documents which showed that the bearers had never been in Russia after 1920.[15] But Bryar and his men, influenced no doubt by General Keightley's order that 'individual cases are not to be considered unless particularly pressed' and that 'in all cases of doubt the individual will be treated as a Soviet national', rejected such appeals and released only four people.

The British report maintains that steps were taken to segregate people who were obviously non-Soviet, the only problem being that 'lack of documents and the speed and secrecy with which the evacuations had to be carried out made a complete individual check impossible.' But even this modest claim falls down in the cases of the senior commanders like Shkuro, Krasnov, Klych Girey and von Pannwitz. These were well-known men. In 1919 Shkuro had been awarded a senior British military honour. He had been made a Commander of the Order of the Bath for his services in the First World War. He had been an émigré since then. Von Pannwitz was a German through and through. He was not even a Russian, let alone a Soviet citizen. One can only conclude that the decision to repatriate these men in violation of the Yalta Agreement was taken on the basis of Keightley's belief that the Soviet forces wanted particularly to lay their hands on the senior Cossack officers, and that they would regard their safe delivery as a sign of British good faith. It was more important to placate the Soviet authorities than to observe the Agreement.

Only in very small ways were the British able to alleviate the horror of that journey. Major K. Rowlette, who was in the quarter-master's department, said, 'I rang up Division and said I wanted tons and tons of vodka.' The drink was duly provided and loaded onto the trucks to assuage the agony of the journey, as was a generous ration of food. A few yards from the gate of the camp a man jumped from one of the trucks, but the column was quickly brought to a halt and he was recaptured. Major Thomas Goode was the officer in command of the armoured escort which then appeared on the scene. He says, 'They were rounded up and loaded into lorries by the time we arrived. My squadron of 21 armoured cars drove fore and aft among them. The machine-gunners were ordered to discourage them from bolting.' In fact another Cossack did try to run away a few miles down the road. In

Goode's words, 'a burst of machine-gun fire made him change his mind.'

Geoffrey Pickard, another officer with the escort, recalls that his orders were to open fire only to prevent escapes, not to shoot to kill.

> I don't think our gunners aimed *at* anyone who ran away. It was quite easy just to make the dirt fly up around their feet a bit. That's usually enough to stop a man running across a field, and it was then. We recaptured them. Mind you, if we'd known what was going to happen to them, we'd have made sure they got away. We didn't quite know who these people were or what we were doing. So we just played 'follow my leader', and it was over before we knew what we'd done. My men were sickened at the thought that we'd delivered the Cossacks to their deaths, and there could well have been trouble if we'd been asked to do it again. But it was just that one day.

Anxious to show the Soviet forces that they were fulfilling their promises over the delivery of Cossack officers, the British ordered their victims to keep their uniforms and badges of rank intact. The Soviets would thus know that these were the leaders from among their enemies, men due for special treatment. But once the Cossacks were in the trucks the order could no longer be enforced. During the journey every man tore the incriminating insignia from his uniform and threw them from his truck, so that the road to Judenburg became littered with shoulder-flashes and silver stars. They also pressed their valuables onto the guards— money, cameras, watches and jewellery. At first there were pathetic attempts to bribe the guards to allow them to escape, but later the Cossacks wished only to get rid of the stuff or to exchange it for a few cigarettes. They knew that the first act of the Soviet forces would be to search their new prisoners and remove every item of value. Lieutenant English writes that some of the guards 'did a brisk trade', giving cigarettes in exchange for cameras and watches.

The convoy entered Judenburg and stopped at the big iron bridge which spans the river Mur, the boundary line between the British and Soviet zones of occupation. The Russians on the other side were ready and the trucks began to cross the bridge one at a time for unloading. Sergeant D. Charters describes in his report what happened next: 'While our trucks were halted one man asked to be allowed to make water. He was given permission to do so. He then jumped over the railing which had a rather great drop on the other side. He was picked up later.' Major Goode did not see the actual incident, but, he says, 'I saw the after-effects of it.' In his report at the time he wrote, 'One officer leapt over a hundred-foot precipice, but was recovered and handed over mangled and dying to the Soviet forces.' He adds, 'As the officers were being debussed and just after the Soviet guard had taken them over, one officer cut his throat with a razor blade and slumped dying across my feet.' Leniwow writes that there were five who committed suicide by the bridge, but Charters reports there were only these two and 'the remainder went across smoothly.'

Goode went across the bridge and watched the Soviet forces receiving their prisoners. The British had provided lists and the Soviet 'reception committee' knew the names of many of the Cossack officers, especially Krasnov and Shkuro, who had been generals on the White side in the Civil War. Goode writes that the Soviet officers seemed delighted at the arrival of such notorious characters, among whom were some of the chief demons of twenty-five years of Soviet folklore. There was a Soviet girl interpreter, a captain who spoke good English. When Goode asked her what was going to happen to the Cossacks, she replied that the senior officers would be 're-educated' and the junior ones put to work reconstructing destroyed Soviet towns.

He asked another officer the same question. This one had only a smattering of English. 'He just made a face and drew his finger across his throat,' says Goode. He had been given two answers which totally contradicted one another, but there was no doubt which one he believed:

It was quite clear to me after that talk on the bridge that there was no hope for any of them. Until then I don't think we appreciated quite what was happening. Certainly I didn't. It hadn't hit me that first night at Spittal. But it did afterwards. With hindsight one should probably have turned the other way and let them escape. But at the time it didn't occur to us to do that. Our orders were so clear.

He remembers some weeks later meeting a Guards officer who had done a similar job. He told Goode that when a group of Cossacks ran away his machine-gunners opened up on them either well high or well to one side. They scattered into the hills and no one tried very hard to find them. Goode says, 'In a sense people like that officer did disobey orders, but maybe they were right.' It might have been possible, he thinks, for some of the officers 'to leave the back door open and turn the other way'. This would have been preferable to an outright refusal to obey the order, which was repugnant to him as a soldier and in any case futile, for it would merely have meant his replacement by someone more pliable.

Many British soldiers involved in the operation still ask themselves such questions, while others are content with the thought that they obeyed orders to the letter. For instance, Lieutenant J. T. Petrie was one of those who (in the words of his own report) 'at point of bayonet encouraged the senior officers to embus' and was a member of Goode's escort. He agrees with Alec Malcolm that the repatriation of the Cossacks was just another job that had to be done:

> It was a very unpleasant thing of course, but one cannot have a war without unpleasant things. And our instructions were quite clear. We were told it was a personal instruction from Churchill, and this was explained to us through local Brigade commanders, and we carried out an operational move of the prisoners from A to B. As for what I felt about the job, I'd rather not answer that question. I've no idea what happened to them after we left Judenburg and I'd rather not get involved because I don't have a view.

This opinion that a soldier's job is to obey orders without question—'theirs is not to reason why, theirs but to do or die'—is shared by most of the senior officers. Musson has said to the author, 'It's Churchill you should be asking about all this, not Musson and Keightley. What we think about it all is really neither here nor there.'

The Cossack officers were now in Soviet hands, about 2,000 of them, 1,500 from Domanov's community and 500 from von Pannwitz's Cavalry Corps. Back in Lienz there was widespread anguish when the officers did not return by the evening of May 28, as had been promised. But the British, afraid of massive attempts to escape, still could not afford to tell the whole truth. One of the Cossacks' woman interpreters, M. N. Leontieva, has written:

By that evening there were rumours that all the officers had been handed over to the Soviets. Major Davies categorically denied this. He was as polite and agreeable as ever, but when it became possible to hide the truth no longer he told us with tears in his eyes that he had himself been deceived by his superior officers. He said he felt very bad about having told lies to the Cossack men and women whom he had come to like very much, but he simply did not dare go against his orders.[16]

But the next morning, May 29, while their officers were being conveyed to Judenburg, the Cossacks in Lienz were still not convinced that this was going to happen. Davies had told them that the officers would not be returning, but this did not necessarily mean they would be handed over. The most likely outcome was that they would be held by the British as prisoners-of-war. And even if the officers *were* to be delivered, it did not mean that the others would be—thousands of ordinary men, women and children. Even after they knew they had been deceived, the Cossacks still would not admit such a possibility.

There were still about a hundred officers who for one reason or another had not gone to Spittal with the main body, as well as thirty or forty priests. That morning loudspeaker vans drove round the area ordering any officer who had not gone to the conference to report to a certain office. Some obeyed the order, others took to the hills, aware that if they stayed it was only a matter of time before they were caught and sent to join their fellows. Then on May 30 the loudspeakers announced that any officer who did not report by twelve noon would be charged with an offence under military law. Dmitri Frolov heard the news and was distressed. Unlike most of his friends, he was convinced that the British were resolved to deliver them to the Soviets. But if he remained in hiding, he would be caught and his family would suffer. He had a wife, two daughters aged fourteen and eleven, and a little boy of five.

Frolov decided that he would have to obey the order, so he packed a rucksack and set out with his family to Peggetz Camp:

There was a truck on the square at Peggetz with two soldiers, a driver and a British officer, a young lieutenant with red hair, about twenty years old. It must have been twelve o'clock, the end of the period by which we had to report, and he was waiting to give the signal for the truck to move off with the Cossacks who were already inside it. I had actually put my rucksack in the truck and was kissing my wife and children goodbye, when this officer took me by the arm and led me away from the truck so that I wouldn't get into it. He gave the signal and the truck drove off with my rucksack, but without me. My wife was crying as we were kissing goodbye. He must have known what was going to happen and taken pity on us. Anyway, he saved my life.

But eighty-three other Cossacks, stragglers from the main party, were not so lucky. Once rounded up, they were dispatched to Spittal and on May 31 loaded into trucks. Lieutenant Dennis Hemming, the officer in charge of this 'cargo of misery', as he called it, has written a vivid account, amusing to the point of flippancy, of what then happened: 'The convoy was comprised of three 3-tonners containing the officers, with a corporal in charge of each. At the rear travelled an armoured car with bren gun mounted and orders to shoot any prisoner that attempted to escape.' The convoy was held up, so Hemming drove ahead to warn the Russians that there would be a delay. He also had with him some swords which had been taken during various searches. Cossack swords are often jewel-encrusted and of great value. Soviet officers in Judenburg knew of their existence and thought they should have been handed over with the prisoners. They made a special request for them.

Hemming drove across the bridge to the barrier, where he was met by a Russian colonel. He gave him a list of the prisoners who were about to arrive. But the colonel's first question was about the swords. Hemming writes:

> These I handed to him, but on seeing they were battle swords he registered much disappointment, as he apparently expected to receive the ceremonial variety. Two Russian officers nearby however took possession of a sword each and charged madly down the road leaping into the air, waving their newly-won possessions and uttering war cries as they went, much to the amusement of the Russian officers and men in the vicinity.

The colonel asked Hemming to hurry the prisoners up, as there was a Soviet general waiting to meet them, and this was duly done:

Almost immediately after the party arrived at the Russian barrier, two high-powered Mercedes-Benz cars drew to a halt and a general got out of each. They saluted all and sundry and ordered that the prisoners be paraded by truck loads. By this time the prisoners evidently felt that Nemesis was overtaking them. This could be seen by the expression on their faces. The generals surrounded by all and sundry spoke to one or two individuals. One general then made a grand speech in which he told them that they had been naughty boys, but provided that they did as was bid of them and worked as every other member of the Russian community, no serious harm would befall them. At this point one could see the immense relief on the faces of the prisoners as they were led away to an enclosure.[17]

Other British officers have commented on the warm, almost friendly reception that the Cossack officers received on the Soviet side of the bridge. Goode says there was about a battalion of Soviet troops who met the main body on May 29, formed them up and marched them off to a factory nearby: 'But there was a group of senior officers also and they must have been surplus to battalion. Whether they were press or political boys I don't know, but they were more educated-looking men than the actual troops. Some of them were taking photographs.' It was indeed a historic moment, the return to Russian control of the Soviet Union's bitterest enemies, and it was only natural for the professional Soviet officers to feel some sympathy towards their defeated fellow-countrymen as well as hatred for their collaboration with Nazi Germany. Their friendliness may have been a trick to convince the British that the Cossacks would be treated humanely, or it may have been partly genuine. After all, it was not the soldiers who would have to deal with these prisoners. In a few days they would be handed over to Stalin's security police, the NKVD, and the friendliness would come to an end.

MASS DEPORTATION
FROM THE DRAU VALLEY

THERE remained more than 20,000 Cossacks camped in the Drau Valley between Lienz and Oberdrauburg: non-commissioned officers, private soldiers, priests, civilian refugees, women and children. One of their interpreters, Olga Rotovaya, was present while the officers were being loaded on May 28: 'Some of their wives were crying and begging me as interpreter to ask the British officer whether their husbands would return. "Of course they will," the officer told me. "We'll be at the conference by three o'clock. It'll last an hour, an hour and a half. By five or quarter-past the officers will be back in the camp. Try to calm the women down. There's no need for them to cry." '[1]

But the evening passed and there was no sign of the Cossack leaders. At eight o'clock Rotovaya was told that some British officers wanted an interpreter. 'Where are the officers?' she asked them. 'They're not coming back,' they told her. 'Where are they?' 'We don't know.' She then said, 'Four times you promised us that they would be back this evening. Does this mean you've deceived us?' To this, according to Rotovaya, the officers replied, 'We are only British soldiers and we carry out the orders of our superiors.'

Not surprisingly the Cossacks began to fear that the worst had happened. The British officers' evasiveness and the absence of the liaison officer, Major Davies, who usually kept in close contact, made the Cossacks suspect that their captors had something to hide. Another woman interpreter, M. N. Leontieva, asked British officers the next day clearly whether or not the Cossack officers were to be handed over. She was assured that this would not happen.[2] They would not be coming back to Lienz, but they were safe and would be accommodated in good conditions. There was no need to send them food or clothes because everything would be provided. Their kit and belongings would be collected and sent on to them.

It was an unlikely story, but the Cossacks could not be sure that it was untrue. Natural optimism kept some of them in a fool's paradise for a little longer. That night, Leontieva writes, 'was a night of sleeplessness and torment.' But from the British point of view it was vital to keep the truth hidden for as long as possible. There simply were not enough troops to guard 20,000 people scattered about a large open area. Already some of them had left the valley and were living rough in the hills. Once the news was out, the trickle would become a flood.

Rusty Davies was given the most unpleasant task of breaking the news and he remembers the moment vividly:

> They had a sort of camp committee and I asked the heads of this committee to come together. They were quite horrified when I told them, and I was petrified myself, to be quite frank with you. Looking back I realise that they could have torn me limb from limb if they'd wanted to. But I was completely naive. I just walked straight into it. They didn't shout at me or attack me, they just pleaded. They couldn't believe that I was doing this to them. You see, they had implicit faith in me. That's the horrifying thing about it. That's why I feel so sick about the whole thing.

Zoe Polaneska, the young Russian girl, remembers, 'I put my arms round my ears and said, "No, I don't want to hear it." ' Davies tried to soothe and reassure. He was authorised to tell them, he said, that the Soviet authorities had promised to treat all those who were repatriated humanely and decently. The Cossacks almost laughed at such naivety. They flung questions at him: did he know what Soviet power had done? Did he know how many millions had been killed in forced collectivisation, or had died in the famines? Did he know about the mass deportations and the purges? Did he *really* think that the word of Stalin could be trusted? Davies could not answer such questions. He knew that for four years the Soviet people had fought bravely against the Nazi aggressor. For four years British newspapers had been singing the praises of Stalin. What was he to believe?

Davies said that he would make things as easy as possible for them. He would see that families were kept together. They would all get good food for the journey and some extra clothing from the stores. He would do everything to help in these matters of detail, but on the main point at issue there could be no argument.

They would have to go back to the Soviet Union. Those were his orders. He remembers then that some Cossacks brought an old woman towards him. She held out her hands and he could see that she had no finger nails. 'The torturers of the NKVD—that's what you're sending us back to!' she told him through an interpreter. Davies was deeply moved, but what could he do?

It was two days before the deportations were due to start. In the words of the official British report, 'the areas of the camps were patrolled in as much strength as the numbers of British troops available allowed, but it was impossible to prevent a considerable number of Cossacks and Caucasians from disappearing into the neighbouring hills during the ensuing few days.' One of these was Gregori Schelest, who now lives in the United States. A British soldier disobeyed orders and told him what had happened to the officers before Davies made his announcement: 'There were a few soldiers who were ready to help us. They told us the truth. I was with my wife and my little boy Gregori, who was only nine months old. So I decided that our only hope was to run away. Hundreds did what I did. We would rather have died in the forest like beasts than be handed over to the communists.' Prokofi Vasilenko did the same. He took a rucksack and ran up into the woods which covered the lower slopes of the mountains. The weather was fine, the nights were warm and life could seem quite attractive. There were plenty of streams that provided fresh water and food could be begged from the local farmers.

But the vast majority, more than 20,000 people, decided to stay in the valley and resist the order. Their officers were gone, so they elected a senior sergeant called Kuzma Polunin to be their temporary 'ataman'. Polunin turned out to be a good organiser. He addressed a petition to Alec Malcolm, commanding officer of the troops guarding the area. It began, 'We Russians, Cossacks, who evacuated from Russia of our OWN WILL and who joined the German army not for the reason to protect the German interests, but bearing in mind EXCLUSIVELY THE STRUGGLE AGAINST THE SOVIET UNION, declare that our return to the Soviet Union is absolutely impossible.'

The petition explained that many Cossacks had relatives in the United States and in Europe, for the existence of which they had suffered imprisonment and torture in the Soviet Union. Many others had suffered and died as prisoners of the Nazi

Germans. This was why they were glad to have fallen into the hands of the British. 'We wished to be protected by the British government, as thus we hoped to find salvation,' they wrote, but if this protection was impossible, 'we prefer death than to be returned to the Soviet Russia, where we are condemned to a long and systematic annihilation'. They asked Malcolm to forward the petition to the British Parliament and the American Congress.

An even sadder document was prepared by the Caucasians in Dellach, a short distance away: 'For the last twenty-five years we have had no place to stay in Russia. We have had to go from one place to another, hungry and cold, with our old men, women and children. If you now have any pity for these peoples, do not send them back to Russia, which is certain death for them.' The Caucasians asked to be sent to some British-controlled territory. They would then obey all orders and serve the British faithfully. But, the petition concluded, 'if our requests cannot be granted and you want to send all Caucasians to a concentration camp in Russia, then please shoot us all here in the fields yourselves.'

Leontieva writes, 'Major Davies accepted these petitions, but we must assume that they went no further than his waste-paper basket.' This is unjust, because Davies did in fact pass all petitions on to his superior officers, though what happened to them after that he does not know, and if they did reach London or Washington it was too late for anything to be done about them. Davies was visiting the camp authorities regularly, pleading with the Cossacks to be sensible and accept the inevitable. The meetings caused him great distress. Now that Butlerov was gone he was using Olga Rotovaya as his interpreter, a girl whose wedding he had helped organise two weeks earlier.

At one such meeting she asked Davies for more details about the proposed deportation: Would the old émigrés be sent back too? Yes, they would. Then she, Olga, would also have to go? Yes, that was correct. Rotovaya asked Davies to turn and look at the others present at the meeting. The men were weeping, she told him. 'I can't look,' Davies replied. Rotovaya continues:

His hands were trembling. He was chain smoking and nervously crunching up pieces of paper with orders written on them. Tears were flooding from our eyes. Even the men were sobbing. I tried

everything I could to convince Major Davies that our return to the
Soviet Union was impossible because the Bolsheviks would inflict
terrible suffering upon us. But it was all useless. He had only one
reply: 'I am only a soldier and I must accept the orders I receive from
my superiors. It does not depend on me. I am ready to do all I
can to help to prevent families being split up.'

This was a strong argument. Davies told the Cossacks that if
they obeyed the order they would be well provided with provisions
for the journey and families would be kept together. If they resisted
they would be loaded by force. Parents would be separated from
their children. Surely they did not want that? But the argument
was nowhere nearly strong enough to influence the Cossacks.
They had already decided what to do on the day of the proposed
move: they would assemble for a huge open-air religious service.
'We would pray in the fields, we would pray continuously,
without pause. We were convinced that the British would not
lay hands on people who were praying,' writes Rotovaya.[3]
It was clear that the British did not want to use force. So long
as she and her friends stood firm, she thought, the British would
not be able to move them. It would be emotionally impossible for
the soldiers physically to attack people whom they had treated
so kindly and come to like so much. The Cossacks were so
impressed by the good treatment they received that they took
it as a sign of British sympathy and approval. They did not
realise that the part they had played in the war was regarded in
London and Washington as base and traitorous. They did not see
that the soldiers of the Argyll and Sutherland Highlanders had
been hardened by years of cruel fighting, that they were a tightly-
disciplined body of men and that they would fulfil their orders,
even those orders which they did not understand and which they
found personally distasteful.
The Cossacks declared a hunger strike. They told the British
that they did not want any more deliveries of food as they were
'resolved to fast in preparation for the sufferings they were about
to endure'.[4] The British brought the food nevertheless: bread,
sugar, biscuits and tins of meat. Some of this the Cossacks
scattered over the ground. Tins were opened and the contents
poured away. The rest of the food was piled into stacks and
guarded to make sure that it remained intact. Food was allowed

only to the sick. The rest remained hungry. Even small children were refused food by their own parents.

They made large numbers of black flags and hung them from their tents. Black flags were also placed to mark the boundaries of the camp and the guarded stacks of unconsumed food. They made placards and nailed them up about the area with such ungrammatical slogans as 'Better death here than our sending into the SSSR!!'. The Russian Orthodox liturgy was read continuously in the many tented churches pitched in the Lienz area. Religious fervour was beginning to mount and the leadership of the Cossacks was now moving into the hands of the thirty or forty priests, the only people of officer rank who remained. By now some of the more devout Cossacks were beginning to accept death as a possibility. To allow themselves or, still worse, their children to fall into the hands of the atheists was the most terrible prospect of all, for it would mean the loss of their immortal souls. Suicide or even murder might be better in the eyes of God than what was being planned for them by the British.

Trucks came to collect the officers' kit. The Cossacks refused to load it, so the British had to do it as best they could, but it was difficult, because no one knew what was whose property or where the officers had lived. After a while the Cossacks began talking to the soldiers. They asked them where the baggage would be sent. The soldiers replied that they did not know, but that it would be delivered to the officers, whereupon distraught wives rushed off to scribble letters to their husbands, and these were handed to the soldiers for transmission, often with pathetic little packets of food. The soldiers took the letters out of kindness, but of course they never reached the Cossack officers, who were already in Soviet hands.[5]

When the time came, Davies thought, the Cossacks would realise that there was no way out and would go voluntarily. He expected trouble and embarrassment, but not serious violence. He had told them that they would have to go, in an orderly fashion if possible but by force if necessary. Surely they must believe him and realise that resistance would only make matters worse. Sadly, though, the Cossacks on this occasion did not believe the Major. The trouble was that he had misled them so many times already. True, he had done this either unwittingly or as a result of direct orders from his superiors. Nevertheless, he had misled them, and their return to the Soviet Union was all the more unbelievable for being unacceptable. Their minds were open to the rumours which raced about the area: that war was about to break out between the Soviet Union and the western powers, that the British soldiers were on their side and would refuse to use force against them, that their officers were being held in a British camp nearby and would soon be returning.[6] It was all untrue. The British soldiers were warned that the job would be unpleasant but told that its proper fulfilment was essential to British interests. They were going to obey their orders.

A few miles east of Lienz the Caucasians were encamped, and they were the ones chosen for the first assault. These units were not so hostile to the Soviet Union as the Cossacks. Some individuals had actually volunteered to go home. It was thought that they would be generally less likely to resist. During the afternoon of May 30, a company of the 5th Buffs, under Major B. McGrath, went to the Caucasian camp to move them to Dellach station, where trains would be ready to take them into Soviet territory. They had been ordered to be ready by 2 pm, but McGrath found that little preparation had been made for the move. Instead, they found a party of about 200—men, women and children—formed into a circular mass. It appeared, writes McGrath, 'that they had no intention of moving for they put up a black flag, and were chanting hymns and wailing.' He continues:

I ordered four three-tonners to back up to them and with about twenty men tried to get them into the vehicles. The wailing increased and a number indicated that they wanted to be shot by us rather than sent to the USSR. With great difficulty a few were forcibly put on one of the trucks, but it was impossible to prevent them from jumping off, which they all did. It appeared that certain men were the ring-leaders of this sit-down strike, and as an example I ordered four men to put one of these ringleaders on a vehicle. However he created such a disturbance that I was forced to hit him on the head with an entrenching tool handle.

The blow had what McGrath called 'a sobering effect' on the rest of the Caucasians, who then dispersed and were moved without further difficulty to a site near the railway station, ready for departure the next morning, May 31. One British officer and forty-five others escorted a train-load of 1,737 Caucasians which left Dellach at 10 am. Eight hours later the train crossed the frontier near Judenburg and the hand-over took place. Another 1,414 Caucasians made the same journey the next day. On May 31, besides the Caucasians, about 7,000 Cossacks from von Pannwitz's Cavalry Corps were handed over. There were few serious incidents that day. The Caucasians were less fervently resolved to resist the move, while the Cossacks from the Cavalry Corps had been successfully kept in ignorance of what was to happen.

Originally the hand-over of Cossacks from the Lienz area was to have begun on May 31 too, but this was postponed for one day at the request of the Soviet authorities, who had their hands full with the other 8,500. It was early on the morning of June 1 that the deportations really began along the length of the Drau Valley. Lieutenant E. B. Hetherington came to a camp near Oberdrauburg with a company of the Royal West Kents and found, like McGrath, that no preparation had been made for the move. He called the local Cossack leader and told him to get his men ready. The Cossack refused, adding that he would rather be shot than go, whereupon two British soldiers took him to the train by force. Hetherington then found the bulk of the Cossacks 'bunched together at the end of the camp, the outer ring linking arms to prevent any infiltration by our troops.'

The Lieutenant ordered his men to fix bayonets 'in an attempt to rouse the Cossacks to surrender', but their only reply was to rip their shirts open to invite the soldiers to stab them. A verbal appeal through an interpreter provoked only jeers and hisses. Hetherington then decided to adopt the classic crowd-control techniques of removing the ringleaders. He told his men 'to pounce on the most undesirable characters'. However, he reported, 'this was easier said then done, for it took four or six men to handle one Cossack.' Entrenching tool handles were used to break the outer ring and get people away from the mob—a policy which 'met with success slowly but surely.' The only problem after that was when one group broke away and tried to escape into the woods. The soldiers opened fire and two Cossacks were shot dead. The loading continued without further incident and another train-load of Cossacks were dispatched into Soviet territory.

In another area the 2nd Battalion, Royal Inniskilling Fusiliers, were having even greater difficulty. David Shaw, their commanding officer, says, 'It was terrible. We had to manhandle them and force them into trains at the point of a bayonet.' Lieutenant R. Shields was in charge of a company which was ordered to load some 800 Cossacks during the morning of June 1. In his report he writes: 'I was witness to many amazing incidents of fanatical fear and dread of the future they [the Cossacks] thought was in store for them—men outstretched on the ground baring their chests to be shot where they lay, women in a state of frenzy.' He and another officer, Captain Campbell, were confronted by a mass of Cossacks, all sitting with arms interlaced, refusing to move and demanding death rather than delivery into the hands of the Reds.

Shields's report makes it clear that a most terrible scene ensued:

> Captain Campbell decided that this was no time to be gentle and to try to coax them to move. It was a case of having to move them by force. The troops fixed their bayonets and started breaking the body into small groups. This proved no easy job. There followed ten minutes of beating with sticks, rifles, and even to the extent of bayonet points being used, and not too gently either. The men were by this time much aroused and it was then someone opened up with an automatic. That gave the troops the thing they had waited for. Weapons were fired above the heads of the Cossacks and into the ground in front of them. Scenes were pretty wild by this time.

Miraculously, no-one was hit by the flying bullets. The demonstration of strength induced only a few Cossacks to make their way towards the trucks which were conveying them to the train. The main body still would not move, in spite of the rough handling. As usual, the soldiers spotted a ringleader urging the Cossacks to more steadfast resistance and made special efforts to subdue this man. According to Shields's report, 'by the time he had been dragged to the trucks he was bleeding from the blows he had received and his leather coat, which was a very good one before the fight started, was in shreds, likewise the jacket and shirt underneath.'

Once this man was removed the Cossacks were no longer able to resist the combined effect of the blows and the bullets zipping into the ground at their feet. Three-quarters of them moved grudgingly towards the trucks. But a group of about 200 made a dash towards some nearby woods. Shields writes, 'They were of course met by bren-gun fire, designed to stop any such attempt.' Hardly any reached the woods and almost all those who did were quickly recaptured. Three Cossacks were killed by the gunfire. It took the soldiers two hours to clear that one camp.

David Shaw says, 'It gave us all a great shock. It was a frightful order to give and there was a lot of feeling among my troops.' After these incidents he went and complained to Robert Arbuthnott, and was amazed to be told that his battalion had been specially picked for the dirty job because they were Irish. The general said he had taken the view that the Irish would be less likely to object or make trouble than an English battalion. Shaw was shocked and insulted. But, he says, 'General Arbuthnott gave me a direct order and I had to carry it out. The men moaned like anything, but in the end they obeyed orders too. It was terrible. I remember these women—some of them pregnant—lying on the ground rolling and screaming. My men were putting their rifles on the ground and lifting the women into the train, then locking the doors and standing there as the train pulled out with women screaming out of the windows.'

Thirty miles north of Klagenfurt Captain J. S. Lowe, of the 12th Honourable Artillery Company, was having similar trouble in persuading his Cossacks to board the trucks. Originally 2,000 of them had surrendered to him personally a few days from the end of May, having waited three weeks after the end of the war before doing so, but security had been less tight than in the Lienz area and many of the original number had vanished before the beginning of June came, with its orders that all ranks were to be handed over. Ten three-tonners were provided to take about 300 of them to Judenburg.

Lowe was in charge of the loading. He remembers:

They knew where we were supposed to be taking them and no one wanted to get on the lorries. They stayed in their tents. So we struck the tents with them inside. Then, when they were out in the camp area, we felt that the only thing was to make a demonstration of strength, so we mounted a flame thrower on a bren-gun carrier and flamed down the alleyway between the tents. After that the Cossacks got into the trucks.

Lowe was no part of the escort, but on its return he was shocked to hear that several of the Cossacks had committed suicide. He says, 'I think there were three who killed themselves in the trucks and one who jumped over the bridge at Judenburg. Judging by the blood one of my men saw in the trucks afterwards, they did it by cutting their arteries, either wrists or throat.' After this, representations were made to the Brigadier, Clive Usher, and all further transports were cancelled. Lowe says, 'We all felt very strongly about it after that one day, what with the flame-thrower and the suicides, so we virtually said, "Not again." ' Those Cossacks who had had the luck to avoid the transport remained with the unit for some days before being sent to general displaced person camps. A few hundred stayed with the British for months, working as grooms or servants.

But these incidents of violence, shocking though they were, seem small when compared with what happened at Lienz, the area controlled by the 8th Battalion, Argyll and Sutherland Highlanders. The special horror of the Lienz events was that they involved some 4,000 women and 2,500 children and were seen almost as an act of genocide, marking as they did the liquidation of a large part of the émigré Cossack nation. The affair was not discussed in the British or American press at the time. It suited both sides, the Soviet Union as well as the West, to keep the whole question of forcible repatriation quiet, and journalists were still receptive to the advice of government officials.

Before the British documents covering 1945 were opened in 1972 there was no accurate information available on what happened. Russian émigrés wrote about the affair in some detail, but their accounts are of course emotional and often exaggerated. They speak of Britain's 'great betrayal' of the Cossacks, without explaining why loyalty or favour should have been shown by Britain to men who fought on Hitler's side. They describe Churchill as a war criminal,[7] without trying to analyse the Yalta Agreement on repatriation or the reasons that compelled it.

The former Cossack ataman, Vyacheslav Naumenko, has called June 1 'the day which, together with the word Lienz, is inscribed in letters of blood in the history of the Cossack nation.' He foresees that 'this day will remain in our memories for all time as the day of unparalleled cruelty and inhumanity perpetrated by the western Allies in the form of the British army against the defenceless Cossack nation on the banks of the River Drau.'[8] But he has not placed the event in the context of the Second World War, or compared it with the greater horrors inflicted on other peoples by the Nazis.

Still, the Cossacks were human beings and, although they had no claim on the Allies' loyalty, they had a right to expect correct, decent treatment from the army which had accepted their surrender as prisoners-of-war. It is on this basis that one examines British documents on the affair which are now open. Alec Malcolm wrote a report which begins:

> At 0730 hours on June 1st I went with Major Davies to Peggetz Camp . . . At the camp I saw a very large crowd of people, number-ing several thousand, collected in a solid square with women and children in the middle and men round the outside. There appeared to be an evenly spaced cordon of uniformed men round the whole crowd. A body of 15 to 20 priests were assembled in one part of the crowd, wearing vestments and carrying religious pictures and banners. At 0730 hours these priests began to conduct a service and the whole crowd to chant. It was obvious that this form of resistance had been highly organised.

Malcolm was right. The previous evening the priests had decided to summon Cossacks to a huge open-air service. Vassili Gregoriev, the senior priest, was against the idea because he did not want too many people to congregate in one place. He thought this would make it easier for the soldiers to collect them and load them. But he was overruled by other priests and Cossack leaders who thought that the religious ceremony would make it impossible for the deportation to happen. It would increase the moral pressure on the British, they thought. No one likes to disturb a man while he is praying. At 6 am the priests walked in procession round the camp, gathering people as they went, until by Davies's estimate there was a crowd of 4,000 gathered in a central square, surrounded on three sides by a tall wooden fence.

Cossacks and soldiers alike have vivid memories of that scene. Towering over the crowd was a wooden platform with a makeshift altar and a large cross. Around this platform were the priests, all in brightly coloured vestments. Vassili Gregoriev was leading the crowds in the prayers of the Orthodox Liturgy. Archie Reid, one of the soldiers, remembers: 'There was one priest and he seemed to be the root of the trouble. He had a tabernacle built and he was giving them a talk. His word was law. They'd have gone more peaceably if he'd have kept quiet.' Others recall an almost carnival scene: the colours of the icons and religious banners, the black flags tied to every available structure, the crowds and the singing.

Davies addressed the crowd through an interpreter and told them it was time to begin loading. He writes that 'the only result was a tightening up of the crowd.' He told them they had half an hour in which to finish their service, and when this time was up he gave them another half-hour. But there was no sign that the prayers were likely to draw to an end. Davies then realised 'that appeal to this crowd for voluntary movement was useless and that they would have to be forcibly evacuated'.

He formed his men up along the unfenced side of the square. Some were armed with pick-helves, others with rifles loaded with live ammunition. The riflemen had bayonets tied to their belts. He gave them the order to fix bayonets. He says:

> I made sure these men were smart and well turned-out. When I ordered them to fix bayonets, I made sure they did it as a perfect drill movement, like guardsmen at Buckingham Palace. I felt sure that this would do the trick. The Cossacks could see those bayonets being clipped onto the ends of those rifles, and I felt sure it would make them realise that we meant business. I really did not think they would resist after that.

Davies was mistaken. Even when the soldiers advanced into the crowd with their clubs and bayonets, the Cossacks carried on praying and refused to move. Like a herd of animals facing an attack by predators, they had hidden their women and children deep in the middle of the crowd, while along the edge was a line of young men resolved to defend the tribe. In Davies's words, 'the people formed themselves into a solid mass, kneeling and crouching with their arms locked around each other's bodies.' The soldiers tried taking hold of individual Cossacks and pulling them away from the mob. Ivan Martynenko remembers how the whole crowd trembled and rocked as the soldiers tugged at it, but they were not able to prise anyone away.

The soldiers had never encountered such a situation and were nonplussed by it. Several of them went back to Davies. 'They won't go, sir,' they told him, almost pathetically. Davies's orders were clear. He told his men that the Cossacks would have to go whether they liked it or not. They obeyed him and returned to the fray, but they were puzzled and confused, looking at Davies as if to say, 'Do you really mean that?' Davies was disturbed by this. He knew from experience that they would never have hesitated for a moment if he had told them to attack a position in battle. Archie Reid recalls, 'We were told that they had done dirty work for the Germans and that we were to regard them as our enemies. But when it came to the point they didn't seem like that. It wasn't a nice job at all.'

Davies's next plan was to send one of his platoons into the crowd to isolate a corner: 'A pocket of about 200 people was cut off. I ordered the remaining two platoons to move between this pocket and the remainder of the crowd to ensure that no one escaped from the pocket, and that no one interfered with the first platoon which was to commence loading these people onto the trucks.' The Cossacks were eventually to be loaded onto a train of covered goods wagons which was standing a few hundred yards away. There was no railway platform there and wooden steps had been built to bridge the gap and enable the Cossacks to climb in. But first of all the problem was to get them into the three-ton trucks and ferry them to the line. Usually the main bodies of these trucks are enclosed by canvas pulled tightly over semi-circular iron struts, but in this case the canvas had been removed. With the sides of the trucks open as well as the backs it would be easier to load the people.

Up to this point the soldiers had used little violence. There had been pulling and tugging, but blows had not been struck. Colonel Malcolm has described the whole episode to the author as 'like one of those demonstrations outside the American Embassy in Grosvenor Square, like a sit-down strike', and up to this point his description is accurate. But what happened next puts the whole matter into a different category. Emigré Cossacks have written about it emotionally and at length. It is natural for them to exaggerate the horror and violence of the scene. The British have stayed silent about it and some are still anxious to minimise its drama. But both Malcolm and Davies described the event at the time, and it is clear from their reports how terrible were the scenes which took place.

Davies described how the isolated pocket of 200 people were loaded onto the trucks:

> As individuals on the outskirts of the group were pulled away, the remainder compressed themselves into a still tighter body, and, as panic gripped them, started clambering over each other in frantic efforts to get away from the soldiers. The result was a pyramid of screaming, hysterical human beings under which a number of people were trapped. The soldiers made frantic efforts to split this mass in order to try to save the lives of those people pinned underneath, and pick-helves and rifle-butts were used on arms and legs to force individuals to loosen their holds.

This scene made a vivid impression on other British soldiers. Duncan McMillan says, 'The whole thing went in and the centre rose up higher than a man stands.' Archie Reid, who is now a farmer in Scotland, says: 'It wasn't the soldiers who smothered them, it was themselves. They were like a lot of sheep in a fog, all piled one on top of the other. I think there were six suffocated to death.' Davies writes in his report that all the Cossacks in this group had to be forcibly loaded and that two died through suffocation.

Dmitri Frolov, one of the few Cossack officers present at the scene, says: 'They threw us into the trucks like sacks of potatoes. I remember seeing the seventeen-year-old daughter of Sergeant Pastryulin. She was a beautiful girl. I watched her being tipped over the side of a truck head first. Then I saw her stand up in the truck, one hand holding onto one of the iron struts, the other holding her head which had banged against the floor.' The priests were continuing the service. Frolov goes on: 'One soldier came up to Father Panteleymon. He grabbed the priest by his robe and tried to pull him out of the crowd. Father Panteleymon held out his wooden cross towards him as if to ward him off. The soldier backed away.'

Frolov then saw a soldier carrying a boy of about five on his shoulders towards one of the trucks. The boy was in Cossack uniform struggling and wriggling, and Frolov thought to his horror that it was his son Volodya. He lost control of himself and ran out of the crowd, but when he got nearer he found that it was not his son, that it was just another little boy who looked like him. He turned back and made for the protection of the mob, but he was grabbed by a couple of soldiers who started marching him to the trucks. He was only saved by a group of young Cossacks who dashed out of the crowd and rescued him. The young Cossacks once again linked arms around the outskirts of the group and did their best to protect them from the soldiers' raids. The women and small children were obviously easier to capture and they could be loaded with less violence. Often the father of the family would see this happening. Like Frolov, he would be momentarily blinded by the thought of his wife or child being taken to the Soviet Union without him. Many Cossack men flung themselves from the mob to save a relative, and once they were out it was easier to seize them.

Zoe Polaneska was at the back of the throng. At first she did not realise what was happening, only that she was being pressed more and more tightly against the huts and the strong wooden fence which partly enclosed the gathering. When she saw the soldiers dragging the Cossacks away, her first reaction was one of amazement. These were the British troops who had treated her so kindly. Why had they now turned so cruelly against her? 'They were behaving so badly that I think their minds must have blacked out,' she says today. But dimly she realised that what the soldiers were doing came quite unnaturally to them. There must have been some compelling political reason, some force beyond their control and understanding making them act in this astonishing way.

In his book *The Great Betrayal*, devoted entirely to the event, General Naumenko writes:

> The soldiers beat the Cossacks about the head with clubs. Blood was drawn, and as the men lost consciousness the soldiers picked them up and threw them into the trucks . . . Some of them regained consciousness and jumped out of the trucks, whereupon they were grabbed, beaten again and thrown back in. Once a truck was full, two machine-gunners got on board and they were driven down to the railway line to be thrown into the waiting goods wagons.[9]

His allegations are rejected most strongly by Colonel Alec Malcolm and by all the officers and men of the 8th Battalion, Argyll and Sutherland Highlanders. Malcolm says, 'The Cossacks were traitors to their country and so they had to pay the penalty. What if Hitler had invaded Scotland and various Scotsmen had volunteered to fight on his side? They would have been punished after the war, of course.' He feels that, given the order to load the Cossacks onto the trains, his men used the absolute minimum of necessary force. He writes, 'I do think that the political decision to repatriate the Cossacks was right, and the only one which could have been agreed then.'

When shown a striking and terrifying painting of the scene done by a Cossack émigré artist in 1957 and portrayed on the jacket of this book, he described the work as 'barmy' and 'an absolute travesty'. Malcolm feels that there is a danger of over-dramatising the whole affair. It occurred only three weeks after the end of six years of war, he writes. In those six years he and his men had many difficult and unpleasant orders to carry out involving the death of friends and comrades in arms. He regards the whole operation as just 'another unpleasant job which had to be done'.

From interviews with British soldiers who took part in the operation it is clear that the Cossack artist S. G. Korolkov took certain liberties with reality in his portrayal of the scene. For instance, no one recalls seeing a soldier swinging his rifle like a club. Davies points out that the rifles carried fixed bayonets and that it would have been dangerous, if not impossible, to swing the weapon in this way. Nor were there any caterpillar-tracked tanks of the type depicted by the artist. Davies does say, though, that apart from these details the painting provides 'a pretty fair picture' of what was happening.

None of the officers or men interviewed for this book share Malcolm's view of the need to send the Cossacks back to Russia by force. Kenneth Tyson, the battalion's padre, describes the operation as 'an evil event'. Davies says, 'I still regard it with horror.' Duncan McMillan says, 'They should never have been sent back.' John Pinching, the battalion medical officer, also says, 'They should never have been sent back. We all felt very badly about it.' These feelings are shared by the ordinary men who feel that the job was 'unsoldierly' and should not have been given to them.

All those interviewed share Malcolm's conviction that there was no *deliberate* or *unnecessary* violence used in order to load the trains, but they recognise that there *was* violence. Their case is that, once given the order, they had no other way of loading the

Cossacks. Their only alternative was to disobey the order, and this they would not do. Tyson writes that the soldiers 'had to make themselves blind and deaf to heart-breaking protests, to act unyieldingly and to use force.' It is the degree of force used which is hard to describe accurately. No one doubts that Cossacks —men, women and children— were pulled, dragged and carried, in fact manhandled, onto the trucks and trains. But, as Malcolm indicated, this sort of work is frequently done by police when dealing with sit-down strikers in peacetime. If this were the full extent of the violence, there would be little cause for anyone to complain.

But this was not the full extent of the violence. Perhaps the most important piece of evidence is contained in Malcolm's own report. He wrote, 'It was necessary to hit the men hard to make them let go.' He makes it clear that the soldiers were hitting the Cossacks, especially the young men in the front who were guarding the rest, in order to clear a way through for soldiers to grab people and load them. He admits too that some Cossacks suffered bayonet wounds, but affirms that these were accidental. Indeed, it seems likely that such accidents could easily have happened once the soldiers began striking Cossacks with the butts of rifles which carried fixed bayonets. All in all, it is clear from Malcolm's own report that the scene bore little resemblance to 'a sit-down strike in Grosvenor Square', and that it was only by attacking and beating with some ferocity that these Cossacks could be loaded.

At the back of the crush Zoe Polaneska was being pushed tighter and tighter against the wall of one of the huts. At the front everybody was pushed inwards, trying to escape the raiding parties, and those at the back were in danger of being crushed. Zoe was lifted up by the mob to the level of one of the windows. She was pressed against the window until suddenly the glass broke. The upper part of her body fell into the inside of the hut, but her legs remained outside, impaled on the jagged glass of the broken window. She says: 'My legs were cut to ribbons. Blood was streaming down and I couldn't feel them—that was my worst worry. I just lay there until someone came and threw my legs over the window and into the hut.'

The crowd was also pressing against the tall wooden fence, and eventually the weight of the bodies was such that it began to give way. Then suddenly it burst. People poured through the gap like lava from a crack in an erupting volcano. Then, in Rotovaya's words, 'they scattered in all directions like hunted hares.' She was thrown to the ground close to the spot where the fence broke:

> People were rushing past my legs, scared out of their wits. Everything was mixed up: the singing, the prayers, the groans and screams, the cries of the wretched people the soldiers managed to grab, the weeping children and the foul language of the soldiers. Everyone was beaten, even the priests, who raised their crosses above their heads and continued to pray. I prayed to God to help me get to my feet. I managed to get up and ran with the crowd through the broken fence into another field outside the camp. There many people, led by the priests, fell to their knees and continued to pray. Others rushed towards the bridge which crossed the river and made for the mountains. Everybody had the same idea: 'Soon it will be my turn. They'll grab me and throw me into a truck. A short journey and there I'll be, face to face with the Bolshevik hangmen.'

Not surprisingly, the nightmare turned many Cossacks to thoughts of suicide. Frolov says, 'I got into the woods and saw several people there hanging from trees.' This is confirmed by several British soldiers, including Davies, and there can be no doubt that a number of Cossacks died in this way. More terrible still were the suicides that took place on the bridge which spanned the river Drau. After the fence broke, many Cossacks found themselves briefly in an unguarded area. True, there were soldiers about the place, but for the moment the crowd was not surrounded. Rotovaya writes, 'The river seemed our only salvation. One jump into the raging stream and all would be ended.' Many people made for the bridge, most of them aiming to escape into the hills, but a few resolved to end their lives.

The soldiers too ran towards the bridge to stop people from crossing it, but many Cossacks had crossed before an effective barrier could be formed. Zoe Polaneska was one of these. She remembers tearing a piece of her skirt to try to bandage her legs, which were streaming with blood, and the soldiers firing machine-guns over the heads of the fleeing Cossacks to try to bring them to a halt. But they poured across the bridge like ants and were quickly in among the trees. It was then that she saw with her own eyes women and children jumping off the bridge into the water.

Memories of this terrible scene are especially vivid. Tyson saw soldiers on the bridge dashing to left and right, holding their rifles sideways like a gate and trying to push people off the bridge. Davies says, 'I think the soldiers got quite rough then and were literally knocking them back to keep them away from the bridge, so that they wouldn't throw themselves into the water.' Frolov says: 'I saw soldiers trying to save people with poles and ropes. One soldier managed to lasso a woman and pull her out. I saw him put his arms around her and embrace her. He was in tears.' The soldiers did what they could, but it was a swift-flowing river in full flood from the snows melted by the recent hot weather. They were not able to save everybody.

What shocked the soldiers most of all was that the Cossacks were not only drowning themselves, but also their children. One such case is described by the émigré writer, Fyodor Kubanski:

A young woman with two small children ran to the edge. She embraced the first child for a moment, then suddenly flung him into the abyss. The other child was clinging to the bottom of her skirt and shouting, 'Mama, don't! Mama, I'm frightened!' 'Don't be afraid, I'll be with you,' the frantic woman answered. One jerk of her arms and the second child was flying into the rushing waters of the river Drau. Then she raised her arms to make the sign of the cross. 'Lord, receive my sinful soul,' she cried, and before her hand reached her left shoulder she had leapt in after her children. In a moment she was swallowed by the raging whirlpool.

Such emotionally written accounts show the depth of the fear and religious hysteria which gripped the Cossack crowd on that day. The terrible and sudden turn of events—the disappearance of the officers, the violent attacks of men they thought were their friends, the prayers and exhortations of the priests, the all-consuming fear of the Soviet authorities—had removed their instinct for self-preservation and made them suicidal. For the moment they were genuinely convinced that life in the Soviet Union was worse than death. The knowledge that their enemies were convinced atheists only added to the religious hysteria, making them fear for their immortal souls as well as for their lives. They hated the Soviet government not only for the physical harm it had inflicted on so many of them in the past, but also for its determination to extirpate the Christian religion. The

Bolsheviks would not only kill them, they thought, but they would also destroy them spiritually, which was worse.

It was this that lay behind the Cossack mothers' decision to kill their own children. They knew that, while they themselves would probably be killed or allowed to die in the labour camps, their young children would not die. Instead they would be taken from their parents, brought up in state orphanages and taught the ideology of Marx, Lenin and Stalin. They would learn to hate the Christian Orthodox religion and to reject everything that their parents had fought for. Their emotions fired by the exhilaration of mass prayer and by their belief that death was near, the Cossacks found such an idea even more intolerable than the physical violence. Both logically and emotionally the situation was ripe for infanticide. General Naumenko estimates that twenty or thirty people were drowned in this way.[10] Probably there were not so many, but there were certainly some, perhaps as many as ten.

Davies's most terrible memory, and one confirmed by many other witnesses, is of a Cossack who first shot his wife and three children, then shot himself. He found them himself by a sharp dip in the ground, the wife and children lying side by side on a grassy bank and the man lying opposite them, a revolver in his hand. Davies says, 'I think it was this that brought the horror of it all home to me, that a man could do such a thing.' He remembers wondering as he looked at the bodies, how could the man have killed these four people? Could he have got them all together and then shot them quickly, one after the other? Davies thought this unlikely. If he had done it this way there would have been confusion and disarray. The bodies would not have been so carefully lined up. What the man must have done, Davies concluded, was to take one child to the bank, kill him, then go off and collect another child, kill him, and so on until all four were dead and he could be sure that none of his family would fall into Soviet hands. Naumenko writes that the man's name was Pyotr Mordovkin and that his wife's name was Irina.[11]

At this point Davies went up to the main group of priests, who he could see were leading the crowd's resistance, and spoke to them through an interpreter. He told them of the terrible sight he had just seen and begged them to help him bring the crowd under control, so that there would be no more deaths. The priests refused absolutely. By this time Davies was on his own, because Malcolm had gone down to where the train was standing to supervise the loading there. He felt deserted and rather alone, a mere major with a mere company of men under his command, expected to control a crowd of many thousands hysterical to the point of suicide. He felt too a sudden twinge of resentment against the priests who were responsible for the chaos and who took what seemed to him a cavalier attitude to the deaths of their countrymen. Truckloads of Cossacks were still departing for the railway line and Davies invited several of the priests to go with them. Every priest refused. Davies felt that having incited their flock to violence, they should have been prepared to go with them, to comfort them on the journey and to share their fate. 'We didn't think a lot of the priests. I'm sure they were the cause of a lot of the casualties,' says Musson. The evidence shows, though, that the priests did no more than follow the wishes of their flock. They were leading the crowd, but the crowd was following them all too willingly towards a state of religious frenzy.

The horror of the scene was having its effect on the soldiers too. Tyson says: 'They were emotionally disturbed by what they had to do.' Pinching too noticed that some of the soldiers were in deep distress, which was all the more surprising with hardened soldiers such as these, who had fought their way through many cruel battles in North Africa and Italy. Soldiers were finding that it is one thing to kill, or to see one's friends killed or to be wounded oneself in battle, but something quite different to be forced to use violence against women and children. As Davies wrote in his report, 'terrified and hysterical people threw themselves on their knees before the soldiers begging to be bayoneted or shot to death as an alternative to loading.' Tyson remembers that a few broke down completely: 'One or two of the soldiers just couldn't take it. There were soldiers pushing people along with their rifle-butts—not hammering them but just pushing them—with tears streaming down their faces. It was the only time I ever saw an Argyll and Sutherland Highlander in tears.'

Nevertheless, the soldiers were under military discipline and they had received direct orders to load the Cossacks, by force if necessary. Having fought together for many years they were conditioned to obeying orders, and although this was a new type

of order, which threatened them emotionally rather than physically, the shock was not enough to make them even contemplate
disobedience. Discipline had become an instinct, a feeling stronger
than the ordinary human emotions which rebelled against what
was happening. In spite of their distress Davies and his men felt
that they had to complete the job. Davies writes:

> We therefore made a second raid on the crowd. When the people
> saw the soldiers again in amongst them they panicked and ran, and
> the soldiers had to use their rifles to prevent themselves from being
> overwhelmed. During this stage one of the crowd clasped at one of
> the soldiers' rifles and deliberately pulled the trigger in an effort to
> shoot himself. The bullet killed a youth standing alongside. During
> the stampede a man was trampled to death.

Zoe Polaneska, her legs still bleeding, was hiding with another
girl in some trees a little way up the mountains. They thought
they were safe because there was thick undergrowth and plenty
of space. But having finally blocked off the bridge, a group of
soldiers went into the hills to look for those who had escaped.
The local Austrian farmers, alarmed at the idea that there were
fugitives in their midst, were willing enough to guide the soldiers
to where the Cossacks were hiding, and it was one of these who
pointed out the two young girls. The soldiers escorted them
down the hill and across the bridge to where the train was
standing.

Donald Smith was a corporal in 'B Company', commanded
by Major C. H. Burn, whose job it was to get the Cossacks onto
the train and then make sure that they did not get off. The train
had stopped on a level crossing across a dirt road down which the
trucks of prisoners were to drive. The camp was only a few hundred
yards away and Smith could hear the commotion. 'Those poor
devils are going back to be shot,' an officer told him. Then the first
trucks began to arrive. They turned and reversed right up to the
train and the specially built wooden platform.

Smith remembers 'frightened, desperate old people and children
crying', as well as 'two or three aged men with white hair and
beards, their heads bleeding from being hit with rifle-butts'.
They began to get down from the trucks. Smith writes: 'We helped
the aged, who were praying all the time. Some of the children
had been separated from their parents. Some were, I think, too

shocked even to cry or pray, but climbed into the vans quietly to squat in a corner. I was at this point sickened.'

Zoe Polaneska and her friend were led to the train and pushed into one of the trucks. She thought of trying to jump off, but there were guards all around, even on the other side of the track to prevent people from diving under the train and escaping. Then, luckily for her, an officer noticed the blood pouring from her legs. He had her taken off the train and escorted to a medical centre. A British medical officer bandaged her knees and she took the opportunity to show him her German identity card (*Ausweis*), which showed her nationality as Yugoslavian. (She had been living there for some months and been given new documents.) She was able to make the doctor believe she was not a Soviet citizen. He directed her to a special part of the camp where non-Russians were being held.

As soon as she left the surgery she was picked up by the soldiers and put back on the train: 'It was really dreadful. It was only after a great argument with the guards that they let me off it. I was waving my *Ausweis* and explaining that I ought not to be there. Eventually an officer said I was not Russian, so I was allowed off. I was very lucky.' Her friend Sonia was not so lucky. She was one of those still in one of the trucks when the sliding doors were pulled shut and locked. The windows were small, about a foot square, so the prisoners were in semi-darkness as they sat on the floor with their few possessions, waiting for the train to move off towards the East.

Davies came down to the train and saw it standing there, full of screaming people, waiting for the signal to depart. Because of the hunger strike and the 'hand-luggage only' order the prisoners had hardly any food with them. This did not bother Davies unduly, for it was only a few hours to Judenburg, where they would be taken over by Soviet forces. It was a hot day, so three 4-gallon water cans had been placed in each truck. This too was satisfactory. But, Davies wondered, what about lavatories? The Cossacks were travelling in goods wagons without any facilities of that sort whatever. They were totally enclosed and their only windows were high up the walls. So what were they to do if they wanted to relieve themselves?

Davies was sufficiently worried that he put this question to an officer responsible for administering the trains. 'Oh, that's all right,' was the reply, 'there's a bucket in every truck.' Davies had a momentary vision of a typical truck-load: thirty people, men and women together, some of the women elderly, the wives of sergeants or senior officers, women whom he had known personally. Was each of these women supposed to take turns squatting on a bucket in the corner of a cattle truck, in full view of the other twenty-nine? He realised that the Cossacks were being treated as something inhuman, as little better than animals. He was horrified.

By now it was 11.30 in the morning. In four hours the soldiers had managed to load only 1,252 people onto the train, 500 less than the figure set down in Malcolm's orders. At this point, writes Malcolm, he did stop the loading 'in view of the inevitable injuries inflicted'. But elsewhere in the valley the operation continued, usually with violence, though not such dramatic violence as at Lienz. In all 6,500 Cossacks were sent to the East on that day.

The train moved off, the soldiers departed, leaving only a few guards, and the remaining Cossacks drifted miserably back to the shambles of Peggetz Camp. Zoe Polaneska describes the scene: 'The flags and the platform where the priests had been had all collapsed. I had a good look round and saw some patches of blood where people had been killed. Everyone was wandering from one barracks to another as if in a daze, looking for their families. Some of the people had lost their husbands, some their children and some their wives.' But she at least was saved. She was now living in a special part of the camp reserved for Cossacks not liable to repatriation. The remainder would be sent back within the next few days.

There were not enough soldiers to guard the whole area, so that night many more Cossacks slipped away into the hills and woods. George Morozoff was one of these. He had been an officer and entitled to carry a revolver, but in fact he had owned two, and when the order came to hand in all weapons he kept the second. He had seen one of the women throwing herself into the river with her child and he was in a state of frenzy. He said to his wife: 'If the English soldiers catch us, I'll shoot you first and then myself. But I won't go back home. They can take us back dead.'

That evening Malcolm went to see his Brigadier and told him he did not want to repeat the operation the next day. But another train-load was due to be collected from the Peggetz area and Musson did not want the timetable disrupted. Malcolm agreed to try to fulfil his orders, and in fact he succeeded because in the days that followed there was none of the violence that had marked June 1, only mild passive resistance. The will of the Cossacks was broken. While some continued to escape into the hills, most were unable to desert the 'tribe' even at such a moment of danger. Only a few were ready to live like beasts in the woods, their only possessions a rucksack of food and perhaps a revolver. The rest were resigned to their fate, their religious fervour and determination to resist replaced by dull acquiescence. On June 2 the soldiers were able to dispatch 1,858 Cossacks and on June 3 another 1,487.

June 3 was a Sunday, and the church service which Kenneth Tyson held that morning has remained in the memories of many. Davies says: 'I remember the "padre" giving us the most tremendous sermon. My God, he chastised the blooming lot of us. We were absolutely numb by the time he'd finished. We were all feeling a bit squashed and he rammed it further home. I'll remember it for the rest of my days.' Like most of the British soldiers who were there, Tyson confirms that 'it was generally understood that all these men would be shot by the communists on arrival at their destination'. He was therefore, he says, 'in a dreadful state' when he addressed the battalion and spoke about 'the impersonal dealing with the Cossacks that was an offence to everyone concerned'.

Tyson recalls that his text was St Mark, Chapter 6, Verse 34: 'When He saw the multitude He was moved with compassion, for they were as sheep not having a shepherd.' In this sermon, he says, 'I expressed more or less my whole mind about the inconsistency of and the necessity for compassion, even in war.' Many soldiers had been to see him in the previous forty-eight hours, gravely disturbed by the thought that they had used such violence against women and children, and that they had sent thousands of harmless people to their deaths. What right had they to treat people in this extraordinary way, and what right had their superiors to expect them to do such things? They told Tyson they thought the whole thing was 'a bloody shame'.

These soldiers did not share the view of Colonel Malcolm that the operation was just 'another unpleasant job which had to be done'. On the contrary, most witnesses have been at pains to explain how the whole thing seemed quite different to the ordinary brutality of the battlefield. For instance, Davies says: 'You might have been in a hell of a battle during the day, you might have captured a position, but when the prisoners started coming in you didn't just cut them down. You'd be much more likely to give the man a cigarette. After all, he'd given himself up and that was the end of it.' He was horrified to think that men who had surrendered voluntarily and who had been accepted as prisoners-of-war were being sent to their deaths. The idea was unsoldier-like.

Such feelings were held even more strongly by the soldiers whose unpleasant duty it was to escort the trains into Soviet territory. One unit which did this in the early days was the 2nd Battalion, London Irish Rifles, probably because of the divisional commander's strange notion that Irish troops were more suited to this type of work than English. The battalion's commanding officer, Lieutenant-Colonel (later Major-General) H. E. N. Bredin, remembers receiving orders that all Russian prisoners were to be 'repatriated' and being surprised at how vehemently these men protested that their return to the Soviet Union was impossible. At first his men were irritated by the frantic complaints and the wild stories of what was likely to happen. He recalls some of his men telling the Cossacks not to be silly and not to exaggerate.

Bredin says: 'The dear old British soldier at that time could not believe that such things were likely to happen. But then our men went into the Russian zone as guards on trains, and it wasn't until the first troops came back that we heard that prisoners were being taken away and shot.' Bredin did not himself see such incidents but, he says,

I spoke to people who had seen prisoners being shot and I think there was clear evidence that shootings took place. Anyway, my men were quite sure of it and we heard enough about it to be sure that it was not the sort of thing that we ought to be having a hand in. We also got reports that there were suicides on the trains, people jumping off or cutting their throats with bits of broken window pane. A fairly serious situation arose with the soldiers very nearly getting to the point of saying, 'Sorry, sir, we won't obey your orders. We will not take these men to where they are just being mown down without any sort of trial.'

The London Irish was a seasoned, hardened regiment. There were 300 men in Bredin's battalion who held the Africa Star and 200 who had twice been wounded in battle. It was most unusual for such men to make representations to their commanding officer in this way. Bredin cannot remember it happening at any other time during the war. 'They'd seen plenty of carnage during the war, but this was one thing they would not put up with,' he says. He consulted his subordinate officers, who confirmed the seriousness of the problem, as well as a few of the German officers, now prisoners-of-war, who had commanded Cossack units. He particularly remembers one of the latter, who spoke perfect English, telling him before repatriation began, 'I don't know if you realise it, but these Cossacks will be cold meat as soon as they're off your train.'

Bredin thereupon went to see his superiors to tell them that feeling was running high and that his men were on the verge of disobeying orders. They made no particular judgment about the merits of the case. Instead they had the London Irish battalion taken off guard duty on repatriation trains and replaced by another unit. Bredin explains: 'They probably thought, "Let's try another lot of troops that are green to it." You see, with that job it took a few days for it to sink in. It wasn't easy to accept that things like that were going to happen. So I think they kept a unit on for just a few days and then rang the changes.'

The deportations continued daily until on June 7 General Keightley was able to report: 'Hand-over of Cossacks complete with exception of stragglers yet to be rounded up and sick still under medical care.'[12] By that date 35,000 Cossacks had been delivered, 20,000 of them from Domanov's units in the Drau Valley and the rest from other parts of Austria. A hasty counting of heads and comparison with various lists made it clear that 4,000 had absconded from their camps during the ten days of evacuation. The Soviet authorities were quick to spot this and complain. The British felt obliged to accept the complaint as justified and to launch the most vigorous action to round up the fugitives. Any reluctance, they thought, would be interpreted by the Soviets as an expression of sympathy for men who had betrayed their country and supported Hitler. At that time of all times the British generals needed good relations with their Soviet colleagues. They were not prepared to provoke them in any way whatsoever.

The British army therefore mounted a search operation along the length of the valley for about sixteen miles. They even permitted the attachment of a few Red Army officers to assist the search parties, and it is a measure of their concern to show that no stone was being left unturned that they were prepared to tolerate such men, who were unpopular with the troops and regarded as no better than spies in the camp. In some ways the terrain was ideal for the fugitives. A few miles either north or south of the river and they were in thickly wooded, mountainous country where a man could easily lie undetected. The days were hot, the nights warm. Life in those hills could seem almost an inviting prospect.

But the Cossacks had little spirit left with which to make the best of their predicament. There were only five roads out of the valley and these were quickly blocked by British units. There was little chance of escape into the chaos of post-surrender Central Europe. They all knew that their friends and members of their families were already in communist hands, so their morale was low, too low for them to endure a long period of survival in the open. Many of the men were encumbered by wives and small children. They would never be able to dodge the patrols, and anyway their children needed proper food.

A few were lucky. Gregori Schelest and his wife decided that they would not be able to keep their nine-month-old baby in good health without supplies from down in the valley. So, carrying the child, he went down the hill towards the bridge in the hope of crossing it and finding food in Peggetz Camp. As he approached the bridge he saw that it was guarded by British soldiers. An armoured car was standing across one end, blocking it. Schelest did not know what to do. His friends in the hills had told him, 'Don't go. They'll catch you and send you back to Russia.' He had heard that at long last the British were trying to sort out the 'new émigrés', the people who had just come from the Soviet Union, from the 'old émigrés' who were not liable to repatriation under the Yalta Agreement. But this was no help to him. Until 1943 he had lived near Krasnodar in the Kuban. He was undoubtedly a Soviet citizen.

He decided to risk it and walked on across the bridge:

The baby was in a very bad state, dirty and all in rags. The soldier in charge saw us and he was very upset. Instead of arresting us or blocking our way, he had one of the cars moved so that we could get past. Then he scribbled something on a piece of paper and gave it to me. I don't know what it was, but it saved our lives. I was able to get into the camp and get something to eat, and so long as I had that bit of paper no one interfered with us.

The soldier had given Schelest a certificate which showed, falsely, that he had not lived in the Soviet Union after 1939 and was therefore not liable to repatriation. It enabled him to move his family into the 'safe area' of Peggetz. When he did this he faced one final problem. The old émigrés in the 'safe area' asked him where he came from, and when they heard that it was from the Soviet Union they were suspicious of him. They asked him, 'How did you escape? Why were you not sent back? Why are you here?' They thought he might be a Soviet agent. But soon he was joined by other new émigrés who had also been given false certificates. He was then accepted as genuine.

It was clear to the Cossacks then that some of the British were sympathetic to them and were trying to help them. 'I owe that British soldier my life. I only wish I could meet him again and thank him,' says Schelest. He and his family were eventually able to move to the United States and now live on a small farm in New Jersey. His little boy grew up there and served in the American army in Vietnam. He is proud to think that he has worked hard, paid his taxes and generally fulfilled his duties as a citizen. He sees this as some repayment for the stroke of good fortune that came his way in 1945.

The rest of the Cossacks did their best to survive in the open but, physically exhausted and broken in spirit, they fell quite easily into the hands of the search parties. Kenneth Tyson accompanied one such party and has described what happened. They climbed several thousand feet up the Spitzkoffel mountain near Lienz and came upon a party of fifty, mostly old men and women, with a few younger women and children. Tyson was amazed at the variety of equipment they had with them:

Trunks, suitcases, bundles of bedding and crude camp equipment—to this day I wonder how they carried such weights, and where they got the strength to lift and to climb no mean mountain. And it was chiefly the women who did so! I don't know how they did it, these

old men and women, carrying quite enormous cases on their backs,
old-fashioned black leather trunks. I helped one old woman coming
down, and in a way I regretted having offered to do so because I
didn't think I was going to get down myself. It was the sheer weight
of this thing. But she'd been carrying *two*, and not downhill, but up
a very steep climb. I suppose they were driven by sheer desperation.

These older Cossacks showed no resistance once they were
surrounded by the British patrol. They just turned round and
walked down the mountain. Tyson detected no hostility on either
side, just a tired acceptance of the roles of prisoner and captor.
The only harsh note was struck by the presence of a Red Army
officer who was with the group and supposed to act as interpreter.
Dressed in British uniform and assigned from Brigade Headquarters, he had been allowed into British-held territory only in
order to show the Soviet authorities what strenuous efforts were
being made to round up the escaped Cossacks and to fulfil the
agreement. He had little to do, merely translating into Russian
the orders issued by George Wood, the British officer in charge of
the patrol. The Cossacks were like sheep and obeyed these orders
at once. But the soldiers objected to the Soviet officer, whose
presence made their job seem all the more distasteful. On the
way down a few Cossacks slipped away and no attempt was
made to recapture them. 'In our hearts we wished them luck,'
says Tyson.

It was the younger men, especially those unencumbered by
wives or children, who had the best chance of remaining at large.
They climbed higher up the mountain and moved along the snow
line during the day in groups of ten or twelve. When they stopped
they posted sentries, who gave the alarm as soon as a patrol drew
near, whereupon the group would scatter into the woods. At
night, when the temperature dropped, they moved down and
camped on the lower slopes, or occupied summer-holiday huts.
Geoffrey Pickard, who also took part in several patrols, remembers
scanning the hills with binoculars early every morning, looking
for plumes of smoke. 'Ah, there's a group of Cossacks having
their breakfast,' they would say when they saw one. They would
then try to mark the spot on the map and would send patrols up
the mountain on either side in the hope of surrounding it.

The Austrians were even more anxious to get rid of the

Cossacks, whose horses were now scattered about the valley by the thousand trampling gardens and consuming pasture. As their provisions ran out they had to steal in order to live. 'Throughout the summer months one often saw camp-fire smoke rising from the depths of the woods and strange figures going about the countryside,' recalls Tyson. To begin with, the Austrians were ready to help them. Gertraud Einetter, an Austrian lady who lives near Oberdrauburg, remembers Cossacks knocking at her door and asking for food. But there were British soldiers searching for them. So, she says, 'We gave the Cossacks signs to run away and hide in the hay huts, where they sometimes spent the night with a few old potatoes to eat and some hot tea without sugar to drink, for we could not give them much, as we had nothing for ourselves.'

But the Austrians soon realised that the situation was likely to get worse. So long as it was summer the Cossacks could survive, but in a few months they would need shelter as well as food. The snows would come and force them down the hills into the inhabited areas. There were fears that these thousands of strange people would become bandits, terrorising the countryside. The British began to receive information on the Cossacks' whereabouts and assistance in capturing them.

For instance, on June 4 an Austrian civilian reported that there were a hundred Cossacks at a certain point in the hills, and Lieutenant C. J. Heather was sent out with eight men to capture them. The Cossacks spotted the patrol as it approached. They ran away down a gully into some dense undergrowth. Then Heather took swift and violent action: 'We fired some shots into the undergrowth and shouted "Kommen sie hier" '. This failed to bring any response, perhaps because few of the Cossacks knew even this amount of German. Heather then gave the harsh order to spray the whole area with bullets. This was done and the desired result achieved, because the fugitives then emerged with hands raised. They were taken down the valley and put into a prison cage to await transport eastwards.

Another such patrol, consisting of two Red Army officers and four British soldiers, set off into the hills on horseback on June 8. They captured one group on the lower slopes and decided to go in search of some of the sturdier Cossacks, who were lurking higher up. Sergeant A. Kennedy, who was in command, told his group to change into some old clothes which they had found in the captured hide-out. They were now wearing Cossack clothes, riding Cossack horses and two of them spoke Russian as their native language. As such they had a good chance, they thought, of getting in amongst the main group of fugitives and making a big capture.

They found the group and were approaching when one of the Soviet officers enthusiastically but foolishly fired his revolver in the air. The Cossacks ran off, leaving just a few, mainly women and children, who were too weak to move. One soldier spotted a Cossack in the distance, aimed his rifle at him, fired and saw him drop. Kennedy reported that 'as the Cossack was not seen to rise again it was assumed that he had been killed.' He and his men were not prepared to pursue the Cossacks into the woods because they had information that some were armed and would resist. So they collected the ones who had stayed behind and marched them down the mountain.

These accounts make it clear that British soldiers, while privately sympathetic to the Cossacks and ready to help them in surreptitious ways, were assiduous in searching them out and even using firearms against them as soon as they were observed by representatives of the Soviet Union. Again one detects the feeling then pervading western political and military thinking that Soviet requests must be fulfilled, even those requests which seemed unreasonable and cruel. During June, therefore, 1,356 fugitives were captured. The War Diaries explain that 'many of these surrendered voluntarily, preferring captivity to the rigours of the hills', but others were taken by force of arms and a greater number, estimated at more than 2,000, remained at large, evading the patrols and surviving in the open, hoping for some miracle that would save them from the tender mercies of Stalin's policemen.

On June 16, a convoy of three British and sixteen German trucks, commanded by Captain Duncan McMillan, took 934 of these recaptured Cossacks into Soviet territory. Strict precautions were taken to prevent any escapes. There were soldiers armed with sten guns in each truck and scout cars at the end of the convoy with machine-guns mounted. But no one tried to run away. Their will was broken and they were resigned to their fate. They reached the border at Judenburg that evening and McMillan was asked by Soviet officers to take the prisoners on to Graz, deep inside the Soviet zone, where large numbers of forcibly repatriated Cossacks were already being held.

They drove through the night and reached Graz about dawn. McMillan remembers being guided to a small railway station where there was a barbed wire enclosure. He saw the Cossacks being unloaded from his trucks. First they were searched. All personal valuables, especially money and watches, were taken from them, even the packets of food they had been given for the journey. Then they were marched away. No British soldier saw them again and, as McMillan says, 'it didn't take much imagination to know what was going to happen to those people.' Many British soldiers who were there have testified that they heard the rattle of machine-guns nearby just a few moments after the prisoners were removed. No soldier actually *saw* any prisoner being shot, so one cannot say conclusively that it happened, but as one of the drivers, James Davidson, says, 'We thought that machine-gunning must be the finish of them. We thought they were just taken back there and slaughtered. That was our general view.'

Exhausted by a whole night of travelling and subdued by the terrible thought that they might well have just handed a thousand people over to execution, the British soldiers faced another problem when the Red Army men made a determined attempt to confiscate the German trucks and arrest the German drivers. In the Soviet view these men and vehicles were part of the Cossack division and therefore Soviet property. 'We had quite an argument. They put a Russian soldier on each truck and I put one of my boys on each truck,' McMillan recalls. Everyone was armed and a violent incident seemed likely to erupt, when the Soviet side suddenly gave up their claim and invited the British to breakfast.

The meal was a jolly occasion, with much talk of Allied unity and many toasts drunk in neat vodka, even though it was not yet eight o'clock in the morning. For the British it was not so bad because it was the end of their long day and they would have to rest before setting out on the road home. For the Russians, of course, it was the beginning of the day, and the British were amazed at their hosts' ability to down quantities of strong drink at such an hour. Afterwards they were taken to a granary where they were allowed to sleep, doubtless all the better for their alcoholic breakfast. A few had been ordered to remain sober and these mounted guard over the trucks to prevent another attempt at confiscation. They were closely watched and not allowed outside the building. That afternoon they got back into their trucks and set off for the Drau Valley, crossing into British territory just before daybreak.

This bizarre episode marked the end of forcible repatriation of Cossacks from the Drau Valley, but in other areas occupied by V Corps it continued. During the second half of June, 13,350 Soviet citizens were handed over to the Red Army at Judenburg, making a total of a little more than 50,000 during the five weeks which began on May 28.[13] About 35,000 of this total were from the Cossack units which fought on the German side. The evidence shows that almost all of these people were unwilling to return to Russia, that many could only be repatriated by the use of physical violence and that some were ready to commit suicide and others to murder their families before doing so, rather than be handed over to the Russians.

After June, the deportations ceased temporarily, but not because of any change in British policy. As the 36th Infantry Brigade War Diaries explain: 'Henceforth, although we were to run to earth many more fugitives, we treated them as surrendered personnel and did not hand them over to the Russians. The reason for this was that the Russians were satisfied with the numbers they had received and did not want any more.' British decisions in the matter were still dependent on requests received from the Red Army. The operation was completed and a message from Musson was read to everyone in the Brigade congratulating them on the speed and efficiency of their action.

A small cemetery was built near Lienz to mark the graves of the Cossacks killed during the violence of June 1, 1945. It contains twenty-seven graves, rather more than the figures quoted in the British documents. These papers show that in the Drau Valley that day five were shot trying to escape, two were smothered to death, and one shot by accident. To this must be added the five victims of the father who shot his own family and the three drowned in the river Drau. (Several people, British as well as Cossack, have confirmed the truth of both these incidents.) Other reliable witnesses have said that even more Cossacks committed suicide by hanging themselves in their huts or in the woods, but one will never know how many of these there were.

Of the officers handed over on May 29 there are five documented suicides: two who hanged themselves on lavatory chains, one who cut his throat during the overnight stop at Spittal; another who cut his throat with a razor blade by the bridge at Judenburg; and the one who threw himself off the bridge onto the rocks below. According to the British guards, an unknown number of Cossacks also killed themselves on the trains that were carrying them into Soviet territory. One will never know the exact figure.

It was the beginning of many years of suffering not only for the Cossacks, but also for several million Soviet citizens who had spent years under Nazi German control—either as prisoners-of-war or as forced-labour workers or as volunteers in the German armed forces. Most of these had not collaborated willingly with the Germans, but Russians and other Slavs were treated so badly under the Third Reich that many found themselves with a clear and terrible choice, either to compromise with their country's enemy or to die of starvation. After the war it was impossible to decide absolutely who had collaborated and who had remained loyal to the Soviet Union. There were so many middle ways.

The Soviet authorities could have no doubts about the loyalty of the Cossack men, because they were in German uniform and ready enough to admit that they had fought on the German side. The generals, especially Krasnov and Shkuro, were famous enemies of the Soviet Union and they were quickly separated from the others. Within a few hours the two 'stars' were ordered to appear before a senior officer. Nikolay Krasnov, the general's great-nephew, was worried that they might simply be shot, but it turned out that the meeting was to satisfy professional curiosity:

> A Soviet general and several elderly colonels were waiting for them in a small house where the officers lived. They had been 'on the other side of the front' during the 1918-20 war and had fought against my grandfather and Andrey Shkuro. There was a lively conversation during which they recalled various battles—the places where they had happened, the units which had taken part and the eventual outcome. The political and moral sides of the question were not referred to.[14]

The generals were treated well and with the courtesy that professional soldiers often extend to their defeated enemies. Nikolay

Krasnov was worried by what he thought was 'excessive politeness'. Most people assumed that these courtesies would cease as soon as the prisoners were in the hands of the security police, but some Soviet officers tried to reassure their prisoners even about this. 'They won't keep you in prison very long. They'll interrogate you, find out what they have to and then let you go,' said the Soviet general as he said goodbye. Nikolay Krasnov was impressed. He thinks that the general may even have seriously believed what he said, that there was a new mood of kindly tolerance in the Soviet Union.

Domanov was in the worst situation of all. For months he had taken precedence over the 'old heroes', Krasnov and Shkuro, but now his status as a Soviet citizen made him doubly hated by the Soviet guards. Many of them saw a distinction between Domanov, who had been brought up and nurtured in the Soviet Union, and the others who had always fought the Bolsheviks tooth and nail. And while they laughed merrily at Shkuro's civil-war stories of how he 'knocked the stuffing out of the Reds',[15] they were bored by Domanov, who had no such tales to tell. The Cossack generals hated Domanov even more, if that were possible, because they blamed him for helping the British with their deportation and suspected him of conniving at the deception. 'Did the English promise him some reward in exchange for his silence?' Nikolay Krasnov wonders.[16] Most Cossacks believe that they did.

On May 30, the morning after their delivery into Soviet hands, the generals were paraded in readiness for the journey to Graz. Lieutenant von Himmenhofen, one of General von Pannwitz's German aides, was executed by firing squad before they left Judenburg because he had tried to escape during the night.[17] This was done before the eyes of the senior Cossack officers as a warning of what would happen to them if they were foolish enough to make any similar attempt. They spent the night in Graz and the next day set out for Baden bei Wien, a resort near Vienna that was being used as a centre of Soviet counter-intelligence. On the way, they were given an excellent breakfast and General Krasnov said he felt like a goose being fattened up for Christmas.

In Baden bei Wien they were briefly interrogated. On one occasion they were brought together as a group to be photographed. Care was taken to see that they were properly dressed in German uniforms with all the appropriate medals and shoulder flashes. A few had lost pieces of their regalia along the way and replacements were procured from Soviet stores of captured material. Thus an authentic picture of these important men was obtained for the archives. On June 3 some of them were loaded into an aeroplane and flown to Moscow. The following day another aeroplane took the rest. They were lodged in the Lubianka prison in clean conditions and with adequate food. Everyone with experience of Stalin's 'justice' knew that this was an ominous sign. The cleaner his cell, the closer a prisoner is to the moment of execution.

But the greatest danger to the lives of the Cossacks was not trial and formal execution, but the conditions of imprisonment in Siberian corrective labour camps. The bulk of the prisoners, officers and other ranks, were held for only a few hours in a factory in Judenburg before being transported to Graz, where there was a large prison. Here they were searched, relieved of watches and other valuables and identified with the help of lists made available by the British.[18] After a week, they were ready for the long journey eastwards. On June 11, they were marched to the railway station and loaded, forty in each truck. For three days trains of prisoners left Graz and made their way into Hungary, then south into Rumania and north into the Soviet Union. By June 25, some of the trains had passed through Kiev and reached Moscow, where there was a three-day wait while the details of their destination were worked out. During these days the prisoners in the trucks heard frequent artillery salvoes and sometimes during the night they would see fireworks. The capital was celebrating victory.[19]

The trains then set out along the Siberian railway to the province of Kemerovskaya, just south of Tomsk and 2,000 miles east of Moscow. The prisoners were given dry bread and pieces of salt fish to eat, but it was high summer and the more experienced prisoners refused to eat the fish, because the water ration was not enough and thirst is a greater danger than hunger. The problem of water is what the survivors remember best about the journey:

Every day our truck got four or five buckets of water for ninety-four people. These were poured into a rusted-through metal drum and as soon as this happened the water would turn brown. I stood by the drum and measured out two German-army mugfuls for each man.

The men always drank it down at once, then stood by waiting for a share of the thick rusty dregs that remained at the bottom of the drum.[20]

Once the engine broke down and the engine stood for more than a day on the parched open steppe waiting for rescue, while the prisoners fried, their tongues swelling inside their mouths. Each truck had one window, a small opening laced with barbed wire. The stronger men would fight their way close to it, blocking the space and plunging the interior into suffocating darkness. A few were killed by the guards during the journey and many others died through disease and general weakness brought on by the terrible conditions. When anything like this happened it was the British whom the prisoners blamed as 'those responsible for our misery'. One survivor has written: 'I never once heard anyone cursing the Americans or any of the other Allies. All our fury, hatred and threats were directed against the English.'[21]

Around July 10, the trains reached the Tomsk area and the Cossacks were sent to various places nearby where prison camps were being built. The influx was such that more accommodation was required. A surviving Cossack officer, M. I. Kotsovsky, has written:

> They unloaded us from the train and took us to a camp surrounded by barbed wire. It consisted of two barrack blocks, a bath house and a cookhouse. Every twenty prisoners were assigned a tent which they had to pitch and live in. Two days later they brought us some planks to make bunks. We got no bedding, but slept fully-clothed on the bare boards. All the time insects were eating us up. The food in the camp was very bad. In the morning they gave us watery soup sprinkled with oatmeal or barley meal. Our midday meal was a so-called vegetable soup made of rotten sour cabbage, with some runny porridge. For supper we got the same as at breakfast. Sometimes they gave us a little salt fish, which often was covered in rust from the inside of the cans. We had a 400-gram daily ration of lowest-quality bread. People began to fall ill, especially the Germans. For the most part it was liver complaints and dysentry. There were fifteen to twenty people dying every day.[22]

A. K. Leniwow writes that mortality among the Cossacks was particularly high during the first year of imprisonment, when they were put to difficult, dangerous work in the coal mines of the Kuznetski Basin. In spite of the nature of the work, they were issued with no proper clothing, so that within a few weeks their clothes were in rags and many were going about barefoot. In November a little clothing arrived, but not much, and the prisoners were in no fit state to face the Siberian winter. A sort of jungle law came to prevail in camp number 7525. The older prisoners grew weaker and could not fulfil their daily tasks. The authorities then cut their rations as a punishment for under-fulfilment of the norm, which of course weakened the prisoner even more. Thieves preyed on these unfortunate people, stealing their clothes and food. Leniwow estimates that more than 7,000 Cossacks died during that first year of various wasting diseases.[23]

This was the main part of the Cossacks' suffering, that along with several million other people of various nationalities who had incurred the anger or distrust of the Soviet authorities they were forced to spend ten years in conditions of such murderous cold and hunger that all but the physically and mentally robust were killed or driven insane. How many of the prisoners managed to survive ten such years one will never know, but most authorities on the subject indicate that it cannot be more than half. So effectively did Stalin succeed in sealing off the Soviet Union that until his death almost nothing was known of these horrors, those few words of information which slipped out being quickly repudiated by the Soviet Union's many whole-hearted supporters throughout the world. Only with the publication of *The Gulag Archipelago* in 1974 was a detailed and accurate picture of the horror made available.

In the two years which followed Stalin's death on March 5, 1953 amnesties were declared which liberated most of those still serving sentences for treason or collaboration with the enemy during the Second World War. Of these there were a few who were not Soviet citizens, who had been captured by the Red Army or turned over to them by the western Allies in violation of the Yalta Agreement. In the mid-1950s these were given the chance to leave the Soviet Union and return to the place where they had lived before the war. Leniwow, who was one of these, estimates that seventy Cossack officers were able to leave in this way.[24] The other 1,400 had either died or were forced to remain.

On the fate of the senior Cossack officers there is the testimony of Nikolay Krasnov, the great-nephew of General Pyotr Niko-layevich Krasnov. He was a young officer and was granted the 'honour' of imprisonment in the Lubianka only because of his connection with the notorious Krasnov family. A year and a half passed before the leaders of this anti-Soviet movement were brought to trial. On January 17, 1947, *Pravda* announced that P. N. Krasnov, A. G. Shkuro, Sultan Klych Girey (the Caucasian leader), S. N. Krasnov, T. I. Domanov and Helmut von Pannwitz had pleaded guilty to 'forming White Guard detachments' and to 'carrying out espionage, diversionary and terrorist activity against the Soviet Union'. They had been condemned to death by hanging and the sentences had been carried out. Nikolay Krasnov was too junior an officer to be included in this select band. After lengthy interrogation, he was sent to a labour camp, then released and allowed to leave the Soviet Union in the mid-1950s. He died shortly afterwards in Argentina.

Of the six men whose execution was publicly announced only one, Domanov, was liable to repatriation under the Yalta Agreement. Von Pannwitz was a German through and through who spoke Russian only because he came from the Baltic States. The other four had not lived in the Soviet Union at any time since its creation. There was only the slenderest legal basis for their extradition by the British or for their execution by the Soviet Union. They were not accused of war crimes, but were condemned for fighting against the Soviet forces, the implication being that this was an act of treason. But of the six only one, again Domanov, was a Soviet citizen and liable to trial as a traitor.

Perhaps in the context of the millions who died during the Second World War the execution of six generals who supported Hitler in his war of aggression was hardly a surprise. Churchill was informed that the Cossacks had 'fought with ferocity, not to say savagery, for the Germans',[25] and this was accurate for, although they themselves claim that they fought not for Hitler, but to liberate their lands from Stalin, the fact remains that they were used by Hitler merely as a contribution to his scheme for world conquest. Philip Longworth has written in his book about the Cossacks:

> Their fate was inevitable and not unjust. Although only a third of
> the officers were Soviet citizens, they were most of them traitors

in the eyes of any law, and some could be classified legally as war criminals ... Men who had sworn loyalty to the Nazis and had accepted the protection of and fought for the ss ought not to have been surprised at the lack of Allied sympathy. And their friends who protested on the grounds of humanity forgot the bestial reputation these men had earned in the Civil War, and how they would have treated the Bolsheviks had the roles been reversed.[26]

But this argument ignores the injustice done to those Cossacks who were innocent of any crime, for example the women and children. It ignores the injustice done to the men who took up arms against Stalin without realising that they were assisting an equal tyrant in the shape of Hitler. These men were perhaps naive, but it can hardly be maintained, in view of the crimes of the Soviet state, the full extent of which has now been revealed by Solzhenitsyn and others, that they deserved the normal traitors' punishment.

THE POLICY UNDER ATTACK

ON 29 JUNE 1945, a terrible incident took place at Fort Dix, New Jersey, a prisoner-of-war camp which contained 154 Soviet citizens, all captured in Europe while serving with the German forces. The only such prisoners remaining in the United States, they were thought likely to resist, having refused to join previous shipments home to Russia from west coast ports. The previous week they had been told what was going to happen. They would be taken to New York and embarked on an American ship bound for Germany. They would then be handed over to Soviet authorities. The prisoners declared that under no circumstances would they go. So when the American guards came to get them at nine o'clock that morning, they were ready to resist to the death.

Their first act of defiance was to barricade themselves inside their barrack block and refuse to emerge. The camp commandant, Colonel G. M. Treisch, made several appeals, inviting them to send out their three highest-ranking officers to discuss the situation. When this offer was refused, he had his men issued with gas masks and tear-gas grenades, and these were fired into the building to force the Russians out into the open. The result was that the rear door of the block swung open and a large number of prisoners rushed out, armed with knives from mess kits and wielding clubs improvised from furniture.[1]

Two American officers were slightly injured, one cut on the hand, the other struck on the head. The mob then ran towards a group of guards who were armed with carbines and sub-machine guns. The guards opened fire, wounding seven Russians. Eventually, the guards managed to bring their charges under control, but it was only after the prisoners had been locked up and an inspection made of the barracks that the most grizzly discovery of all came to light. They found belts and ropes hanging from the rafters of the barrack room, and from three of these dangled the bodies of men who had hanged themselves.

The three suicides and one severely injured man were left at Fort Dix, but the rest were forced into buses and ambulances and taken that same evening to Camp Shanks in New York State. Each prisoner was guarded individually by a military policeman and there were extra guards in each vehicle. The 150 prisoners were escorted by a total of 200 armed men. The next morning they were taken from Camp Shanks to Pier 51 on New York's North River and, the guard now augmented by eighty military police armed with sub-machine guns, marched to the ship 'Monticello', a former luxury cruise liner of the Italian merchant marine.

Accounts differ as to whether the Russians actually boarded the 'Monticello'. According to some reports, they began to fight furiously as soon as they were on board and, in spite of their guards, to inflict damage on the ship's engines. In any event, a sudden order arrived cancelling the repatriation and at 3.30 that afternoon (June 30) they were loaded into their vehicles and taken back to Fort Dix.[2]

In spite of this sudden reprieve, the Russians seemed to know that the plan to repatriate them had not been abandoned, but merely postponed. Henry Stimson, Secretary of War, wrote in a letter of explanation to the State Department that 'these prisoners were opposed to their repatriation to Russia because of their individual fears that it would mean death for themselves and suffering for relatives and friends.' Indeed, Stimson was understating the case, because many of these prisoners had come to the conclusion that delivery into the hands of the Soviet authorities was a fate *worse* than death. The reason why they had rioted, they said, was not that they wanted to harm their captors, but that 'they wanted the Americans to shoot them all.'[3]

For the next few weeks amazing precautions were taken at Fort Dix to discourage the prisoners from further suicide attempts. They were housed in six 25-man barrack rooms under constant guard, twenty-four hours a day. Brigadier General Madison Pearson wrote a report on the arrangements:

The prisoners have sufficient clothing to protect them from the elements, but are not allowed to have any article which could readily be used as a noose without attracting attention, such as shoe laces, belts, suspenders or other simi!ar items. Each has a mattress, mattress cover and blanket. There are no beds in the buildings, as parts of the beds could be used as weapons or implements of self destruction.

The Russians ate off paper plates and drank out of paper cups. The only eating utensils they were allowed were spoons, and these were collected and counted after each meal. They were allowed to visit the latrines only one at a time. Shaving also was organised on an individual basis. One prisoner would be given a safety razor. Then, when he had finished shaving, the razor was returned to the guard and inspected before being issued to the next prisoner. For one hour a day they were allowed to take exercise in the yard. They were then issued with tobacco and cigarette papers, but not with matches. A guard would light the cigarettes of two or three prisoners and leave the rest to obtain lights from these.

On July 19, a party of four Soviet officers came to Fort Dix to interview the prisoners and investigate the riot. The Americans were happy to allow this. They wanted to show that it was not they who had provoked the riot by ill-treatment. And there was the faint hope too that some of the prisoners might by persuaded to give up their resistance and go home voluntarily. Colonel Malkov, the senior Soviet officer, told the Americans 'that he would explain to them [the prisoners] that they would not be persecuted on their return to Russia.'

The Soviet officers interviewed the prisoners one by one in the company of four Americans. Like other repatriation officers, they were conciliatory and did not threaten the prisoners. But this kind approach made little impression. The prisoners were sceptical, implying that the kindness would cease as soon as they were safely back in the Soviet Union and away from American eyes. Several of the prisoners refused to answer any questions at all, even to give their names. Colonel Horatio Rogers reported after the interviews:

> Those who did talk said that they did not wish to return to Russia because they knew they would be shot. They did not believe any statement to the contrary, as the order issued earlier in the war that a prisoner-of-war was a traitor had never been revoked to their knowledge. In some instances their families have been killed or

deported and they would rather commit suicide than return. They further stated that they had no complaints to make against the American authorities, that the riot was organised for the sole purpose of inciting the American guards to shoot them.

The prisoners were pathetic, desperate men with terrible stories to tell. One said that his parents had both been shot by the Soviet authorities in 1941, another that Russian women had been executed for such minor collaboration as taking in washing from German soldiers. If that was indeed the situation, what hope could there be for these 150 men who had actually carried arms against Soviet power? Malkov tried to reassure them. He told one prisoner, quite falsely, that the law had been changed and that the two million Russians from Germany were returning freely to their homes. He added, 'I want to instil into all of you that no harm will come to you.' The prisoners who heard such promises showed little inclination to believe them. In spite of all the persuasion, by the Americans as well as by the Russians, and in spite of the obvious implication that they would have to go anyway, and that those who went voluntarily would in the end be better treated than those who had been dragged by force, Malkov and his men were unable to persuade any of their fellow-countrymen to relent.

Meanwhile, the incident had led to an investigation of American policy at the highest level. But there was nothing to be done, unless the United States was going to abrogate the agreement signed by its representatives at Yalta, and this it was not yet ready to do. The most it would do in defiance of Soviet wishes was to refuse to return by force the Balts and the western Ukrainians, the people who had not been Soviet citizens before the Red Army's seizure of those areas in 1939 and 1940. Otherwise, as Secretary of State Byrnes confirmed in a letter dated August 9, 'under commitments made at the Crimea Conference, the United States Government undertakes to return to the Soviet Union all Soviet citizens.'[4]

The Russians at Fort Dix were most carefully investigated yet again and seven were judged to be Balts or Poles. The remaining 146 were eventually put on board a ship at New York on August 31, together with a guard of two officers and fifty others, and handed over to Soviet representatives in Europe. No details of this last successful repatriation are given in available documents, except that it took place 'without incident'. One source claims that a barbiturate drug was put into the prisoners' coffee and that they were carried on board in a state of coma.[5] The strange fact that the operation passed off without difficulty, whereas previous attempts had led to extreme violence, lends some weight to this serious allegation, but no way has been found to confirm or disprove it.

This was the last batch of Soviet citizens repatriated from the United States. In Germany and other American-occupied areas a little more than two million had been handed over by the end of August. In the words of an American report,[6] 'the principle of forcible repatriation did not come into issue' during this mass movement. Rough and ready methods had been used to persuade the unwilling to go quietly, but amid the chaos of those early days of peace they made small impression on the press or public opinion. The movements of the Russians were mixed up with normal military mopping-up operations: corralling German prisoners, crushing those small groups that had refused to surrender, sorting out the ss men from the ordinary soldiers. After this was over and some semblance of order restored, no more than 20,000 acknowledged Soviet citizens remained in the American areas. Large numbers of others, no one knows how many, managed to escape the net and pass themselves off as non-Soviet.

The problem was that these were the hard core of the resistance to returning home. Most of them had carried arms against the Red Army and knew they could expect no mercy from Stalin. But the international agreement was quite clear. They had to go back. Many British and American commanders sympathised with these men. After weeks of frustrating contact with their opposite numbers from the Red Army they were beginning to understand why so many people should have hated the Soviet government so much that they were ready to join with Germany. These commanders indeed helped many Russians to escape. But whatever their personal feelings, their orders were clear. They were obliged to give Soviet officers access to displaced person and prisoner-of-war camps in their areas, to help them identify Soviet citizens and then to repatriate them, by force if necessary.

One of the first operations took place at a camp near Kempten, a small town seventy miles south-west of Munich, which housed about a thousand Russian and Cossack prisoners who had fought on the German side, a few of them with Vlasov's Russian Liberation Army but most of them with von Pannwitz's Cossack Cavalry Corps. Some of them, for instance the veteran of the Civil War General Vyacheslav Naumenko, were old émigrés and not Soviet citizens. The Americans had no intention of repatriating these. But several hundred had come from Russia only a year or two earlier. According to the Yalta Agreement they would have to go.

The prisoners did their best to conceal their origins and show solidarity. Old as well as new émigrés refused to cooperate with the mixed Soviet-American commission which endeavoured during the first two months of peace to sort the 'condemned men' from the rest. But eventually a more or less accurate list was compiled. Soviet officers had been able to recruit agents among the prisoners. The joint commission had obtained the cooperation of their senior officer General Danilov. They were able to obtain details about who had been born where and when. Other details were extracted from the UNRRA relief organisation, with whom the prisoners had been forced to cooperate in order to obtain clothes and rations.

On June 22 the new émigrés were ordered to parade in readiness for transfer to a camp nearer Munich. The idea of separation from the others terrified them out of their wits. It would only be a matter of days, they thought, before they were handed over to the Red Army. They explained their fears to the American authorities, making it clear that they would never go back to Russia, that they would rather the Americans shot them dead on the spot. Their pleas were heard and the decision taken on the local level to cancel the movement to Munich. Their relief knew no bounds.

The American commandant Major Legrand did not yet know of the Yalta Agreement, but as soon as this was explained arrangements were put in hand for another transport towards the Soviet zone, this time in the full knowledge that there was likely to be violent resistance. But there was one serious problem which faced the American authorities. Many of the guards had come to know the Russians and Cossacks. They liked them and felt sympathy towards them.

On August 11 the prisoners were told what was to happen.

Some were resigned to their fate. They proceeded to act like condemned men before the day of execution. They took Holy Communion and made their wills. Others, about half of the 410 on the 'condemned list', escaped from the camp that night and took refuge either in the woods nearby or with German families. But others were determined to resist. Around 7 o'clock on the morning of August 12 several hundred of them, together with some old émigrés who were pledged to assist, went to the camp church and began to sing the Orthodox Liturgy.

As the morning progressed religious fervour grew among the prisoners. They finished the Liturgy and stood in line to receive the Sacraments, many in the belief that it would be for the last time. Then the interpreter came into the church and asked Vladimir Vostokov, one of the priests conducting the service, how much longer it was going to last. He told the interpreter that it would end in about ten minutes. Shortly afterwards the senior Russian officer General Danilov entered the church with an American officer. Silence fell and he began to read out the names of the 410 'condemned men' who would have to go back. He invited them to come out of the church and to climb into the trucks which waited outside, advising them not to make any fuss or do anything which would induce the American guards to resort to violence.

Vasili Boshchanovsky, another of the priests, describes what happened then: 'Hardly had he finished the last name when the whole church burst into indescribable sobbing and weeping. Everyone was crying, old and young, men and women, and especially the children as they gazed up at their defenceless and inconsolable parents.'[7] The American officer immediately withdrew, ordering the guards to remain outside the church and await further instructions, and went to Major Legrand's office to report. After telephoning and receiving instructions, Legrand ordered the guards to dismiss. This they did, according to Cossack witnesses, with great delight, for they had spent three months with their charges and did not want to use violence against them.

For a short period the church remained unguarded and anyone who wished could probably have escaped. But nobody did, either because they were afraid of leaving the community, the only one they knew, or because they thought that now the guards had withdrawn the danger had passed.

Nikolay Nazarenko, today a leading anti-communist activist and Naumenko's son-in-law, was present at the scene. According to him, as soon as the guards withdrew, Soviet repatriation officers and Soviet agents inside the UNRRA organisation protested violently to Allied Headquarters and extracted from them the order to resume the operation by different means. All sources agree that within half an hour of the guards' withdrawal a dozen trucks arrived at the church containing between a platoon's and a company's strength of Military Police.

This new force was of course trained to deal with rowdy scenes. Its men had no knowledge of the prisoners or their problems and saw no reason why they should refuse to obey American orders. Their commanding officer entered the church, spoke to Danilov and ordered the 410 on the list to leave. The result was the same as before: cries and screams of distress. The Russians and Cossacks shrank away from the American officer and bunched into the far corner of the church. The young men moved to the front of the crowd and tried to form a cordon to protect the women and children.

The American officer thereupon called his men into the church and ordered them to drag the prisoners out. Boshchanovsky writes: 'The soldiers dragged us by our arms and legs, pulled us by the hair and beards. Fists and rifle butts were freely used. Shots were fired. Those who fell to the ground were beaten and kicked. The church was filled with wailing and cries of despair.'[8] The altar was overthrown, icons torn off the walls and the floor littered with pieces of torn clothing, shoes, combs, buttons and other debris. In émigré literature it is these acts of sacrilege which are described most bitterly, which seem to have caused more outrage even than the physical violence.

Once outside, the prisoners were divided into two groups by the MPs with the help of the Soviet repatriation officers and agents. They were checked against their documents, identified and dispatched, some to safety on the first floor of a nearby school, others towards the trucks. Nazarenko writes that some of the latter ran and managed to reach a wall which divided their camp from another camp which housed displaced persons from the Baltic countries who were safe from repatriation. The Balts climbed onto the wall and held out their hands to pull the Russians and Cossacks into their camp. The MPs rushed in to stop this wielding their rifle butts and, according to Nazarenko, wounding twelve people, two seriously.

So many of the original 410 had run away the previous night or escaped during the actual operation that only about ninety of them were actually loaded and transferred to Kempten railway station. There they joined a further ninety Soviet citizens who had been grabbed from other camps nearby. All 180 were loaded into a goods train where they were to spend the night. A guard was mounted, but it consisted of men from the camp. Nazarenko writes that these men 'from the very beginning closed their eyes to those Cossacks who, after nightfall, began to creep away one by one.' The train moved off the next morning with only about fifty prisoners on board, some of whom also managed to escape 'thanks to the mercy of the American guards'.

Those actually repatriated were therefore only a token number out of the original 410, a sop to the Soviet officers who were demanding rigorous implementation of the Agreement. 'Kempten was only a small episode compared to Lienz, which was a great tragedy,' says Naumenko. Nevertheless, many of the prisoners were severely beaten up and those few who were returned faced the possibility of execution and the certainty of ten years in a labour camp.

This incident convinced senior American officers in Europe that it would be dangerous to continue the policy. Large numbers of American soldiers had disobeyed orders and allowed Russians to escape. To punish them was difficult, for their defence at a court martial would inevitably be to attack the Agreement as inhumane. There would be publicity and public opinion would be outraged. The result would be to strain even further the alliance with the Soviet Union. On August 25 the United States Seventh Army requested further instructions from Headquarters about forcible repatriation. The matter was thought important enough to be referred to Washington and in the meantime soldiers in the field were ordered to stop sending people back.[9]

The controversy was equally acute in Britain. News of the terrible events at Lienz had been kept out of the newspapers but had reached the ears of senior officers in Germany and Austria, and in Whitehall. At the end of June there were still several thousand Russians in British-occupied territory. What was to be done with them? Legally the answer was plain. Under the Yalta Agreement they had to be sent back. But after the events in Austria this prospect was viewed with trepidation by the men whose duty it would be to do the work. Europe had now been at peace for nearly two months. The men were becoming less hardened to violence. Many units had been on the verge of disobedience during the repatriation of the Cossacks. There was a real risk that they would refuse to carry out a similar operation.

Cyril Gepp, Director of Prisoners-of-War, received a letter from a senior officer at Allied Forces Headquarters telling him that 'this was a very serious problem and that the British soldier would not be used to push into trains 2,000 men who did not want to go back to their country and who might be "done in" when they got there.'[10] It was decided to discuss the matter with the Foreign Office. On July 6, Colonel V. M. Hammer, an officer from Gepp's department, told John Galsworthy of the Foreign Office that he thought British soldiers might refuse to do such jobs. It was then that the Foreign Office came up with a possible solution—to invite the Red Army to send its own people to use whatever force was necessary. The Foreign Office felt that this was the best way out of the problem. The Yalta Agreement could thus be preserved without asking British soldiers to commit acts which were distasteful to them and risking a possible mutiny. They would arrange matters so that Soviet soldiers, not British, did the job, and any violence used would be none of Britain's business.

Hammer saw practical difficulties in this plan. The Red Army had no trained guards stationed near the relevant camps. Galsworthy replied that 'in that case they would have to provide a scratch team from their orderlies and drivers.' He felt that 'the more difficult it was made for them, the more hope there was that they would not be able to take possession of these miserable folk.' Hammer then said that he thought that Allied Forces Headquarters would dislike 'on principle' the use of Soviet guards on their territory. Galsworthy's reply to this was 'that they would have to balance this principle against the British soldier's conscience.'[11]

On July 28, Christopher Warner wrote to Hammer setting out the Foreign Office's views in greater detail. Their legal advisor had made it clear, he said, that British troops must 'exercise the necessary measures of constraint as part of the process of repatriation'. Although force had been used occasionally to load Soviet citizens onto ships in Britain, he added, this had usually been unnecessary because 'the toughness of their [the British soldiers'] appearance has been enough to make most of the recalcitrants go quietly.'[12] He agreed that every effort must be made to avoid the use of force in Germany and repeated his suggestion that the Red Army should be invited to provide an armed guard to convey the prisoners out of British territory.

Meanwhile the 'miserable folk' had found a staunch protector in Field-Marshal Alexander, the Supreme Commander of the Mediterranean theatre. In June, he sent a telegram to the War Office about fifty-five Soviet citizens, including twenty-seven women and children, who were refusing to return home from Italy. The Soviet Mission in Italy had specifically requested their transfer, he wrote: 'This would require use of force including handcuffs and travel under escort in locked box cars. We believe that the handing over of these individuals would almost certainly involve their death. There are likely to be many more such cases.' He asked the War Office to give him further instructions.

Alexander had spent the year 1919, as a young officer, organising forces to resist the Bolsheviks in Poland and the Baltic States. It may well be that his sympathy for people who feared the revenge of the Soviet government stemmed from this period in his life. Anyway, he was taking a firm stand in writing such a note because he already had his orders—that all Soviet citizens should be repatriated—and it was under these orders and under his command that the Drau Valley and other operations had happened. The War Office was sympathetic to his protests, but it was not they who had negotiated the Yalta Agreement. The best they could do was to refer the matter to the Foreign Office for a ruling on its legal interpretation, suggesting that force should no longer be used against Russians who would under normal circumstances qualify as political refugees. If this was accepted, there would be a return to Britain's traditional policy of political asylum.

The Foreign Office prepared a case for submission to the new Secretary of State, Ernest Bevin, which emphasised the legal situation and took little account of changed circumstances. This memorandum pointed out that any proposal to vary the Agreement 'might well be regarded by the Soviet Government as a breach of our pledged word and might possibly be taken by them to indicate a general change of policy.' The diplomats felt that Britain's tradition of granting political asylum applied to people who reached the United Kingdom or British territories, but not to people who fell into British hands through military operations. The document concluded that 'it is rather misleading to describe them as political refugees' since they had not fled from the Soviet Union but had been moved westwards, either willingly or unwillingly, by the Germans. It was because of 'their association with the Germans' that they were unwilling to return.

By such moral hair-splitting it was shown that Britain's traditional policy remained intact. But of course everyone agreed that morality was not the important issue. What counted was the Agreement. Humanitarian considerations merely clouded the issue. 'I am afraid there is no doubt that this is the correct legal interpretation,' wrote Alexander Cadogan. He hoped, though, that Britain would use a 'a minimum of force' in carrying out her obligations. Ernest Bevin agreed. On August 14 he scribbled on the document one short sentence—'Let them go.'[13] It was a delphic judgment, but everyone seemed to know that it was to the Soviet Union that they would go, not to freedom.

Christopher Warner wrote to Major-General A. V. Anderson, his War Office opposite number, to tell him of this decision: 'In view of this Ministerial ruling we presume . . . that you will now be able to proceed with the transfer of these people.' He advised Anderson that Britain was not obliged to find large numbers of troops to escort reluctant Russians by force and that British soldiers should 'use the very minimum of force'. In a very grave situation, he suggested, British commanders 'should invite the local Soviet authorities to make the necessary arrangements for their removal under guard.'

Thus a conflict arose between the Foreign Office, which was frightened of the deterioration in British-Soviet relations that would follow any unilateral breach of the Agreement, and the War Office, which did not relish the distasteful task of using force against unarmed prisoners, including women and children.

Even after Bevin's decision Alexander continued his attempts to have the policy changed. On August 18, four days after the decision and the day after the dispatch of Warner's letter, Alexander met Major-General Y. D. Basilov, who had been sent on a special mission from Moscow to discuss repatriation. He told

Basilov that his instructions on the use of force were unclear: 'The present situation was that of the Russian citizens in the theatre some wished to return and some did not. He was not however at present empowered to make people return to Russia against their will.'[14]

Basilov protested, pointing out that Article One of the Yalta Agreement had always been interpreted to mean repatriation irrespective of the wishes of the individuals concerned. To this Alexander made a cautious and devious reply: if ordered to do so, he would use force to effect repatriation. At present however he had not received orders to this effect. Basilov asked him to send a telegram to his superiors requesting further instructions, which Alexander agreed to do.

Alexander described the meeting in an interesting letter to Alan Brooke, then Chief of the Imperial General Staff, who was in constant touch with the Prime Minister:

> It was very correct and formal, but not in the least matey. I had to be very firm as some of their demands were in my view outrageous. For example, they wanted to visit all my prison camps to find their nationals, as if we were not able to do this efficiently. Of course I flatly refused this, as in any case our interpretation of Soviet citizens differs from theirs. Their request to visit Polish units is just damned cheek and I told them so in different words. Their request to visit Crete is just another excuse to do a bit of spying and slip in some Soviet propaganda. I propose, if you agree, to be absolutely firm in dealing with these people and give them nothing to which they are not strictly entitled.[15]

He concluded his letter with an astonishing admission: 'So far I have refused to use force to repatriate Soviet citizens, although I suppose I am not strictly entitled to adopt this attitude.' His correspondence with Brooke was an intimate one, and he felt able to confess that he was, if not disobeying, at least bending his orders. Instructions for the use of force had already been given, and he was deliberately misleading Basilov in pretending that the situation was otherwise. He was indeed planning to write on the matter, though in different terms from those indicated to Basilov. He was planning a strong protest against the whole principle of forcible repatriation.

He wrote to the War Office on August 23:

A large proportion of these Russians have been repatriated, but there remain a certain number who, because they fear the fate that awaits them on arrival in Russia, refuse to be repatriated. To compel them to accept repatriation would certainly either involve the use of force or driving them into railway coaches at the point of the bayonet and thereafter locking them in, possibly also handcuffing a number of them.

Such treatment, coupled with the knowledge that these individuals are being sent to an almost certain death, is quite out of keeping with the principles of democracy and justice as we know them. Furthermore it is most unlikely that the British soldier, knowing the fate to which these people are being committed, will be a willing participant in the measures required to compel their departure . . . In view of the circumstances I recommend that efforts be made to obtain some modification of the Agreement which would allow these people to be treated as stateless persons for the time being. The matter is urgent.[16]

A special correspondent of the *Manchester Guardian* wrote an article about the same problem a few days later, and in the same issue a leading article made one of the first veiled references to the still secret Yalta Agreement, expressing concern: 'Here surely is a case where the Labour Government would be justified in asking for some revision. Unless these wretches are accused of some definite crime against the Soviet they should be given the same free choice as the other displaced persons.'[17] These reports were carefully noted by the Foreign Office, which was alarmed to note that the matter was beginning to creep into the press and even more alarmed that the War Office was challenging a decision taken by the Foreign Secretary himself. In the Foreign Office's view the War Office had no right to interfere in a matter which was essentially diplomatic and political.

The American press was beginning to discuss the matter more frankly. On 9 September, the *New York Herald Tribune* quoted senior Allied officers to the effect that Britain and the United States would soon be pressing for abrogation of the Agreement. The article claimed that British soldiers might mutiny if they were asked to use force against Russian prisoners, that 'American blood may be shed in skirmishes with unwilling repatriates' and that 'one British officer had already been court-martialled for refusing to obey an order to aid the Russian agents.' The *Christian Science Monitor* was also concerned at the thought of Red Army officers prowling about the British and American areas: 'Fifty special agents have been sent into the American zone to round up hesitant Russians and there is plenty of apprehension over the kind of men and tactics that may be employed.' Up to now, it went on, any idea of differences or quarrels between the Soviet Union and her allies had been mere Nazi invention, but in this matter 'fundamental concepts of life and society were involved.'[18]

But while the British and American officers in Europe were concerned about the ethics of the matter, the State Department and the Foreign Office had a different preoccupation—the need to maintain good relations with the Soviet Union and respect for international agreements. The Foreign Office was particularly embarrassed because on 26 August, in reply to a complaint, they assured the Soviet Embassy that instructions for the removal of Soviet prisoners were about to be sent to Italy. This they did on the basis of Ernest Bevin's August 14 decision, only to be told that Alexander had informed Basilov yet again that 'he was not allowed to use force to effect repatriation.'[19] The Foreign Office was now under attack from Soviet diplomats not only for violation of the Agreement, but also for giving confusing and contradictory information. On September 2, the British Embassy in Moscow wired London along the same lines: 'Soviet Government would inevitably take strongest exception to any attempt to discriminate between Soviet citizens who wish to go home and those who do not, and distasteful though it is I can see no reason for making any exception in Italy to policy already approved.'[20]

Sure enough, on September 2 the Soviet Ambassador, M. Gousev, handed Cadogan a note protesting that 'fascist organisations' were carrying out 'agitation among Soviet citizens for their non-return to the homeland'. He demanded an immediate end to such 'flagrant violations of the Yalta Agreement'.[21] Cadogan protested about the tone of the note, but could hardly complain about the content. It was true that the British *were* in breach of the Agreement. Alexander had admitted as much in letters to London. He had refused to use force against Soviet prisoners and had refused to allow Red Army officers to visit his camps. It was all quite illegal, as Christopher Warner pointed out in a pained letter to the War Office. There was now another reason why he and his colleagues wanted the matter sorted out. At the end of September there was to be a conference at Lancaster House in London of the three main Allied foreign ministers—Bevin, Molotov and James Byrnes. The Soviet Union announced that at this conference it intended to raise the repatriation issue. The Foreign Office would be exposed as having broken an international agreement.

The London conference was not a success. Charles Bohlen, a State Department official, who later became American Ambassador in Moscow, wrote that 'it was our first experience with the extraordinary ability of Molotov to frustrate and delay.'[22] During the discussions on the repatriation issue on September 24 and 25, Bevin reminded Molotov of the 'traditional British reluctance to compel persons to return to their countries'. During the last years of Tsarist Russia, he said, Britain had given sanctuary to many prominent Bolsheviks, including Lenin.[23] It was an argument which Molotov found unconvincing, and in a sense it was irrelevant because the Agreement was so clear. Molotov 'pressed very hard for the repatriation of all Vlasov's men', to which the American Secretary of State said that 'if there were any in American hands there would be no sympathy for them.'

The problem was that Bevin could not order Alexander to fit in with Soviet wishes. The Mediterranean theatre was still under joint British-American command, and any orders to Alexander had to come from the Joint Chiefs of Staff, who were American as well as British. The British government was therefore in the strange position of needing American approval before it could issue an order to one of its own generals. Therefore on the day of the second meeting Bevin informed the British Embassy in Washington by telegram that 'great play was made by Molotov of the fact that they were withholding from the Soviet authorities large numbers of Vlasov-men.' He wanted 'immediate instructions' issued to Alexander to end the trouble.

Meanwhile, he said, 'the delay in the issue of necessary instructions is causing considerable embarrassment to His Majesty's Government and seriously weakening the strong case which we would otherwise present to the Russians.' Bevin also wrote to Byrnes personally, reminding him of his assurance to Molotov that 'no sympathy' would be shown to the Vlasov men, and concluding that 'it is most important to get rid of these people as soon as possible . . . using such force as may be necessary.'[24]

One can therefore imagine the dismay of Bevin and his subordinates when on October 4, a few days after the letter had been sent, they heard that General Eisenhower had suspended the forcible repatriation of Soviet citizens. An American spokesman told the press that they thought some of the Russian prisoners might have hidden arms and 'we are not eager to risk the lives of American soldiers trying to make them go.' The order was described as 'a temporary abrogation of the Yalta Agreement'.[25] Thomas Brimelow wrote to Colonel Hammer, 'we are both mystified and alarmed by this statement which is of course quite contradictory to His Majesty's Government's policy.'[26]

Forcible repatriations had ceased at the end of August, and it was only towards the end of 1945 that a new policy began to emerge from the confusion. For months there was bureaucratic conflict, the Americans against the British and the Foreign Office against the War Office. Then, mainly under American initiative, a compromise solution was worked out. It was now proposed to return by force only those Soviet citizens who had once been in the Red Army or who had collaborated actively with Nazi Germany. Ordinary civilian refugees would be allowed to remain in the West, if they wished.

The British Embassy in Washington sent Bevin an early American reaction to his letter to Secretary of State Byrnes:

> They are much concerned over the general principle of return to the Soviet Government of Soviet civilians, of whom there are about 15,000 in the American zone of Germany. State Department feel no difficulty about handing back to Soviet Government civilians who were at any time members of the Soviet Army, but they anticipate strong criticism from the public and in Congress here on grounds of humanity and of traditional American views of asylum if United States Government uses force to return others against their will. There have already been cases of suicide.[27]

The Foreign Office saw little merit in this suggestion. The main objection of course was that it would still constitute a clear breach of the Agreement, which applied to 'all Soviet citizens' and allowed no distinction between categories. 'We would like them to show how they propose to justify their action,' wired Bevin to his Embassy in Washington. He thought that the proposal 'will serve no purpose other than to aggravate existing difficulties.' His other objection was on practical grounds. How would the western Allies ever be able to work out who was a 'traitor' and who a mere refugee?

The telegram to Washington ended:

> We consider that it would be difficult in practice to draw a line between traitors and political refugees. The Cossacks are acknowledged traitors. But amongst the civilians there may be many whose conduct has been no less reprehensible. In our view it would be illogical that such persons should enjoy immunity while others, who have displayed their colours, are being sent home for punishment. Moreover, any attempt to draw a line between traitors and refugees would lead to interminable wrangles with the Soviet authorities. We are therefore in favour of avoiding discrimination.[28]

On the legal and practical points the Foreign Office was correct. The Agreement and the negotiations which had preceded it were clear. Any attempt to discriminate would be a breach. There could be no doubt about that. Nor can one easily see how the British and Americans would have tackled the task of sorting out the Soviet citizens they held, of separating the 'traitors' from the refugees. Here were large numbers of men, speaking for the most part only Russian, confused and suspicious about the intentions of their captors and in no way anxious to help in any enquiry or give details of their pasts. During interrogations, which could be conducted only occasionally because of the shortage of reliable interpreters, they changed their stories and even their identities. One of the British officials most closely involved in the Agreement and the practical problems of its implementation had said firmly that any idea of sorting the war criminals from the innocent victims was 'just not on'. It would have taken years.

Still, not content with these two powerful points in their favour, the Foreign Office felt obliged to seek moral justification for their view that all the prisoners should be sent home. They claimed that 'amongst the civilians there may be many whose conduct has been no less reprehensible' than that of acknowledged traitors.

But they could equally have claimed that there were many who had committed no crime, who had suffered appalling persecution at the hands of Stalin's policemen and yet had resisted the temptation to fight for Nazi Germany. Now that the war was over they wanted to stay in the West, to enjoy some of the freedoms for which the Allies had supposedly been fighting. Britain and the United States believed that to give them this freedom would be to damage their relations with the Soviet Government and that this would be against their national interest. They did not foresee that relations were going to deteriorate anyway, whatever they did. They therefore proposed to deny the Russian civilians this freedom and this elementary right, and not content with committing this act, which was perhaps inevitable and perhaps correct on political grounds, they were trying to justify it morally as well.

On December 13 the Foreign Office heard from Vienna that there were several hundred Soviet citizens still awaiting repatriation. Brimelow wrote that same day to Hammer complaining strongly that 'no progress had been made since September last' over their transfer. In a few days there was to be another Bevin-Byrnes-Molotov meeting, this time in Moscow. Brimelow thought it 'very likely that this question will be raised', in which case 'our Secretary of State would certainly be put in an extremely awkward position.' Once again the War Office were asked to treat the matter as one of 'the utmost urgency'.[29]

Field Marshal Alexander had given up his command of the Mediterranean theatre and was shortly to go to Canada as Governor General. But other senior officers carried on protesting against forcible repatriation. General Richard McCreery, the General Officer Commanding British Forces in Austria, sent a long and moving telegram to the War Office on December 16. He confirmed the fact which the Foreign Office had discovered only in October—that Allied Forces Headquarters had ordered the suspension of forced repatriation as far back as the end of August. He revealed that, from the Foreign Office's point of view, the situation was worse than they had imagined, for the number of Soviet citizens in Austria numbered not hundreds but thousands. There were 3,100 in camps, 2,500 domiciled outside camps, and an estimated 1,500 who had run away into the hills.

McCreery explained his objections to British policy in detail:

A high percentage of Soviet displaced persons consists of women and children against whom the use of force by British soldiers would be contrary to normal British practice . . . Troops are also not available for the rounding up of the 1,500 (or 1,800) Soviet citizens believed to be at large. The Commander in Chief [General Eisenhower] believes that the practice of forced repatriation of Soviet citizens will inspire such displaced persons to become deserters, who would almost certainly become bandits in preference to dying of starvation. There is also a danger that such a policy might likewise lead to desertions of other displaced persons such as Poles, Yugoslavs and Hungarians.

It was not the first time that this danger had been mentioned. On December 4, the *New York Herald Tribune* had printed an article under the alarming headline—'Renegade Reds roam Balkans, spread terror'. It revealed that remnants of Vlasov's army were wandering about Austria near the borders with Hungary, Yugoslavia and Czechoslovakia, 'fully armed and desperate'. There were apparently several thousand people moving about in wagon trains, and they had 'not hesitated to murder farmers from whom they steal food'. Eisenhower thought that it would not take much to induce the 5,600 Soviet citizens under British control to abscond and join the bandits. McCreery was obliged to tell the War Office that 100 prisoners had run away from one of his camps the night after the Soviet Military Mission had visited it. Two days later the British authorities made a search for arms in the camp. The Soviet prisoners took this to be a preliminary to repatriation and another 200-300 of them took to the hills.

On December 19, Brimelow wrote to Colonel Hammer, 'The arguments advanced by General McCreery against forcible repatriation seem to us quite unconvincing.' He repeated the legal argument that political asylum is normally granted to refugees who manage to reach British territory, not to people who fall into the hands of British armed forces. He saw no merit in the suggestion that the use of force against women and children was 'contrary to normal British practice'. This could not be, he said, because 'the situation which gave rise to the Yalta Agreement is without precedent in British history.'

Meanwhile the Foreign Ministers had met in Moscow for discussions on France, the Balkans and nuclear fission. Charles Bohlen writes, 'The conference had been hastily improvised and was thoroughly disorganised. Items were put on the agendas without proper preparations.'[30] Brimelow concluded his letter: 'In view of the possibility that this matter may come up at any moment in the current discussions in Moscow, we should like our Secretary of State to know as soon as possible that he would be safe in saying that urgent measures for the repatriation of these people are now being taken.' A telegram was sent from the Foreign Office to Vienna: 'I appreciate that the task is difficult and distasteful ... I am well aware of the complexity of the problem. But the job must be tackled.'[31]

The Moscow meeting, like the London one, was a failure. Only ten months had passed since the conference in Yalta, but already the warmth had gone out of the Grand Alliance. Victory seemed to have brought nothing but problems between the Soviet Union and the western powers. Most people now saw that the world was about to become seriously divided, an ideological battleground, and that the Soviet Union had lost none of its single-minded approach to internal and international events. For a few months there had been hopes, but most people saw that these hopes would not be fulfilled.

Naturally, it was the diplomats, the men whose job it had been to try and build up good relations, who were the last and the most reluctant to admit that their professional skills had failed to provide the answer. For a few months longer than the others they were ready to persevere in their attempts to woo the Soviet government with sweet reason, to treat the Soviet leaders like gentlemen, to trust their word of honour.

To break the Agreement would set, they thought, an appalling precedent. It would also encourage the Soviet government to break other clauses of the Yalta Agreement—for instance the one on Poland—which were, in political terms, far more important. They did not appreciate that Stalin was planning to break many of these clauses anyway, that this could not be prevented, however scrupulous they were in sending him his citizens. They believed that by cajoling him they would induce him to treat his subjects and the countries he had occupied in a civilised way. It was because of the sad and incorrect belief that they might be able to tame the beast that they urged British and American soldiers to commit acts which were, in Field-Marshal Alexander's words, 'quite out of keeping with the principles of democracy and justice as we know them'.

THE LAST OPERATIONS—
DACHAU, PLATTLING,
KEELHAUL, EASTWIND

ON NOVEMBER 15, a committee representing three United States departments—Army, Navy and State—prepared a paper which modified the policy of forcible repatriation. 'The United States has long had a firm policy against repatriation of unwilling individuals merely on demand of their country of origin,' the committee declared. They recalled that before the war Soviet sailors who jumped ship in American ports had always been protected and concluded that it would be wrong to surrender large numbers of people merely because they were Soviet citizens.

There were now to be only three categories of person whom American forces would continue to deliver to the Soviet Union, by force if necessary. The first was 'Soviet citizens captured in German uniform' because they were *prima facie* traitors to their government'. The second was former members of the Soviet armed forces, because 'they may be regarded as deserters from an Allied force.' The third was people who, though not captured in German uniform, 'have voluntarily rendered aid and comfort to the enemy.' With this last category the Soviet authorities, if they wanted any individual, would be required to give the Americans details of the alleged offence and 'each case should be decided on its own facts.'

This policy directive arrived in Europe from Washington on December 20, by which time most Soviet citizens had slipped through the net, concealing their Soviet status often with the connivance of British or American soldiers. Of the 20,000 acknowledged Soviet citizens remaining in American hands no more than 4,000 had been taken in German uniform, but it was recognised that all of these would have to be delivered. A series of operations was therefore instituted in the camps in Germany where these 'traitors' were held. As an American report explains, 'It was natural that the most tenacious resistance to repatriation came from within this group . . . as these persons had the worst to fear in terms of retribution'.[1] More alarming scenes of violence were about to take place.

The first operation took place at Dachau, the site of one of Nazi Germany's most horrible concentration camps. Early in January 1946, a few days after the new policy came into effect, Soviet officers came to Dachau and addressed the prisoners. 'The Motherland has forgiven your crimes,' they told them, but the latter were sceptical and all refused to go to the Soviet Union of their own will. Then on January 17, the prisoners were paraded and told to collect their belongings and be ready for the move into Soviet territory. They refused to move, even when ordered at pistol point by American officers. That evening, after several hours on parade in the cold, they were dismissed and allowed to go to their huts. Some of the Russians thought this meant that the threat had passed, that the Americans would no longer insist. It had, after all, been five months since force was last used against a large number of Russian prisoners, and during that time American officers had told them again and again, no doubt in good faith, that the Yalta Agreement on repatriation was a dead letter.

For thirty-six hours no attempt was made to dislodge the prisoners, but many of them were suspicious and fearful. One of them has described what they did:

> They felt that the decisive moment in their lives had come. They set up a table in one of the rooms and covered it with a white cloth. They placed a cross on the table and ikons on either side. All night and all the next day people came to the table to say prayers. They sang hymns and entrusted their last hopes to God. Several officers and men swore oaths that, if force were used, they would commit suicide in order to show by the shedding of their blood that their cause was just, and to prevent other forcible repatriations in the future.[2]

During the morning of January 19 large numbers of military police arrived from nearby Munich. They surrounded the block and ordered the Russians to come out. There was no movement, so the policemen broke into the hut and began dragging the prisoners out one by one. Although they had deliberately not packed any of their belongings, and although many had stripped to their underwear in the belief that the Americans would not then be able to move them into the open, they were pulled or carried towards the railway line and loaded into trucks. But one room the police had difficulty in entering. The Russians had barricaded the door. Eventually they broke it down and when they entered they came upon a scene of indescribable horror.

The American Army newspaper *Stars and Stripes* described the scene after interviewing eye-witnesses. 'Red Traitors Dachau Suicide described as Inhuman Orgy', the article was headed. Soldiers told their reporter that the Russians 'had fought like beasts to destroy themselves'. As soon as they broke into the the tear-gas filled room, they said, two prisoners tried to disembowel themselves with broken glass. Others stood side by side, slashing with pieces of glass at each other's throats. It was apparently easier to cut someone else's throat than to cut one's own. Another struck his head straight through a pane of glass, then shook it from side to side pressing his neck down against the jagged edges. American and Russian witnesses agree that the whole room was flowing with blood.

One of the guards told a reporter: 'It just wasn't human. There were no men in that barracks when we reached it. They were animals. The GIs quickly cut down most of those who had hanged themselves from the rafters. Those still conscious were screaming in Russian, pointing first at the guns of the guards, then at themselves, begging us to shoot.'³ Russian émigrés have protested strongly against the tone of this description. There was nothing animal-like about what the victims did, they claim. On the contrary, it was a logical and noble reflection of their determination not to be handed over like lambs to the slaughter. It was also a demonstration aimed at American public opinion. The more people succeeded in killing themselves, the more publicity the affair would receive in the American press and in official memoranda, and the less chance there would be of similar operations being mounted in the future. Many Russians who escaped forcible repatriation later feel that they owe their lives to the men who killed themselves at Dachau.

The wounded men fought like demons to prevent the Americans from patching their bleeding necks. The guards were reduced to beating them into insensibility with their sticks. It was the only way of quietening them and sewing them up. These men were carried to the trucks on stretchers, but some of them regained consciousness along the way, whereupon they leapt up and ran, opening their wounds and staining the ground with blood.

The number of suicides was announced in the American press as ten, with twenty-one seriously injured, but there may have been more deaths because some of the wounded were put into the train in a serious condition and may not have survived the journey into Soviet territory. One of the injured died later in an American hospital. The *New York Times* announced this in a small paragraph headed 'Russian Traitor Dies of Wounds'.[4]

Of the 271 prisoners in Dachau, about 135 were delivered to the Red Army that day, those that remained being old émigrés not liable to repatriation. A few days after the events of January 19, the survivors were transferred to the main camp for Russian prisoners at Plattling, a small town ninety miles north-east of Munich and Dachau. Their stories quickly spread among the 3,000 Russians who lived in the camp. For months their lives had been boring, but apparently safe. They had spent their time playing games, putting on plays and learning languages—the traditional pastimes of prisoners-of-war.

The stories of the men from Dachau caused great alarm at Plattling. Some of them went to see the American commandant, Colonel Thomas Gillies. An émigré journal has printed a letter dated February 10, and allegedly signed by him, which assured the Russians that they had nothing to fear, and even apologised for the unauthorised presence in the camp that day of a Soviet officer.[5] Some of the prisoners were calmed by this, but others feared the worst, especially when the American guards ordered them all to fill in questionnaires about their past lives in the Red Army and in Russia.

The Russians did not know how best to reply to these questions. Many of them had suffered repression at the hands of the Soviet police and for this reason had decided to fight on the German side. But should they reveal these facts to the Americans? Many of the prisoners did not do so, fearing that the replies would find their way into Soviet hands, in which case their relatives would suffer, and so would they if by any mischance they were indeed handed over. In their worried and precarious state they were unwilling to supply any biographical data, even though the Americans had promised to protect them. In fact, the smart thing would have been to fill in the most lurid sufferings imaginable, because it was then American policy to save some of those who had suffered particularly badly in the Soviet Union.

For a few weeks all stayed quiet at Plattling, then little things began to happen which made the Russians even more suspicious. The prisoners of other nationalities were loaded into trucks and taken away, nearly 10,000 of them, leaving only the 3,000 Russians. An American guard replaced the one normally manned by the prisoners themselves. All men were locked in their barrack huts from 7 pm until 6 am. Army photographers came round taking pictures of the huts and of the prisoners. The Greek Orthodox Metropolitan of Bavaria visited Plattling and addressed an appeal to the authorities stating that most of the men were in complete despair. He said that the Russians had asked for the right to have their cases tried by United States courts. Many of them, anticipating the hand-over, asked him to give them the last sacraments.

On February 20, Pope Pius XII published an allocution protesting against 'the repatriation of men against their will and the refusal of the right of asylum'. Senior Vatican officials told American reporters that the Yalta policy was 'a betrayal of the morality and ideals for which the Allies fought' and 'against humanity and justice'. The Vatican claimed to possess information that when Russians arrived home 'only too often they end up in Siberia.' Many of these Russians had fought for the Germans, the Vatican admitted, but 'whether they did or did not, they are treated alike.'[6] This information was correct.

On February 22, an American State Department official called Murphy sent a moving telegram from Germany to Secretary of State Byrnes in Washington. Of the 3,000 Russians who had just been screened, he said, 1,800 were found eligible for forcible repatriation. They were the largest group to be dispatched, and in view 'of the number of suicides and attempted suicides attendant upon recent forcible removals and the reaction of United States soldiers thereto, the United States Army authorities approach their impending trip with considerable foreboding.'

The blow fell at 5.45 am on February 24. American military policemen, armed and carrying sticks, burst into the huts while the Russians were still asleep and drove them out into the open air. A Russian witness has described what happened:

> Many of us were barefoot and clad only in our underwear, though some had managed to snatch up a blanket. Any dawdler received a rain of blows from the soldiers' sticks. Many of us had to stand in six degrees of frost from 6 am until four o'clock that evening. We were in small groups surrounded by guards, two for every prisoner. They began shouting people's names out from lists and dividing us into two groups. Each of the groups was told, 'Don't worry, you're only going to be moved to another part of the camp. It's the other group that's being sent to the Soviet Union.'[7]

The Russians were loaded into trucks, twelve or fifteen in each, with a guard of six military police. The account continues: 'The prisoners, who were sitting down or lying on the bottom of the truck, could not see where they were being taken. It was only by the length of the journey that they realised they were going outside the camp, and only at the railway station, when they saw the bars on the carriage windows, that they realised they were doomed. It was then that several people began to commit suicide.' An American report states that 'in spite of the elaborate precautions taken during this transfer, five of the men succeeded in committing suicide and a number of others attempted to do so.'[8] In all, 1,590 Russian prisoners were handed over to Soviet officers that day at Schönberg, north of Munich. There was one more suicide on May 13, when a further 222 Russians were repatriated by force from Plattling.

Meanwhile, relations between the Soviet Union and the western powers were steadily deteriorating. On March 5, 1946, Winston Churchill made his famous 'Iron Curtain' speech at Fulton, Missouri. In Berlin and Yugoslavia tension grew as the West came to realise that the communist governments of eastern Europe planned to rule on Soviet lines, allowing no opposition at all. In Poland violence was widespread, almost reaching the proportions of civil war, and the elections promised at Yalta had still not taken place.

But still Britain and the United States felt obliged to make some show of willingness to fulfil the Yalta Agreement on repatriation. True, by now large numbers of individual officers were bending their orders and allowing Russians to slip through the net. Obviously this was known to higher authority and tolerated. But until the West was ready to renounce the Agreement entirely, they would have to carry on sending back a token few. Interrogations would have to be held and a few unfortunates extracted in order to demonstrate to the Soviet government that that Agreement was to some extent still being observed.

The repatriations of 1946 had been done by American troops, not British, but on June 6 the British Cabinet agreed to fall in with the American modification and send back only the three categories of Soviet citizen defined by Washington. Almost all the Soviet citizens in the West had now, under one pretext or another, been released or resettled. There remained, however, about 1,000 people in camps in Italy who had not been properly screened and processed. Most of these were Soviet citizens, a few of them Yugoslav Croats, and all of them suspected of having fought with the German army. Soviet and Titoist Yugoslav authorities knew of their existence and were constantly pressing for them to be handed over.

Between August 11 and 14, these people were loaded into trains at two camps at Aversa and Bagnoli, near Naples, some to be delivered to an American camp near Pisa, others to a British camp at Riccione, just south of Rimini. For the next few months they were kept under close observation and to become a separate category of prisoner, destined for probable delivery to the communists, their every move to be planned in great detail and on the highest authority. A man with a colourful imagination had worked out the plan. Their move to Pisa and Rimini was labelled 'Operation Keelhaul'.[9] The delivery of the Soviet citizens was called 'Operation Eastwind' and the delivery of the Croats 'Operation Highjump'.

The British camp was a huge complex covering many square miles and containing displaced persons of many nationalities. It was only lightly guarded. The inmates were often allowed to work outside the camp, in which case they could come and go quite freely. Many of the Russians had wives and children. Families were accommodated in large barrack rooms, each unit separated from the other by blankets hung over lines. Though originally alarmed by the idea of moving from Naples, they were quickly reassured once they arrived at Pisa and Riccione. British and American officers told them repeatedly that there was no question of forcing them back to the Soviet Union. The Russians knew that such promises had been given before and not honoured, but this time they found the relaxed approach of the guards quite convincing.

A British officer wrote a report on events at Riccione which was eventually leaked and in 1973 published anonymously in an American newspaper.[10] Captain A, as he will be called, was involved in the screening process and was disturbed by the deception which he and his colleagues had to practise in order to lull their charges into a state of false security: 'The Russians had such blind faith in the British not throwing them to the wolves that they did not realise they were being repatriated until it was too late to resist.'

A few of the Russians absconded soon after arrival, but most of them stayed and submitted to the questions of British intelligence. They were encouraged to co-operate by their senior officer:

> Major Ivanov's tactics were based on the belief that if the Russians in his charge behaved themselves in an exemplary manner and made a good impression on their custodians, they would eventually stand a better chance of being accepted as permanent immigrants with proven qualities of good citizenship. Major Ivanov miscalculated, however, and actually played into our hands by adopting this policy.

The screening officers' job was to talk to the Russian officers at length, to try to gain their confidence, then to use this trust to trap them into the admission that they were Soviet citizens who had fought in the German army. Once this was established they were men marked for forcible repatriation. It was, Captain A wrote, an extremely distasteful task: 'Knowing as one did what the future had in store for them, one was virtually living a lie in attending to their welfare and compassionate problems . . . The bulk of these men were not war criminals . . . They were mainly simple peasants with a bitter personal grievance against the Bolsheviks.' Some of them had been subjected to extreme threats in Nazi camps. Others had endured vicious persecution in the Soviet Union. These were the compelling reasons which had induced them to join the German army. Captain A thought that 'it would be an impertinence for an outsider to set himself up lightly in judgement of their actions during the war.'

Interrogations continued during the winter of 1946-47 until a number of unfortunates had been earmarked for delivery to the Soviet authorities—75 from the American camp at Pisa, 180 from the British camp at Riccione. Of course this decision was not communicated to the prisoners. They still had no idea what was going to happen to them. The questioning indicated to some that they were going to be separated from the rest, but many thought that it was designed merely to determine in which country they would all be resettled. The relaxed attitude of the guards continued, convincing most of them that no serious harm would befall them.

This time every detail of the journey was to be carefully planned and the prisoners delivered by train to St Valentin, a few miles east of Linz on the border of Austria's Soviet zone. There would be none of the confusion and violence of earlier repatriations. This time the move would be made only after scrupulous and intense preparation to ensure that no man was able to commit suicide. What happened to them *after* they were delivered was, of course, none of Britain's or the United States's business.

Nevertheless it was recognised that there probably would be suicide attempts. On March 26, 1947, British headquarters in Rome received a worried message. Everything possible would be done to make sure that the prisoners reached Soviet territory safe and sound, but it was vital that the Soviet authorities be ready to accept the dead bodies of any who died *en route* and to count them against the nominal roll. On March 31, Colonel Pavel Yakovlev, a Soviet liaison officer in Rome, confirmed that the Soviet authorities would accept bodies and count each one as a delivered prisoner.

Two special trains were prepared to take the prisoners from Riccione. Squads of Royal Engineers modified a number of open-plan passenger carriages specially for the journey. All metal objects, hooks and luggage racks, for instance, were unscrewed from the walls in case they might be used as weapons. Heavy grilles made of expanded metal (known in the Army as XPM) were fitted over all the windows to stop any prisoner from leaping out. A complete company of about a hundred men was available to escort each train across the zone border. One carriage carried a quantity of food and drink, two or three weeks supply altogether, and was equipped with cooking stoves. Lastly, just in case any

Russian did succeed in killing himself, each train included a mortuary van.

Instructions issued to the escorting officers made it clear that the men being sent back were traitors who had been selected only after careful screening. Handcuffs, strait-jackets, tear gas and truncheons were available to prevent suicides, and as a last resort firearms were to be used to prevent escapes. In case of any trouble, the escorting officers were advised, firm action was to be taken immediately. There would then be less chance of the trouble spreading or becoming serious. And it was most important that each prisoner, whether delivered dead or alive, be signed for personally by a Soviet officer at St Valentin.

The job was given to the 1st Battalion, the Royal Sussex Regiment. Ben Dalton, one of their company commanders, says: 'Probably our battalion was chosen to deliver them because they had been on the opposite front to us around Orsogna. These Russians fought jolly well for the Germans. This was one of the facts that I put across to my company, because this is the sort of job that a line battalion does not relish at all. But the fact that they'd fought against us made it not quite so unsavoury as it would otherwise have been. The men just accepted that these were men who had changed sides and were being sent back to their owners.' Dalton nevertheless found the job 'the most unpleasant that I had to do during or after the war'.

The battalion had been brought in from outside Riccione and before the move had never come into contact with the Russians socially. They knew nothing of their personal problems or of what had induced them to fight for Nazi Germany. There was thus no chance of their showing the Russians too much sympathy. The British and American authorities had learnt from previous experience that soldiers who became personally involved with Russian prisoners might allow them to escape. Every precaution was taken to prevent this happening during this operation.

It was decided that the first train would leave Riccione on May 8. In spite of the attempts to keep the move secret, the interrogations had made many of the prisoners suspicious. Not all of them were ready to accept Ivanov's advice and obey the British orders to the letter. John Stanton, another company commander from the same battalion, remembers scenes of violence taking place when his men came to take prisoners for entrainment: 'The women were the worst. They became very fierce and hysterical. Several of our men were wounded with knives by women who went berserk at the idea of their man being taken away.'

It was decided that a strong display of force was the best way of preventing suicide or escape attempts. Several hundred British soldiers were therefore in attendance on the morning of May 8, when the 180 doomed men were brought from the camp to Riccione station. To begin with, they were all searched by military police, not very effectively as it turned out. Major Dalton was the officer in charge of the train. He says, 'My prisoners certainly weren't told they were going back to Russia. They were told they were going to another camp.' After all that had gone before, the prisoners were thoroughly suspicious, especially when they were told they would have to leave all their personal luggage behind them, but they could not be sure that they were being told a lie. The previous August, during Operation Keelhaul, they had suspected that their captors were taking them into Soviet territory, but their suspicions had been groundless.

What complicated everything that morning was the new policy of the western Allies not to repatriate by force anyone except Soviet citizens who had fought for the German army or deserted from the Red Army. This raised the question, what about the prisoners' wives and children? If the train was merely going to another camp, there was no reason why they should not go too. But to trick the women and children into going to the Soviet Union with their men was contrary to instructions. It was therefore decided that morning to remove from the train all the nine married men, as well as their nine wives and seven children. After the train had left, these married men were told the truth, that the men would have to go back to Russia. They were then given twenty-four hours in which to decide whether their wives and children should go too.

One can hardly imagine a more terrible dilemma for a wife and mother. Captain A wrote in his report:

> As soon as this macabre proposition was put to them, it was immediately obvious that husband and wife, by being required to make a decision of such fatal importance, had been placed in an intolerable position. The husband could not in good conscience require his wife and children to accompany him to his doom. His

wife on the other hand, by volunteering to go with her husband, would have her own blood and that of her children on the husband's hands. While by declining to accompany him she would place herself in a morally indefensible position according to the tenets of her religion and her marriage vows. Very painful scenes of real agony ensued and were endured for twenty-four hours.

The first train left Riccione soon after noon on May 8. It consisted of Major Dalton, five infantry officers, a medical officer and three orderlies, two interpreters, 151 other British soldiers and 171 Russian prisoners. The train passed through Ravenna and Ferrara, then crossed the river Po. During the late afternoon the prisoners began to realise, by the setting sun on their left, that they were travelling north. Then, as they began to climb into the Dolomites, they suddenly came to the conclusion that they were going into Soviet territory. Dalton says: 'Knives started appearing and they began doing injuries to themselves. They began cutting their wrists and one chap cut his throat. Several of them asked me to shoot them. It was terrible—the noise and the screaming.'

But Dalton had a whole company at his disposal and was able to subdue the hysterical men before anyone was seriously injured. He says: 'I wouldn't say my men didn't strike any blows. They probably did.' After peace was restored he had some of the most violent men handcuffed to the metal struts of their seats. Then he ordered another search. He was annoyed at having to do this because he had been assured that the prisoners were thoroughly frisked before entrainment and were 'clean'. His men found plenty of dangerous objects: razor blades, open razors, knives and phials of pills. He felt that the military police had done a bad job and reported accordingly.

After this episode the prisoners realised that both suicide and escape were impossible. They lapsed into apathy. Dalton and his men talked to them and, although they avoided all political topics, they began to sympathise with them in their predicament. Dalton was particularly impressed by the senior Russian officer, probably the Major Ivanov mentioned in Captain A's report, who spoke some English and struck Dalton as 'a man of fine bearing, a good type of officer'. Clearly the prisoners were no unruly mob of good-for-nothing traitors, as Dalton had first assumed, but soldiers who must have had some strong reason for turning against their own country.

The Russians then began handing over their valuables to the British guards. Dalton says: 'They started giving away everything worth having—watches and money and things. They told us, "The Soviet soldiers will only steal them anyway, so you might as well have them." And we parted on good terms, if one can say that under the circumstances. I don't think they bore us any ill will personally, although in general they obviously thought they had been badly treated.'

Darkness fell as the train travelled through Padua and Udine towards the Austrian border. The doors of the carriages were locked, the lights left burning and guards posted outside each door. The rest of the escort tried to get some sleep. A few minutes after crossing the frontier the train stopped to take on water at the main station at Villach in southern Carinthia. Lieutenant G. F. Hope Hall, a British officer stationed in the town, was ordered to go to the station in the middle of the night:

> My instructions were to ensure that nobody left the train while it was at Villach, to ensure that nobody except authorised Austrian railway staff approached the train, to contact my commanding officer if for any reason the train was delayed. Normally, one knew certain details about military trains passing through one's area— station of origin, destination, personnel on board. This train however seemed to be shrouded in secrecy.

Hall remembers standing on the platform and looking at the mysterious train. No one got on or off. But he could hear people shouting inside the locked carriages. He could not distinguish any words, but the shouts seemed to him like 'cries of anguish or despair' and entirely fitted in with what he had been told in strict confidence, that these were Russians who had fought for the German army being returned to the Soviet Union. He remembers turning to the man next to him and saying, 'Poor bastards!'

The train-load of crying men left Villach and reached St Valentin during the morning of May 9. It was met by a Soviet colonel and, after a few questions, moved to a camp a few miles inside the Soviet zone. The train was then unloaded, one carriage at a time. Dalton says:

The Russians were courteous and efficient. They were meticulous about identifying every officer and warrant officer from the nominal roll of prisoners. When it came to the other ranks they weren't interested, they just ticked them off in batches of ten. But they isolated the officers and moved them into a separate corral. I got the impression that they were going to be dealt with pretty summarily.

No fewer than fifty Soviet officers, as well as a reporter from TASS, the Soviet news agency, watched the unloading. The colonel and his interpreter then accepted a cup of tea on the train with Dalton. They invited him to visit the site of a Nazi concentration camp nearby, which they were preserving as a museum. Dalton was suspicious of this idea. He had heard stories of Soviet soldiers stealing the engines from British and American trains. He says, 'I looked out at the engine and decided that it would cost me £30,000 at least if I lost it. So I decided to go home.' They got up steam and set off back to Italy that afternoon.

By then a second train was on its way from Riccione to St Valentin. At 9 am on May 9 the nine wives were asked the appalling question, did they wish to travel with their husbands into Soviet territory? All of them refused to go—a fact which, as Captain A wrote, 'is sufficient proof of the terror with which they viewed being handed over to the Soviet authorities'. The men were then given a short time in which to say goodbye to their families, presumably for ever. At 11 am the nine wives and seven children were taken away under escort to a displaced persons camp at Reggio Emilia. Fifteen minutes later the men were taken to the station, searched and put on board the train. Major John Stanton had a forty-man escort with which to guard his nine prisoners, so it was clear to them that escape was impossible. The show of force was too impressive.

The train left Riccione at 12.30 pm. Stanton remembers that his prisoners were 'very gloomy from the start'. They were given frequent drinks of tea in paper cups and meals which they ate with spoons off paper plates. There was only one incident: 'One chap started shouting and screaming that they were all going to be killed. He was unsettling the others.' Stanton had all the prisoners handcuffed to their seats and told the hysterical prisoner through an interpreter, 'Look, if you don't shut up you'll remain manacled, all of you.' He did this so that the other prisoners would talk to the man and induce him to be quiet. The idea worked. There was no more trouble and after about an hour Stanton was able to have the handcuffs removed. It was a small incident, but, Stanton says, 'it made the whole thing just that bit more disagreeable.'

The two trains passed in the night not far from the Italo-Austrian frontier and Stanton's train reached St Valentin during the morning of May 10. A Soviet lieutenant met the train and accompanied it to a point in open country a short distance away, where it stopped opposite a semi-circle of Soviet soldiers. Stanton remembers being very impressed by them: 'They all looked very young and fit and hard.' About a dozen Soviet officers were there too, and Stanton remembers their fury when it emerged that all he had to offer them was nine men, without one single woman or child. 'Where are the families?' they wanted to know.

Stanton explained that none of the wives had opted to go with their husbands, but the Soviet officers were unconvinced and it was only after they had called upon a civilian for advice—'a great fat man straight out of James Bond'—that the matter was resolved and permission given for the train to return. The Soviet side's displeasure was all too plain and for a time Stanton was glad indeed to think that he had three weeks supply of food and water. He had armed men placed on the footplate of the engine and was ready to deal with a serious confrontation.

The situation became worse when one of the prisoners began complaining that the British had refused to allow his wife to come with him and had actually beaten her with sticks. Stanton explained that this was nonsense, that the women had all been given the chance to travel on the train, but the man was obviously concerned to ingratiate himself with his new captors and to denounce the British who had betrayed him. The allegation was certainly false, but it became the basis for an official Soviet complaint and caused the British much embarrassment. It was thus with some relief that Stanton at last got permission to leave Soviet territory. He vividly remembers the atmosphere of artificial gaiety as, at the end of all the tension, they sped back towards Italy: 'We felt a bit like one does when one's coming away from a funeral. And we probably *were*.'

Unlike previous operations, this final act of forcible repatriation was mentioned briefly in the British and American press, which emphasised the positive fact that the delivery of this small number of men, 180 by the British and 75 by the Americans, had allowed the resettlement and release of several thousand other Russian prisoners whom the screening officers had not selected. Clearly, the 255 victims of Operation Keelhaul and Eastwind were delivered as a sop to the Soviet government. The British and United States governments had signed the Agreement voluntarily and even as late as May 1947 they felt they had to go through the motions of observing it.

But there were some who objected to the cold-blooded sacrifice of 255 people in order to preserve the semblances of an empty treaty. After all, Stalin had by the spring of 1947 violated several important sections of the Yalta Agreement. Most notably, he had orchestrated elections in Poland which bore little resemblance to the 'free and unfettered elections' which he had promised. In January 1947, the British and United States governments had both protested against the violent and dishonest methods used by the Polish communists to win this unequal contest. But in spite of this undemocratic act by the Soviet government, which was convincingly documented by numerous witnesses as a violation of the Yalta Agreement, the British and Americans had still felt obliged to proceed with Operation Eastwind four months later. Even though the Soviet government had broken the Agreement, the West persisted in observing it.

On May 21, Richard Stokes asked a question about Operation Eastwind in the House of Commons. How many attempted suicides had there been, he wanted to know. Christopher Mayhew, then a junior minister at the Foreign Office, told him that there had been no attempted suicides—an answer which was incorrect, as Dalton's evidence shows. It was the second time that Stokes had been given wrong information on this subject in the House of Commons. On June 7, 1945, he had asked if there were any agreements concluded at Yalta and Teheran which were not yet disclosed to the public. Winston Churchill told him incorrectly that 'there were no secret agreements'.

On June 11, 1947, Stokes returned to the subject and was supported by another Member, Godfrey Nicholson, who suggested that 'the whole idea of repatriating people to any country against their will is foreign to this country'. This time the answer was given by the Foreign Secretary, Ernest Bevin:

It is abhorrent to this country. On the other hand, I cannot allow
these people to exploit that fact. Really, we are carrying a very heavy
burden. I am ready to give asylum to the utmost, but I cannot
tolerate people exploiting it by being permanently on our backs . . .
On the basis of the Yalta Agreement my duty is quite clear.

Bevin's comment on this, the final act of forcible repatriation
under the Agreement, summed up much of the official attitude.
The British and United States governments had for nearly
three years carried out a policy which was abhorrent to their
peoples' tradition and moral values. But they had felt obliged to
continue because of their duties under a solemn treaty. There had
been valid practical reasons for signing the treaty: the need to
protect British and American prisoners in Soviet hands, fear of
making the Soviet Government suspicious and so damaging the
war effort, fear of the difficulties involved in absorbing and
resettling large numbers of Soviet citizens in the West.

Today few would deny that the Agreement inflicted a severe
injustice on those Soviet citizens who were repatriated having
in no way collaborated with Nazi Germany. The evidence shows
that many of these people, quite innocent of any crime even under
the harsh Stalinist criminal code, were convicted by makeshift
courts and spent ten years in corrective labour camps. Perhaps
even more shocking is the fate of the rest, several million people,
who though not brought to court were imprisoned for many years
in so-called 'filtration camps'. The camps differed from the labour
camps in that the prisoners were allowed to call the guards
'comrade', but this was the extent of the difference. The filtration
camps were supposed to last only a short time, to allow the
collaborators to be sorted out from the honest men, but in fact
they existed for years and no attempt was made to process and
release the innocent inmates. Meanwhile they suffered the same
cold, hunger and life-sapping hard labour that the convicted
men endured. And they died in the same huge numbers.

The case of those who collaborated with Nazi Germany is more
difficult. There can be no doubt that they were guilty of treason
under Soviet law, as they would be under the law of any country.
There are those who will feel that this is the end of the matter,
that they were traitors who deserved no better fate than the one
they received, either execution or years of torment in the camps.

But there are also those who will feel that morally, if not legally, the Soviet judges had no right to condemn these men. Rebecca West in her book *The Meaning of Treason* has put forward the idea, now supported by many lawyers, that a citizen owes loyalty to the country which gives him protection, and that consequently a citizen cannot commit treason if his country has given him no protection by its laws. By this standard there would certainly be many millions of Soviet citizens who owed no loyalty at all to the Soviet Union under Stalin. The repressions, confiscations and deportations were so massive in that country during the 1930s that the Soviet Government can well be said to have sacrificed the loyalty of large numbers of citizens. With actual war criminals, Soviet citizens who committed atrocities and murders against their own people, the moral issue is plain, they deserved retribution, but many lawyers would acquit those who merely joined Nazi Germany in order to fight against the Soviet system. The Soviet Union had given them no protection. It therefore had no claim on their loyalty.

These people faced a severe moral dilemma in that they could not fight against Stalin, whom they hated, without also fighting against the Soviet people to whom in spite of everything they belonged. And although more than a million of them made this choice and fought with their enemy, they were always a minority. The majority, and by the end of the war almost the whole Soviet people, fought bravely and nobly against the Nazi aggressor, even, one must assume, many people who hated Stalin and all he stood for. It is a thought that may well disturb those survivors of Vlasov's army and of the Cossack Corps now living abroad in sad disillusionment.

Only someone familiar with the pro-Soviet atmosphere of those years and the reality of world war can judge whether or not the violence that they suffered at the hands of Britain and the United States was unavoidable, whether one can justify the cold decision to sacrifice Russian lives, initially in order to save British lives, subsequently in order to advance American and British foreign policy. 'If the choice is between hardship to our men and death to Russians the choice is plain,' wrote P. J. Grigg to Eden— a statement which many people today will find shocking but which made perfect sense amid the slaughter of war. Those were ruthless times and one detects more than a touch of ruthlessness

in the words of Foreign Secretary Anthony Eden who recommended the Agreement to his Cabinet colleagues, who acknowledged that it would mean sending Russians to their deaths but
concluded that 'it is no concern of ours what measures any Allied
government, including the Soviet government, take as regards
their own nationals', that 'we don't want them here' and that 'we
cannot afford to be sentimental about this.'

Once this policy was laid down the suicides and violence which
followed could only have been avoided if there were widespread
disobedience in the field—an unlikely eventuality at such a time.
One must assume, though, that the American and British leaders
who took the decision did not realise that the violence would be
quite so bad. They anticipated having to hand Russians over to
rough justice and possible execution, but they did not realise
that hatred of the Bolsheviks was so strong among the hard core
of recalcitrants. They did not foresee that thousands would resist
repatriation in pitched battles, that many would commit suicide,
that a man would murder his wife and children and that mothers
would drown their babies rather than have them returned to the
Soviet Union.

One must hope that, had they foreseen this, they would not have
signed such a rigid agreement. But once it was signed, once they
were committed to sending back 'all Soviet citizens', they had
little room for manoeuvre. Either they had to break the treaty
—an appalling prospect—or they had to order their officers
and men in the field to carry out the policy as agreed. The
matter was then in the hands of individual soldiers who in
theory had even less room for manoeuvre, for they were under
military discipline which obliged them to obey orders without
question.

For many of the soldiers involved, particularly the professional
and senior officers, this was the overriding consideration. General
Keightley writes that his orders to repatriate the Cossacks came
directly from Churchill and that therefore what he thought about
the matter did not affect the issue. His subordinate General
Musson, then the brigade commander most closely connected
with the main operation, agrees with this view entirely:

I can't envisage a case where an officer would ever disobey an order.
A soldier is an agent of government policy. He can't judge the rights

and wrongs. He doesn't have enough information. He can represent his views, and we did this, we made it perfectly clear how ghastly the job was. But the ultimate decision must lie with the political leaders. I don't see how you can run an army or anything else if your soldiers refuse to carry out orders.

This point of view has been stated so firmly by professional soldiers that it seems to be little less than an ethic. Such men would no sooner disobey an order than would a doctor reveal secrets of his patient's illness or a priest violate the confessional. Obedience is one of the foundations of the soldier's craft and has remained unchallenged in modern armies—until the Nuremberg Trials. It was here that lawyers refused to acquit German defendants who had committed cruel acts and pleaded that they were only obeying orders. This defence was not considered sufficient to absolve them. They were convicted and many suffered the death penalty.

When the West German army (the Bundeswehr) was founded in 1956 these Nuremberg verdicts had their effect on the new military code. In the Bundeswehr a soldier need not obey orders which require him to do something which is a crime against German law. Nor need he obey when asked to do something which is a 'violation of human rights'. This is a vague term, and it remains to be seen how lawyers would approach the problem of deciding what exactly 'human rights' are. But it probably does mean that the old soldiers' ethic is under attack and will probably be altered in other armies in due course. In 1945 at Lienz and Kempten soldiers were on the verge of disobedience. Today they might in the same circumstances rebel openly.

Of course, most British and American soldiers were less professionally committed than Keightley or Musson. Generally speaking they obeyed orders throughout the war, but they did not like being ordered to use force against unarmed men, women and children. Many have said that at first they felt little sympathy for men who had betrayed the Soviet Union. For years their newspapers had been full of pro-Stalin propaganda. They came to believe that to oppose Stalin was to oppose the Allies as a whole. They did not accept that a man could be violently anti-Stalin and yet neither pro-Hitler nor opposed to western democracy. They knew nothing of the internal affairs of the Soviet Union—why should they?

Most of these soldiers have made it clear that when first ordered to load Russians into trains or trucks for repatriation they embarked on the job willingly enough, but without realising its full implications. However, in some instances they had time to talk to their victims and get to know them. Disillusionment with the Red Army grew steadily during the second half of 1945. Western soldiers were suddenly receptive to the stories they heard of the viciousness of Stalin's regime. In some cases they rebelled against their orders, either by complaining to their superiors or by allowing their victims to escape.

The true professional soldier would disapprove of such people. They allowed their personal feelings to get the better of them, their hearts to triumph over their heads, without adequate knowledge of the wider picture, the political necessities which had provoked the order in the first place. But others will feel admiration for the men who challenged their orders, at some risk to themselves, in order to protect Russians and Cossacks from the wrath of Stalin. What they did accomplished little good in the short term. Only a few were saved by the guards who 'turned a blind eye'. And as for those who complained, no operation took longer than a few days and there was never time for a complaint to climb up the chain of command, thus allowing the operation to be cancelled. The policy had been decided at too high a level for that. But the distaste felt by British and American soldiers for this type of work soon became a factor in the minds of the decision-makers in London and Washington. It affected them and induced them finally to modify the policy, thus allowing more to escape.

Solzhenitsyn writes in *The Gulag Archipelago:* 'What military or political reason can there have been for the delivery to death at Stalin's hands of these hundreds of thousands of Soviet citizens?' Now that he is in the West and can study the archives he will be able to see that the decision was only taken after some thought and on a balance of good and evil. It may have been a wrong decision—in the author's view it was wrong—but it was certainly debatable and in no way easy. Solzhenitsyn also writes: 'These prisoners were handed over in a perfidious way, typical of traditional English diplomacy.' This is a wild generalisation, but it is true that many will be shocked by the way in which western diplomats urged the sacrifice of human lives in order to keep good relations with the Soviet Union, and this months after the war was over.

Perhaps the kindest thing one can say about the diplomats is that they were out of their depth. Accustomed to handling matters of state and regarding it as their duty to bring nations together by negotiation, they were confused by problems which involved the life or death of actual human beings and they were aghast at the idea of breaking a solemn treaty in order to protect individuals. But one cannot deny—and here Solzhenitsyn is half right—that it was the diplomats who administered the policy, that many of the operations involved trickery as well as brute force, deceit as well as blows on the head.

Solzhenitsyn's views reflect the fact that his main source of information on this matter was the victims of forcible repatriation whom he met in the camps during his eight-year term. Their bitterness against the British (mainly) and the Americans is still very strong. Amid the cruelties of pre-war Soviet rule many Russians had developed an idealised picture of Britain and the United States. They had heard that an Englishman's word was his bond, they had heard that the United States was the haven of the poor and the oppressed. So naively they accepted it as an absolute truth that the Anglo-Saxons would never tell a lie and would never violate the sacred principle of political asylum.

They did not appreciate the odium which they had brought upon themselves by fighting on Hitler's side. They thought that this was unimportant, that it would soon be forgotten once they explained their readiness to serve the West loyally in the coming conflict against the Soviet Union. This optimism was nurtured by the kindnesses which they enjoyed from the American and British soldiers to whom they surrendered. They interpreted decent treatment as sympathy or approval. Then, when violence was used against them, they did not understand that even good people can behave harshly when under pressure and that even liberal governments act ruthlessly when they believe that their vital interests or the lives of their citizens are threatened. They felt, and still feel, horribly betrayed.

The West too made a serious miscalculation. They thought that relations with the Soviet Union would remain good and that the wartime alliance would endure. In fact during 1947 and 1948, too late to save the bulk of the victims of forcible repatriation, relations deteriorated very seriously. On March 12, 1947, in the face of a communist threat to overthrow the Greek government, President Truman told the American Congress that in future it would be his policy to assist free peoples who were threatened 'by armed minorities or by outside pressures'. In June 1947 the Marshall Plan was launched and three months later Stalin reacted by founding his 'Cominform' of communist parties. In February 1948 a Soviet-organised coup d'état established permanent communist government in Czechoslovakia. In 1949 a play by the hard-line writer Sergey Mikhalkov enjoyed huge success in Moscow. Entitled *I Want To Go Home*, it told the story of Soviet citizens in the United States who wanted no more than to return to their beloved motherland, but who were kept prisoner in America by capitalists intent on subverting them into the great anti-Soviet conspiracy.

The Grand Alliance was finished. It was now the Cold War, and from now on any Soviet defector or deserter, far from being repatriated by force, was welcomed with open arms and put to work in the fast-growing anti-communist industry. The dream of the anti-Bolsheviks had now almost come true. For the moment there was only an ideological battle and a diplomatic confrontation, but few of them doubted that this would soon turn into open warfare. Once again hopes were raised that an invasion of free Russians would sweep the Soviet system away. The excesses which followed were symptomatic of the extremism of Russia's political heritage, the fanaticism of her internal hatred. In this context it is perhaps not surprising that for a few years the noble principle of political asylum was shelved, compelling liberal governments to behave with the cruelty normally reserved for dictators.

General William Morgan, who as Field-Marshal Alexander's Chief of Staff saw forcible repatriation in practice and whole-heartedly detested it, says today, 'There is nothing we can do to help these poor wretches now, but we can at least learn something from their fate.' There was in fact one lesson which Britain and the United States learnt. In May 1952, after several years of the Korean War, the communist side pressed the United Nations hard during peace talks, demanding the return of *all* Chinese and North Korean prisoners, without regard to their individual wishes and by force if necessary. The American negotiators rejected this demand outright and, as a result, the final settlement was considerably delayed. *The Times* wrote in a leading article: 'Whatever was done in 1945 and 1946, it is repugnant to liberal and Christian sentiment to force a man to return to a country against his will.'

Anthony Eden said in the House of Commons on May 7, 1952:

> I am sure the House will feel that the United Nations Command has had no alternative but to resist the forcible repatriation of communist prisoners-of-war who have shown such a strong determination to remain in the free world. I will not dwell on the practical difficulties of forcibly repatriating more than 62,000 men, many of whom could be expected to commit suicide on the way. It would, I think, clearly be repugnant to the sense of values of the free world to send these men home by force.

It would be heartening to think that it was his experience as the architect of forcible repatriation in 1944 that brought Eden to this noble conclusion and that, to this extent at least, the dismal story has a happy ending.

NOTES

In the following references to documents available in London the prefix 'FO' designates Foreign Office records, 'WO' War Office records, 'CAB' Cabinet Office Records and 'PREM' Prime Minister's Office records. I am grateful to have permission to quote from the documents, the copyright of which rests with the Crown.

CHAPTER ONE: *The Decision to Use Force*

1. FO 371 43382.
2. WO 32 11137.
3. ibid.
4. PREM 3 364/8.
5. ibid.
6. WO 32 11137.
7. CAB 65/43.
8. WO 32 11137.
9. FO 371 50606.
10. WO 32 11119.
11. WO 11137.
12. WO 32 11119.
13. WO 32 11137.
14. Harold Nicolson: *Diaries and Letters*, December 20, 1944.
15. WO 32 11137.
16. *Foreign Relations of the United States, Diplomatic Papers, 1944.* Volume IV, Europe. p. 1264.
17. FO 371 43382.
18. *Foreign Relations of the United States* (as above), p. 1258.
19. ibid., p. 1262.
20. ibid., p. 1272.
21. G-1 383.6, Section 6 (National Archives, Washington).
22. FO 371 47899.
23. *Foreign Relations of the United States* (as above), p. 1273.
24. ibid., p. 1264.
25. *The Conference at Malta and Yalta 1945*, p. 455.
26. FO 371 43382.

CHAPTER TWO: *The First Unpleasantness*

1. *The Conference at Malta and Yalta 1945*, p. 691.
2. PREM 4 78/1.

3. FO 371 50839.
4. FO 371 50607.
5. FO 371 50839.
6. *The Conference at Malta and Yalta 1945*, p. 946.
7. FO 371 50607.
8. *The Second World War*, Volume VI: Triumph and Tragedy, p. 351.
9. PREM 4 78/1.
10. *The Diaries of Sir Alexander Cadogan*, February 11, 1945.
11. PREM 4 77/1B.
12. WO 32 11139.
13. ibid.
14. WO 204 897.
15. PREM 3 364/9.
16. ibid.
17. WO 32 11119.
18. FO 371 47898.
19. 371 47897.

CHAPTER THREE: *Death on the Quayside*

1. FO 371 47897.
2. FO 371 47901.
3. ibid.
4. FO 371 47907.
5. *New York Times*, May 6, 1945.
6. *New York Times*, October 5, 1945.
7. *Chicago Daily News*, June 19, 1945.
8. *New York Times*, May 14, 1945.
9. This information comes from a document, to be known hereafter as the 'Wiley Report', which was requested by United States Senator Alexander Wiley in a telegram to Secretary of Defense Robert A. Lovett on November 20th, 1952. It is available in the National Archives, Washington, under the heading G-1 383.6, Record Group No. 218.
10. *The Times*, July 6, 1945.
11. *Daily Herald* (London), September 6, 1945.
12. *New York Times*, June 9, 1945.
13. *New York Times*, June 10, 1945.
14. *Andrey Andreyevich Vlasov, Kratkaya Biografia* (A. A. Vlasov, A Short Biography), published by the Propaganda School of the Russian Liberation Army, Dabendorf, 1944.
15. B. Dvinov: *Vlasovskoye Dvizhenie v Svyetye Dokumentov* (The Vlasov Movement in the Light of Documents), published by the author, New York, 1950, pp. 78-81.

16. *Trial of Major War Criminals*, Vol. XXXVIII, p. 88.
17. George Fischer: *Soviet Opposition to Stalin*, Harvard University Press, 1952, p. 45.
18. *Nazi Conspiracy and Aggression*, Vol. IV, p. 559.
19. Wilfried Strik-Strikfeldt: *Against Stalin and Hitler*, Macmillan, London, 1970, p. 228.
20. ibid., p. 248.
21. Alexander Solzhenitsyn: *The Gulag Archipelago*, YMCA Press, Paris, p. 261.
22. The file containing this letter was, at the time of going to press, about to be placed in the Public Record Office, London, in the WO 32 class. Its Ministry of Defence reference number is 0103/8571.

CHAPTER FOUR: *The Croats and the Cossacks*

1. Nikolay Krasnov: *Nyezabyvayemoye* (The Unforgettable), published by 'Russkaya Zhizn', San Francisco, 1957, p. 18.
2. WO 170 4467. This file, which contains the War Diaries of the 36th Infantry Brigade, is the main documentary source for the events of this and the following two chapters. In the absence of any other reference note, it may be assumed that quotations come from this file.
3. WO 170 4988.
4. WO 170 5045.
5. WO 204 7211.
6. WO 170 4465.
7. *Faugh-a-Ballagh* (The Regimental Gazette of the Royal Irish Fusiliers), July 1946.
8. Joseph Hecomovic: *Tito's Death Marches and Extermination Camps*, Carlton Press, New York, 1962, p. 23.
9. FO 371 47902.
10. WO 170 4241.
11. Vyacheslav Naumenko: *Vyelikoye predatelstvo* (The Great Betrayal), published by Vsyeslavyanskoye Izdatelstvo, New York, 1970, Vol. I, p. 161.
12. ibid., p. 122.
13. WO 204 7211.

CHAPTER FIVE: *The Conference that Never Was*

1. Naumenko (op. cit.), Vol. I, p. 141.
2. *Chasovoy* (The Sentry), April 1949.

3. A. K. Leniwow: *Pod kazachyim znamyeniem v 1943-45 godakh* (Under the Cossack Banner during the Years 1943-45), published by the author, Munich, 1970, p. 307.
4. *Obshchekozachi Zhurnal* (All-Cossack Journal), New York, August 1953.
5. Krasnov: *Nyezabyvayemoye* (op. cit.), p. 27.
6. ibid., p. 28.
7. Naumenko (op. cit.), Vol. I, p. 13.
8. Krasnov (op. cit.), p. 30.
9. Naumenko (op. cit.), Vol. I, p. 164.
10. WO 170 5025.
11. Leniwow (op. cit.), p. 241.
12. Krasnov (op. cit.), p. 33.
13. Leniwow (op. cit.), p. 242.
14. ibid., p. 243.
15. ibid., p. 244.
16. Naumenko (op. cit.), Vol. I, p. 123.
17. WO 170 5025.

CHAPTER SIX: *Mass Deportation from the Drau Valley*

1. Naumenko (op. cit.), Vol. I, p. 181.
2. ibid., p. 123.
3. ibid., p. 185.
4. ibid., p. 124.
5. ibid., p. 184.
6. ibid., p. 187.
7. ibid., p. 159.
8. Rossiya (New York), June 12th, 1957.
9. Naumenko (op. cit.), Vol. I, p. 11.
10. ibid., Vol. II, p. 112.
11. ibid., Vol. II, p. 111.
12. WO 170 4241.
13. ibid.
14. Krasnov (op. cit.), p. 45.
15. Naumenko (op. cit.), Vol. II, p. 281.
16. Krasnov (op. cit.), p. 47.
17. Leniwow (op. cit.), p. 257.
18. ibid., p. 262
19. ibid., p. 267
20. Naumenko (op. cit.), Vol. II, p. 258.
21. ibid., p. 260.
22. ibid., p. 304.

23. Leniwow (op. cit.), p. 281.
24. ibid., p. 283.
25. F. S. V. Donnison: *Civil Affairs and Military Government North-West Europe 1944-46.* Her Majesty's Stationery Office, London, 1961, p. 289. See also Winston Churchill: *The Second World War,* Vol. VI: Triumph and Tragedy, p. 647.
26. Philip Longworth: *The Cossacks,* Constable, London, 1969, p. 338.

CHAPTER SEVEN: *The Policy under Attack*

1. *New York Times,* June 30th, 1945.
2. ibid., July 1, 1945.
3. G-1 383.6, Record Group 319.
4. ibid.
5. Julius Epstein: *Operation Keelhaul,* Devin-Adair, Connecticut, 1973, p. 104.
6. Wiley Report.
7. B. M. Kuznetsov: *V ugodu Stalinu 1945-46* (In the Interest of Stalin 1945-46) published by 'Voyenny Vyestnik', New York, Vol. II, p. 8.
8. ibid., Vol. II, p. 9.
9. Wiley Report.
10. WO 32 11119.
11. FO 371 47901.
12. FO 371 47903.
13. ibid.
14. WO 204 440.
15. WO 214 63A.
16. WO 204 359.
17. *Manchester Guardian* (England), August 31, 1945.
18. *The Christian Science Monitor* (Boston), September 11, 1945.
19. FO 371 47906.
20. FO 371 47905.
21. ibid.
22. Charles Bohlen: *Witness to History,* Weidenfeld and Nicolson, London, 1974, p. 245.
23. FO 371 47906.
24. ibid.
25. *New York Times,* October 5, 1945.
26. FO 371 47910.
27. FO 371 47907.
28. ibid.
29. FO 371 37910.

30. Bohlen (op. cit.), p. 248.
31. FO 371 37910.

CHAPTER EIGHT: *The Last Operations—Dachau, Plattling, Keel-haul, Eastwind*

1. Wiley Report.
2. Kuznetsov (op. cit.), Vol. II, p. 32.
3. *Stars and Stripes* (Darmstadt, Germany), January 23, 1946.
4. *New York Times*, January 22, 1946.
5. Kuznetsov (op. cit.), Vol. I, p. 103.
6. *New York Times*, February 25, 1946.
7. Kuznetsov (op. cit.), Vol. I, p. 36.
8. Wiley Report.
9. WO 204 1593. This is the file on 'Operation Keelhaul'—a term which because of its macabre and vivid character is often applied incorrectly to the whole policy of forcible repatriation. In fact the term applies only to the move of a few hundred people to camps in Pisa and Riccione in August, 1946, for screening and possible repatriation.
10. *The Sunday Oklahoman*, January 21, 1973. The document was given to this newspaper by Julius Epstein, author of *Operation Keelhaul* and other works about forcible repatriation. The anonymity of the writer of the document and the irregular circumstances under which it fell into Epstein's hands inevitably give rise to doubts on its authenticity, especially as the article is headed 'Document Tells Allied Part in Deaths of Thousands' —a fanciful exaggeration in the context of 'Operation Eastwind'. But there is strong evidence to support the idea that the document is based on fact and essentially genuine. It refers to the Riccione camp as '218 Sub Area' and to the Russian prisoners as 'PW/SEP'. These names were not known to outsiders. Several of the salient facts of the document, including the 24 hours given the victims' wives to decide whether or not to travel, are confirmed by British officers involved in 'Eastwind'.
11. Solzhenitsyn (op. cit.), p. 264.

INDEX

Alexander, Field-Marshal Sir Harold, 181, 187; repatriation of Cossacks, 73, 74; and Croats, 84, 85; confrontation with Maj-Gen Basilov, 176, 177-8, 180; leaves Mediterranean theatre, 184
Allied Forces Act (1940), 19
Anderson, Maj-Gen A. V., 177
Arbuthnott, Maj-Gen Robert, 80, 133
Attlee, Clement (Earl Attlee), 51
Austria, 63, 78-9, 84, 89, 151, 175, 184, 185
Aversa, 194

Baden bei Wien, 160
Bagnoli, 194
Bailey, E. Tomlin, 26
Bannister, Captain (Master of the 'Almanzora'), 56
Basilov, Maj-Gen Y. D., 177-8, 180
Bates, Jack, 79, 80-2
Belcham, Ronald, 88
Belgium, 29
Bevin, Ernest, 176-7, 180-3, 203-4
Bleiburg, 84, 87, 88
Bohlen, Charles, 181, 186
Boshchanovsky, Vasili, 172, 173
Boyle, Colonel, 56
Bracken, Brendan, 33
Bradley, General Omar, 68
Bredin, Maj-Gen H. E. N., 80, 150, 151
Bridgeman, Viscount, 14
Bridges, Edward, 34
Brimelow, Thomas, 33, 45, 49-50, 182, 184, 185-6
Britain, Russian prisoners in, 6, 10-11, 19, 24, 37, 40; political asylum, 7, 177, 181; status of Soviet nationals in, 20; and forcible repatriation policy, 21, 174, 176; and US, 24; problem of dual nationality, 43; Allied dis-unity, 66; and Croats, 88; Yalta Agreement, 179, 184; disaffection with USSR, 193
Brooke, Field-Marshal Sir Alan (Viscount Alanbrooke), 178
Bryan, General B. M., 25, 26
Bryar, Lt-Col B. L., 112-17
Bulgaria, 20
Bunyachenko, General Sergei, 71
Burn, Major C. H., 146
Burrows, Major A. G., 16
Bury POW camp, 51
Butlerov, M. K., 90, 96, 97, 105, 108, 127
Butterwick camp, 13, 17
Byrnes, James, US Sec. of State, 169, 181, 192

Cadogan, Sir Alexander, 34, 36, 50, 177, 180
Campbell, Captain, 132
Canada, 184
Caucasus, 75, 79
Charters, Sergeant D., 118, 119
Cherbourg, 41
Chicago Daily News, 63
Christian Science Monitor, 180
Christie, Ethel, 42, 45, 48, 49
Churchill, Winston, 8, 9, 12; and Stalin, 20, 31, 32; Sidorov case, 45; and Cossacks, 73-4, 92, 107, 114, 120, 134, 164, 206; Yalta conference, 97, 203; 'Iron Curtain' speech, 193
Cockell, P. C., 100, 101
Cooden, camp, 14
Cossacks, anti-Soviet, 73, 75, 76; wrongly repatriated, 74, 101-02, 117; fight for Hitler, 77-8, 81, 85, 91; first contact with British, 79; Domanov's surrender, 80; in Drau Valley, 82, 124-9; surrender at Lavamund, 83-4; British admiration for, 89-90, 93; repatriation order, 92; disarmament of,

95; trick conference plan, 96, 103-16; eligibility for repatriation, 97-8; Germans in Corps, 99, 100; handover to Russians at Judenburg, 118, 119, 121-3; British army involvement with, 121, 152, 153; use of force against, 130-3, 158; resistance in Peggetz camp, Lienz, 134-50; hide in Austrian mountains, 154-6; future in USSR, 151, 157, 159, 161-5

Cregeen, Major S. J., 23

Croatia, 87

Cunningham, Admiral of the Fleet Sir Andrew (Viscount Cunningham of Hyndhope), 73

Czechoslovakia, 185, 210

D-Day, 1, 4, 29, 41

Dabendorf, 70

Dachau, 189, 190, 191

Daily Herald, 62, 63, 65

Dalton, Major Ben, 197-9, 200, 201, 203

Danilov, General, 171-3

Dardanelles, 35, 56, 57

Davidson, James, 111, 112, 157

Davies, Major 'Rusty', liaison officer, 90, 94, 124; trick conference plan, 96, 97, 105, 121; and repatriation order, 125, 126-7; Cossacks' resistance, 128, 129; Peggetz camp, Lienz, 135-6, 137, 140, 143-50

Dean, Patrick, legal adviser to FO, 6, 31, 43, 47, 49, 50, 55

Deane, Maj-Gen John, 31, 32

Dellach, 127, 130, 131

Dobrovolyets, 70

Domanov, T. I., 90, 97, 120; Soviet officer, 76, 91; retreat, 78; surrender, 80; in Drau valley, 82; trick conference, 98, 103, 105, 108, 112, 113; possible traitor, 104; resistance at Spittal, 115, 116; in Soviet hands, 160, 164

Donskow, Pyotr, 77, 104

Douglas-Home, Sir Alec (Lord Dunglass), 50

Eastwind, Operation, 194, 203

Eberstein, 99

Eden, Sir Anthony (Earl of Avon), 29, 37, 211; views on forcible repatriation, 7-11, 13, 22, 110, 205-6; and Russian alliance, 12; and Gousev, 15, 16, 20; in Moscow, 21, 23; Yalta conference, 31, 32, 34, 35; Sidorov case, 50, 52

Einetter, Gertraud, 155

Eisenhower, General Dwight, 1, 24, 61, 62, 182, 185

English, Lt V. B., 100, 101, 118

Estonia, 37

Fairfield, Letitia, 53, 54

Firebrace, Brig R., 38-40, 42-3, 54, 60-61

Forni Avoitra, 79

Fort Dix camp (USA), 25, 166-9

Frolov, Dmitri, 81, 94; first contact with British, 79; disarmament of Cossacks, 93, 95; trick conference, 96, 98, 105, 108; resistance at Peggetz camp, Lienz, 121, 138, 142, 143

Galsworthy, John, 15, 43, 48, 175

Geneva Convention, 1, 25, 27

George VI, King, 33, 114

Gepp, General E. C., 19, 25, 175

Germany, 6; surrender, 61, 80; British POW's in East Germany, 9, 20; repatriation of Russians in, 62-3, 67, 170, 176, 182

Gibraltar, 57

Gibraltar, Straits of, 35

Gill, Colonel Robert J., 68

Gillies, Colonel Thomas, 191

Girey, General Klych, 97, 117, 164

Goess, Leopold, 102

Goode, Major Thomas, 117-20, 123

Gorsky, Colonel, 17

Gousev, M., 9, 15-16, 20-1, 180

Graz, 157, 160, 161

Great Betrayal, The (V. Naumenko), 139

Greece, 20

Gregoriev, Vassili, 135

Greig, John, 106, 107

Grigg, Sir James, 10, 205

Gromyko, Andrei, 24, 26

Gryzlov, Lt-Gen, 32

Gufler, Bernard, 24
Gulag Archipelago, The (A. Solzhenitsyn), x, 73, 163, 208

Hall, Lt G. F. Hope, 200
Hammer, Col V. M., 175, 182, 184-5
Harbord, Lt-Col, 18
Harriman, Averell, 28, 35
Haydon, W. T., 49
Heather, Lt C. J., 155
Hemming, Lt Dennis, 122
Hetherington, Lt E. B., 131
Himmenhofen, Lt von, 160
Himmler, Heinrich, 70, 71
Hitler, Adolf, 29, 61, 69, 70, 92, 164; invasion USSR, 76, 78
Hodgson, Robert, 46
Holland, 4
Howard, Major R. S. V., 89
Hull, 54
Hungary, 161, 185

I Want to Go Home (S. Mikhálkov), 210
International Red Cross, 1, 114
Ismay, General Sir Hastings (Lord Ismay), 73
Istanbul, 56
Italy, 78, 82, 93, 109, 176, 180, 194, 202
Ivanov, Major, 195, 197, 199
Izvestiya, 92

Jackson, Robert H., 27
Japan, 91, 94
Jesman, Czeslaw, 18, 55, 56
Judenburg, 100, 102, 113, 118, 120-2, 131, 133, 134, 147, 156, 158, 159, 161

Katyn Forest massacre, 12
Keelhaul, Operation, 194, 198, 203
Keightley, Lt-Gen Charles, 84, 207; interpretation of Yalta Agreement, 91, 92, 97, 98, 117; attitude to Cossacks, 120, 206; repatriation completed, 151
Kemerovskaya province, 161
Kempten, 170, 174, 207
Kempton Park camp, 17, 41, 46, 51
Kennan, George, 28
Kennedy, Sgt A., 155, 156

Kerr, Sir Archibald Clark, 2, 4
Kirkham POW camp, 51
Korolkov, S. G., 140
Kotsovsky, M. I., 162
Krasnodar, 152
Krasnov, Nikolay, 78, 104, 108, 111, 159-60, 164
Krasnov, General Pyotr, 97, 104; fights for Hitler, 76, 77, 78; at Spittal, 114, 117; handed over to USSR, 119, 159, 160, 164
Krasnov, S. N., 164
Krotov, Soviet Consul, 38
Kubanski, Fyodor, 143

Latvia, 37
Lavamund, 83
Lavers, Capt G. A., 112
Leahy, Admiral William, 24
Legrand, Major, 171, 172
Leipzig, 65
Leipzig Agreement, 65
Lenin, Vladimir Ilyich, 144, 181
Leniwow, A. K., 113-17, 119, 162, 163
Leontieva, M. N., 120, 124, 125, 127
Lienz, 81, 89, 94, 96-8, 103 *et passim*
Lithuania, 37
Liverpool, 35, 54, 55-7
Longworth, Philip, 164
Lorenzago, 79
Lowe, Capt J. S., 133, 134

Malcolm, Lt-Col Alec, 82, 90, 94, 126; possible operation against Cossacks, 79, 80; trick conference, 96, 120; receives Cossack petition, 126, 127; resistance at Peggetz camp, Lienz, 135, 137, 139, 140, 141, 145, 148, 149
Malkov, Colonel, 168, 169
Manchester Guardian, 179
Marseilles, 60
Marshall Plan, 210
Martin, James, 56, 57, 58, 60
Martynenko, Ivan, 136
Marx, Karl, 144
Mauthen, 78, 79, 81
Mayhew, Christopher, 203
McCreery, Gen Richard, 184, 185
McDermott, Geoffrey, 73

McGrath, Major B., 130
McMillan, Capt Duncan, 138, 140, 156, 157
Meaning of Treason, The (Rebecca West), 205
Mihajlović, Draža, 88
Mikhalkov, Sergey, 210
Miroshnichenko, Colonel, 56, 57
Molotov, Vyacheslav, 2, 4; and Eden in Moscow, 20-3; Russian defectors, 29; Yalta, 32, 35; British POW's, 37; London conference, 181
Mordovkin, Irina, 144
Mordovkin, Pyotr, 144
Morgan, General William, 210
Morozoff, George, 148
Moscow, 20, 21, 161
Murmansk, 23, 28, 61
Musson, Brig Geoffrey, Cossack surrender, 79, 80, 81; trick conference, 94-8, 108, 109, 120; resistance at Peggetz camp, Lienz, 145, 149; end of repatriation, 158; soldier as Government agent, 206-7

Naumenko, General Vyacheslav, 171, 174; anti-Soviet, 75, 76; and Domanov, 104; on Peggetz resistance, 134, 139, 144
Nazarenko, Nikolay, 173, 174
Neumarkt, 106, 107
New York Herald Tribune, 179, 185
New York Times, 62, 68, 191
Newlands Corner camp, 38, 40, 42, 53
Nicholson, Godfrey, 203
Nicolson, Harold, 21
Norway, 23
Novikov, Kiril, 31

Oberdrauburg, 80-82, 94, 96, 124, 131, 155
Odessa, 35-7, 40, 48, 55, 56, 58, 59-61, 65, 82
Osokin, V., 68

Page, Eddie, 31
Pannwitz, Lt-Gen Helmut von, 82, 120, 131; commands 15th Cossack Cavalry Corps, 77, 82, 97, 99; handed over to Russians at Judenburg, 100-02; not eligible

for repatriation, 117; executed, 164
Panteleymon, Father, 138
Paravicini, Vincent, 65
Pavelić, Ante, 85, 87
Pavlov, Atamin, 77, 104
Pearson, Brig-Gen Madison, 167
Peggetz camp, 121, 135, 148, 152, 153
Peterman, Ivan, 71
Petrie, Lt J. T., 120
Phillimore, Henry, 31
Pickard, Geoffrey, 118, 154
Pinching, John, 140, 145
Pisa, 194, 196
Pius XII, Pope, 192
Plattling, 191-3
Poland, 29, 33-8, 47, 62, 91, 176, 186, 193, 203
Polaneska, Zoe, 82, 125, 139, 141, 146-8
Polunin, Kuzma, 126
Polyachenko, Major, 57, 58, 60
Prague, 70, 71
Pravda, 72, 92, 101, 164
Price, Colonel Cedric, 73
Pugachov, Emilyan, 75

Rastenburg, 70
Ratov, General, 38-40, 42, 43, 48
Rayner, Charles, 35, 36
Razin, Stenka, 75
Red Army, 9, 12, 20, 92, 170; officers visit camps in Britain, 17; liberators of Allied POW's, 21, 27, 31, 35, 59; desertion from, 29; in Poland, 29-30, 36, 39; postwar influence, 62, 65, 66, 182, 208; and Vlasov, 72; and Cossacks, 76, 81, 93, 152, 154-5, 157, 158; used in repatriation, 175-6, 180
Reid, Archie, 110, 135, 137, 138
Retford hostel, 41, 42, 44, 45, 51
Riccione, 194-9, 201
Rogers, Col Horatio, 168
Roosevelt, President Franklin, 20, 37
Rosenberg, Alfred, 78
Rotovaya, Olga, 124, 127, 128, 142
Rowlette, Major K., 117
Rumania, 20, 161
Rundstedt, Field-Marshal Gerd von, 29

Rupert camp (USA), 25, 26
Russian Civil War, 75
'Russian Liberation Army', 41, 69, 171

St Valentin, 196, 197, 200-02
Salm-Horstmar, Prince Carl zu, 83, 102
San Francisco, 27
Sargent, Moley, 47, 55
Scarsbrook camp, 55
Schelest, Gregori, 126, 152, 153
Schönberg, 193
Scott, Brig T. P., 83-8
Selborne, Lord, 8, 9, 10, 12
Serbia, 87
Shaw, David, 132, 133
Shershun, Major, 56
Shields, Lt R., 132
Shkuro, Gen Andrey, 97, 117, 119, 159, 160, 164
Shparengo, Alexander, 94, 111, 112
Siberia, 75, 101
Sidorov, Ivan (pseudonym), 40-4, 46-8, 51-2
Sidorov, Nataliya (pseudonym), 40-51
Silkin, Maj-Gen, 98, 114
Slovenia, 87
Smith, Corp Donald, 146
Solomakhin, General, 98
Solzhenitsyn, Alexander, 73, 165, 208, 209
Spittal, 108, 110-12, 119, 121, 122, 159
Stalin, Joseph, attitude to forcible repatriation, 1, 2, 3, 4, 21; Russia under, 12, 69, 163, 205; and Churchill, 20, 31, 32; Yalta conference, 33-5, 97, 203; and British POW's, 37; 'Russian Liberation Army', 70-2; and Cossacks, 74, 81, 91, 92, 110, 125, 144; 'Cominform', 210
Stanton, John, 64, 197, 201, 202
Stars and Stripes, 190
Stettinius, Edward, 24, 26, 31
Stimson, Henry, 27, 28, 167
Stokes, Richard, 203
Strachey, John, 53
Strik-Strikfeldt, Wilfried, 71
Svinyev, Colonel, 103
Switzerland, 98

Tamplin, Col C. H., 35, 53
The Times, 34, 65, 211
Thorp, Major J. S., 25
Tito, Marshal, 73, 74, 77, 84, 87, 88, 91
Tolmezzo, 78-80, 82, 89
Tomsk, 161, 162
Treisch, Col G. M., 166
Truman, Harry S., 210
Tyson, Rev. Kenneth, 140-42, 145, 149, 153-5

Ukraine, 41, 61, 75
Unforgettable, The (N. Krasnov), 78
Union of Soviet Socialist Republics (USSR), under Stalin, 2, 3, 4, 205; and 'traitors', 9; distrust of Britain, 11; Vlasov and, 68, 69; and Cossacks, 81, 83, 91, 94, 97-8, 100, 103, 109-10, 114-15, 126, 128, 130, 139, 150, 159, 164; Allied disunity, 186, 193, 209
United Nations, 33, 114, 210
United States, POW camps in, 6, 24; political asylum in, 7; policy to expatriate Russians, 24-6, 169, 170, 182, 184; recognition of non-Soviet citizens, 37; Fort Dix camp, 166; Yalta Agreement, 179; modified policy, 188; disaffection with USSR, 66, 193
Usher, Brig. Clive, 134

Vasilenko, Prokofi, 126
Vasiliev, General, 17, 18, 19, 25
Villach, 200
Vlasov, General Andrey Andreyevich, 41, 43, 68-72, 171, 181, 185
Vostokov, Vladimir, 172

Warner, Christopher, 15, 38, 50, 175, 177, 180
Warsaw, 29
Washington Post, 34
Weddendorf, 65
West, Rebecca, 53, 205
Western Byelorussia, 37
Western Ukraine, 37, 38
Wiley, Senator Alexander, 64
Wilson, Geoffrey, 23, 43

Winchester camp (USA), 25
Wood, George, 154

Yakovlev, Col Pavel, 196
Yalta Agreement (1945), 33-4, 43-50, 52, 55, 67, 71 *et passim*

Yalta Conference, 31, 62
Youmatoff, Capt George, 14, 15, 48, 56-60
Yugoslavia, 77, 85, 87, 93, 185, 193

Zarya (newspaper), 70